IVORY TOWER BLUES:
A UNIVERSITY SYSTEM IN CRISIS

North American universities are facing a deepening crisis: in recent years class sizes have become significantly larger, while government funding has been slashed and tuitions have escalated at a phenomenal rate. At the same time students have arrived at university with greater expectations, cultivated in part by inflated high school grades and promises of rewarding, well-paying careers upon completion of their degrees. While many do in fact achieve their academic and vocational goals, increasing numbers of students are disengaged, losing interest and doing poorly in their courses or finding themselves underemployed if and when they do graduate.

In this book, James E. Côté and Anton L. Allahar provide a frank account of the contemporary Canadian university, drawing on their own research and personal experiences as well as conversations with students, counsellors, professors, administrators, educational researchers, and policy-makers past and present. The authors also examine educational and employment statistics and various academic studies and administrative records, which raise important concerns about the social and economic implications of 'credentialism' and increased post-secondary education participation. Challenging official reports and accepted wisdom, the authors argue that many students have been falsely promised, hampered by insufficient preparation at the secondary school level, and indulged in a variety of ways that set them up for failure and disappointment, either in university or as they make their way into the workplace.

Timely and controversial, *Ivory Tower Blues* is essential reading for students, parents, educators, policy-makers, and indeed anyone with a stake in our current education systems.

JAMES E. CÔTÉ is a professor in the Department of Sociology and the University of Western Ontario.

ANTON L. ALLAHAR is a professor in the Department of Sociology at the University of Western Ontario.

JAMES E. CÔTÉ AND ANTON L. ALLAHAR

Ivory Tower Blues

A University System in Crisis

UNIVERSITY OF TORONTO PRESS
Toronto Buffalo London

© University of Toronto Press Incorporated 2007
Toronto Buffalo London
Printed in Canada

ISBN 978-0-8020-9181-9 (cloth)
ISBN 978-0-8020-9182-6 (paper)

Printed on acid-free paper

Library and Archives Canada Cataloguing in Publication

Côté, James E., 1953–
Ivory tower blues : a university system in crisis / James E. Côté and
Anton L. Allahar.

Includes bibliographical references and index.
ISBN 978-0-8020-9181-9 (bound)
ISBN 978-0-8020-9182-6 (pbk.)

1. Universities and colleges – Canada.   2. Education, Higher – Canada.
I. Allahar, Anton L., 1949–   II. Title.

LA417.5.C675 2007   378.71   C2007-900370-2

University of Toronto Press acknowledges the financial assistance to its
publishing program of the Canada Council for the Arts and the Ontario
Arts Council.

University of Toronto Press acknowledges the financial support for its
publishing activities of the Government of Canada through the Book
Publishing Industry Development Program (BPIDP).

Contents

Acknowledgments

We would like to thank the staff at the University of Toronto Press for bringing this book to life, from initial discussions about the potential for this book to final production. In particular, we thank Virgil Duff for signing the book and for his patient and expert stewardship in taking it through the rigorous review required by the dreaded Manuscript Review Committee. We are also grateful to the reviewers and committee members who gave their valuable time, and provided their expert advice, to help shape the book to its current form. We would also like to thank the editorial staff, including Ian MacKenzie and Anne Laughlin, for cleaning up our errors and excesses, and shaping the prose to its current, more readable form. Of course, we take full responsibility for any errors or misstatements that might have survived the extensive reviewing, editing, and proofing this book has received.

IVORY TOWER BLUES:
A UNIVERSITY SYSTEM IN CRISIS

Introduction

Canada's World-Leading University System: Image versus Reality

Once the preserve of the privileged classes, universities today have become a major focal point in the lives of many young people. Just three decades ago, only about 10 per cent of the baby boom generation attended; today, 40 per cent of their children do so. Consequently, while in the 1970s just over 5 per cent of the adult labour force had a university degree, now some 20 per cent have at least one degree.[1] According to Statistics Canada, this makes Canada a 'world leader' in the percentage of the working population with a completed undergraduate university education, putting the country just behind the United States (28%), Norway (26%), and the Netherlands (21%).[2] If we include community college diplomas, Canada tops countries of the Organization for Economic Co-operation and Development (OECD), with 41 per cent of its labour force twenty-five years and older having either a post-secondary degree or diploma.

This is a laudable achievement for all of these countries and for the many other countries that are steadily increasing their university and other higher-educational enrolments. Indeed, many countries, including Canada, have a policy goal of achieving 50 per cent higher-educational attendance among their youth populations.[3] However, when we examine the entire situation and go beyond the public-relations mentality of speaking only positively about higher education, there are many different stories to tell about contemporary Canadian universities.

This book tells stories that are relevant to the constituencies affected: professors and administrators (chapters 1 and 2), students (chapter 3), parents (chapter 4), and policymakers (chapter 5). For example, the contemporary reality is that young people – the so-called millennial generation – are under tremendous pressure to go to university, and a certain percentage are *pushed* into university, rather than *pulled* by the allure of higher learning. This pressure comes in no small part from government policies and public relations campaigns designed to create positive public opinion about the merits of post-secondary education. While there is obvious value to these government campaigns, it appears that many of those young people who are pushed into post-secondary education are not prepared for the rigours of the university curriculum that have been the standard for the past few generations. At the same time, many of their parents feel both an anxiety about their children's futures and an obligation to at least partly finance what has become a new rite of passage for white-collar jobs.

For the first time, a sizable proportion of a generation of parents is compelled to support their children well into their twenties while they pursue higher-educational studies, again as a result of yet other government policies that have downloaded many of the costs of post-secondary education to students and their parents. Many of these parents, especially baby boomers who had children late because of the time it took them to launch their own careers, are deferring plans for their own retirement in order to finance their children's university education. Other parents cannot afford this expense, and they must make other sacrifices if they are to subsidize their children's education. Regardless of whether this is a financial burden that parents did not count on when they first had their children, it appears that most parents do not have full knowledge about how best to subsidize their children's education and to take advantage of the means of saving money that the Canadian government has made available to them. We provide this information for them in chapter 4.

Meanwhile, university administrators and professors have been scrambling to accommodate increased demand for their services, but they have had to do so with steadily declining budgets. And behind the scenes, policymakers are intent on doing what they believe is necessary to ensure that the Canadian economy is highly competitive while at the same time attempting to keep society running as smoothly as possible. Regrettably, the youth labour market began to collapse in the late 1970s and early 1980s, and continued to decline during the 1990s through to the present. Against the alternative of tackling the sources of the problem in the labour market, like developing employment policies such as wage subsidies to help integrate young people into the workplace,[4] policymakers have encouraged young people to pursue a post-secondary education, in the hope of preparing them for the 'new economy,' or at least diverting them from the unemployment lines. As we see, a regrettable ripple effect of this policy push is that, as a group, those who do not acquire a post-secondary education are at a disadvantage far greater than was the case in past generations.

Media attention to this dramatic change in the way people prepare for the labour force has been largely positive, echoing government announcements on the importance of a university education for jobs of the future. For example, in 1994, Statistics Canada predicted that 'almost two-thirds of *new* jobs between 1991 and 2000 will require at least 13 years of education or training and 45 percent will require more than 16 years.'[5] Note that this statement refers only to new jobs, not existing ones; also note that sixteen years of education is normally associated with an undergraduate degree, not all forms of post-secondary education. As it turns out, during the 1990s, about 1.2 million new jobs were created in a labour force of about 15 million, but of those new jobs, only about 800,000 required any form of post-secondary education.[6]

Indeed, while the prediction about the importance of education was true in general, these numbers are misleading, because only 16 per cent of all *existing* jobs required a university degree in 2000, up from just 13 per cent in 1990. And this percentage is for all levels of university education, not the bachelor's degree alone. Moreover, only 30 per cent of existing jobs required community college or an apprenticeship in 2000 – a figure that was actually down from 33 per cent in 1990.[7]

Taken together, then, only about 46 per cent of jobs in the Canadian labour force required *all* forms of post-secondary education in 2000. An almost equivalent number (43 per cent of existing jobs) required just high school or less, down from only 45 per cent in 1991. Clearly, we are *not* now in a position where almost half (45%) of jobs require a bachelor's degree, as the Statistics Canada prediction of 1994 implied. And this story becomes more complex as we dig deeper. For instance, Canada actually graduated twice as many university students in the 1990s as the number of jobs created during that period that required a university credential. Moreover, over four times more community college graduates were produced than could be absorbed in new jobs.[8] This mismatch between Canada's expanding post-secondary participation and the realities of the labour force is but one example of how our massive diversion of young people to post-secondary education is not a simple story with a happy ending for all.

We find it curious that the media have missed the story we are trying to tell.[9] One American observer argues that 'higher education is Teflon-coated, remarkably immune to criticism' from the media. Moreover, while 'higher education's weaknesses and shortcomings remain largely out of sight of reporters, many ... are quick to seize on almost any foible at the elementary or secondary level.'[10] This observer argues that 'it is not a question of exposing scandal or wrongdoing so much as ensuring that people understand and are able to rely on something more than blind faith in determining where and how quality manifests itself in higher education, as well as where and how it does not.'[11]

We could not agree more about the situation there as well as in Canada, but one recent sign of change in this tendency in Canada can be found in the 26 June 2006 edition of *Maclean's* magazine. In a change of course from previous editions, which 'sold' post-secondary education through rankings, this edition begins to expose some of things we write about in this book. For example, a caption for a picture heading the editorial, 'University Students Finally Have Their Say,' reads, 'Speaking up: Many are less than impressed with the post-secondary system.' And a feature story follows a York University undergrad who epitomizes students who use their university experience mainly as an opportunity to party. Moreover, a 'centrefold' titled 'The Average Student: SWF, 22, Some Debt, Seeks Degree, Job,' tells us that the typical Canadian university student can earn a B to B+ by spending about thirty-two hours on schoolwork (fifteen hours of classes and seventeen hours of studying) – basically by treating university as one would a part-time job. This turn of *Maclean's* coverage may have something to do with the fact that many Canadian universities are refusing to release data on student and graduate engagement, as well as institutional data for their rankings, as we discuss in chapter 5.[12]

In listening to media proclamations, especially from governments and their agencies, then, one must be very careful in interpreting statistics and rankings, particularly those that appear to be predicting massive shifts in the economy leading to bright futures for everyone who embarks on a higher-educational journey. We understand the need of policymakers to put a positive spin on trends to encourage people, but people must also learn to be informed consumers of this sort of information. A shift is underway, but it is hardly as large or as promising as many of the pronouncements from governments imply. Accordingly, the optimism that higher education will be the panacea for Canada's labour force challenges, especially among the young, has been somewhat exaggerated. At one level, this book is an exposé of that overstated optimism, as it has affected professors, students, and their parents, and those in charge of the system – administrators and policymakers.

As an indication of how an unbridled optimism about the contemporary university is affecting people, we can examine three aspirations parents have for their would-be scholarly progeny – that select minority of young people who earn seats in today's universities. It is fair to say that virtually all parents' aspirations for their university-bound children can be boiled down to three hopes. Their children will:

- Begin university well-prepared by their high school education
- Fully apply themselves to their courses
- Find interesting and rewarding employment after they graduate

On the basis of our experiences with this system in several capacities since the 1970s, however, we have directly and indirectly witnessed these hopes shattered with increasing frequency, in the daily grind of the university system and in the harsh reality of the job market afterwards. Because our experiences are supported by many studies and other recent data sources, we bring this information to readers' attention in the hope that a public debate will emerge about the reforms necessary to fix a university system in crisis.

This book is thus about how the hopes of parents and students alike meet the gritty realities of the contemporary school system and the job market, and how these realities are changing the university and what goes on within it. We flavour this book with our experiences as participants in this system for virtually our entire lives: first as students making our way through all levels of education including completion of our PhDs, and then as instructors making our way from teaching assistants to the top academic rank (full professor) at a major, well-respected Canadian university. Having each taught at the university level for the last twenty-five or so years, we have found that fewer and fewer students experience their education in the ways that parents hoped they would. In fact, we submit that the majority of students are hampered by *at least one* of the following:

- Not being prepared by their high school education for the rigours of university learning
- Not earnestly applying themselves in their courses while at university so that they can fully benefit

- Not finding employment that is as interesting or rewarding as they were led to expect before they began the prolonged process of acquiring university credentials

Outsiders to the contemporary university scene – especially parents hoping their children will attend one day – tend to assume that a university education is uniformly beneficial, and they are likely unaware of the crisis universities are, and have been, facing. In our experience, and we shall present research evidence to support these claims, a declining proportion of students find it so in terms of the three parental aspirations for their children that we have listed. While those students who meet all three aspirations do well in university and go on to rich and rewarding careers, their story is told over and over again to the public, so we feel there is no need for us to dwell on those success stories here. Instead, we focus on students who do not appear in the public discourse, and whose experiences do not match the stereotypes that have been perpetuated by university administrators, the media, and governments.

Let us not be misunderstood: we cannot stress enough that the university system works well for a certain proportion of students. Unfortunately, perhaps because people are used to a one-sided coverage of the university system that claims everything is fine as it is, it is apparently easy for readers to misunderstand our intention. We shall state here, and reinforce throughout the book, that our intention is not to 'bash' students. Instead, our goal is to expose all aspects of the university system that contribute to the crisis of which we speak.

For example, we believe that the public needs to know that the above three problems experienced by students can become compounded, so that when a student enters university unprepared, he or she is less likely to be fully engaged while there, and to fully benefit from the university *if* she or he graduates. This sequence suggests that the roots of the crisis of the university lie in part with factors outside of it and beyond its control. Accordingly, the crisis should not be blamed on the hapless students who are caught up in it. The more obvious factors creating the crisis are: a wider society that provides myriad hedonistic distractions that make book learning boring in comparison; high schools that push students through to graduation without attending to their skill levels; a corporate-driven youth culture that distracts young people from higher-order goals of self-improvement; government policies that have downloaded more of the costs of the university education to students; a workplace where a minimum wage does not allow young people to live independently or pay for their educations; a debt load in the twenty to thirty thousands of dollars upon graduation; job uncertainty; and a labour force that does not need the number of highly skilled workers that universities ostensibly produce.

In the chapters to follow, we choose not to gloss over the facts and instead to describe the crisis in the university system that is neglected in the good-news stories that dominate reporting about this system by governments, the media, and professors who are content not to rock the boat. This coverage shields the public from the dysfunctional and gloomier side of what university students, and those who teach them, experience. The following highlights from each chapter illustrate how this crisis is affecting each of the constituencies affected.

Chapter 1 describes the increasing disengagement of students and professors from the deep and intense learning that traditionally characterized higher education. On the student side of the 'disengagement compact,' many students now expect high grades for relatively little effort. Indeed, grade inflation has become rampant in many institutions throughout Canada and the United States, from high school through university (see the appendix for details and data), and as we show, grade inflation feeds academic disengagement. Disengagement has become such a concern that hundreds of schools in the United States, and more recently many in Canada, have elected to monitor it annually with the National Survey of Student Engagement (NSSE, pronounced the 'Nessie').[13] In fact, all Ontario universities were recently ordered to use the NSSE in a report by Bob Rae, with the reasoning that 'institutions have responsibility for teaching standards, curriculum design, strategies to improve student engagement and the development of teaching expertise in their faculties.'[14] Were there not problems in these areas, such an expensive proposition would not have been required of all universities in an entire province.

Students can be classified with NSSE research into roughly three groups: the fully engaged who do the full amount of work that professors expect of them (10% or so), the partially engaged (the roughly 40% who do less than what is expected, but enough to get by), and the disengaged (the other 40–50% who do the minimal required to play the system or do nothing at all). Of course, these percentages will vary by department, faculty, and school, but these are averages that have been found among the hundreds of thousands of students surveyed in hundreds of schools.

On the faculty side of the equation, Canadian professors as a group now face three times as many students as they did a generation ago, so there are now fewer professors per student with fewer resources. Canadian professors now teach some 1 million students and have had to adapt to often large and impersonal classes by watering down their curriculum and methods of assessment. This deteriorating state of affairs only feeds student disengagement, because in many courses there is little academic substance in which students can engage themselves other than in glossy and expensive but dumbed-down textbooks. In these cases, disengagement in foisted on students, and NSSE research suggests that most students begin university with high expectations of the workload, but revise them when they see how little is often required of them.

With so many students being passed on from high school with inflated grades (in certain regions the majority are now certified as 'A students' when they arrive at many universities), new functions have emerged for university faculty to perform. Professors increasingly find themselves having to sort out, weed out, and cool out students who in previous generations would not have been pushed to attend university. Until recently, high schools performed these functions, and universities concentrated on *higher education* involving deep and higher-order learning experiences. The lack of public unawareness of these problems masks the failure of the system to teach all students effectively, and the potential long-term harm to society as the old mission of the university is threatened.

Chapter 2 delves deeper into how the crisis is experienced by professors, who have found themselves placed in the role of gatekeepers to the world of middle-class, white-collar work. Their crisis is illustrated in the recent case of a professor who promised students (in a class that he felt was too large) final course grades of 70 per cent (Bs) if they would stop coming to class, handing in assignments, and taking tests, and simply pay their tuition to the university. Twenty per cent took him up on his offer. His motivation for making the disengagement compact so public was his frustration in trying to teach a large class where so many obviously disinterested (disengaged) students were enrolled. The large numbers of students who now want high grades for little effort exacerbates this frustration, as does the adversarial relationship that develops when professors do not kowtow to pressures for easy grades from students who are accustomed to putting out little or no effort.

At the same time, faculty members are but employees of what have become the large business operations we call universities. As employees of these businesses, many professors find their jobs difficult when working with undergraduate students who have been implicitly promised a product (degree) in exchange for their tuition. Sources of stress include dealing with the many students who have consumer mentalities (they pay their money and expect high grades in return), and who are armed with teaching evaluations to punish professors who do not deliver the product to their liking. Professors are thus put in the trenches to fight it out with, and take the flak from, students who are now sorted, weeded, and cooled by the contemporary university system.

Chapter 3 goes on to examine how contemporary students of the so-called millennial generation experience a university system that has suffered years of financial neglect and pedagogical crisis, and in a sense are paying for these years of neglect with higher tuition fees, are working while studying, and are offered watered-down courses in return. Fleeing a job market that is the worst for young people since the Great Depression, this generation is the first to attend university in such numbers, but those who attend have been enticed and cajoled by high grades and a relatively easy ride in high school. However, the problems we identify did not suddenly start with this generation and are not due to some generational failing. Rather, the process has been more gradual and is at least traceable to the experiences of the late baby boomers and so-called Generation Xers, who passed through the university system in the 1970s, 1980s, and 1990s.[15] Higher standards in secondary schools in past generations weeded out most who would not have taken the academic demands of the university seriously (other than the most wealthy). Regardless of how the problem evolved over generations, when current students enter university, those who took the easy ride in high school often find themselves in over their heads, even in a watered-down curriculum, and more and more universities must offer remedial courses to bring them up to speed with those classmates who actually learned how to read and write effectively in high school. All manner of remedial courses, writing-skills workshops, calls for mentors and private tutors, and assorted learning support centres on university campuses testify to the veracity of this charge.

This chapter goes on to examine reactions that students from this generation have to university, which on the one hand is a business promising a product, and on the other hand is structured to test their mettle as part of its mandate to sort, weed, and cool them out. Students react in a variety of ways to the contemporary university system, and we attempt to capture some of their experiences. We repeat again that there are still excellent students in the system who benefit from it, and in our experience they are aware of the problems of which we speak, including how the system is dumbed down for their disengaged classmates. At the same time, a good number are angry at what now passes for higher education and their low status in it. Others have been affected by political correctness, and expect that a set of self-made rules will be applied to them. And yet others are simply lost, having been pushed into an experience for which they are not prepared academically or emotionally. In our desire to be fair and accurate, we attempt to relate the experiences of all these types of students.

Chapter 4 then moves on to issues that are of interest to the parents of contemporary university students. Generational comparisons are presented between baby boomer parents and their millennial offspring, including the tendency of some parents to be over-protective 'helicopter parents,' who micro-manage their children's lives. This over-protection can be understood in part because this generation of parents is the first to be expected to invest so much financially in their dependent children for so far into their adult lives. Indeed, we see that the Canadian government has been downloading the costs of higher education directly to students, and indirectly to their parents. At the same time, the youth labour market is now more exploitive than in the past, and lower relative wages in conjunction with higher tuition means that it takes about three times longer in summer jobs – the whole summer in fact – to earn enough to pay annual tuition costs, leaving little or nothing for other expenses. Consequently, in an attempt to avoid accumulating higher debts in their student loans, more Canadian students now work during the school year, taking time way from their studies.

We provide advice to parents about the current costs of university, and draw their attention to information that would help them invest their money more wisely. For while many parents may otherwise be savvy investors in the stock market or real estate, when it comes to their children's education, they are not always as well informed in how best to disperse the tens of thousands of dollars they may spend. This advice ranges from how to counsel young people who may be aimless or have misaligned ambitions, to the downside of their holding jobs during the school year (for example, taking up to two years more than the average to complete their degree). Above all, we are trying to reach the parents of fully or partially disengaged students to alert them to the problems their children may be experiencing and where these problems may lead them if they are not redirected.

Chapter 5 concludes the book with an in-depth look at policy-relevant issues, including what might be value-added to people's personal and occupational development by a university education, beyond other forms of experience – like working in meaningful and challenging jobs, or undertaking journeys of self-exploration through travel and volunteer work in developing countries. Years of academic research on this topic are reviewed, including the good news about the expected personal rate of return for university graduates, and the bad news about the underemployment that many graduates experience. This chapter, and the book, ends with a comparison of the U.S. and Canadian 'soft-sorting' system that filters large numbers of people into post-secondary educations by giving them high grades with other more directive sorting systems around the world, and a call for the public to recognize and support the crucial role of the old liberal-arts mission of the university that is being over-ridden by other personal-, and institutional-economic agendas.

Finally, we provide an **appendix** in which we speak to potential critics of our book about our approach and methodologies. After laying out four possible points of contention, we call for those in other universities and with other insights and data to add to the debate on the crisis in our university system. We also provide readers with a discussion of how grade inflation is conceptualized, and present evidence showing that Canadian universities exhibit levels of grade inflation almost as high as American universities, where this aspect of the crisis was identified several years ago and has been debated there since.

Who Should Read This Book?

This book is written for several audiences, all of whom we would like to involve in a public debate on the crisis of the university system involving the interrelated problems of poor preparation, grade inflation and academic disengagement, and graduate underemployment. Those associated with districts and/or schools where these problems are suspected should be especially interested.

First and foremost, it is written for the general public that does not have ready access to academic journals, government reports, university records, or a window to the day-to-day aspects of university life that is afforded to professors like us. Within this audience, we speak most directly to the parents of today's university students to help them better understand what their children are experiencing. And among parents, we hope that those with children who are struggling in the system can better understand their children's experience. We believe that many of their difficulties can be understood in terms of the lack of preparedness for the rigours of university-level learning, the perceived need to work for pay during the school year, the myriad distractions that are now found in student cultures, and the widespread disengagement we now find in contemporary universities.

The second audience is thus the million university students in Canada's universities, some of whom will read this book in their courses. Frankly, however, unless this book is assigned them as required reading, we believe that it will be read mainly by those from among the 10 per cent of fully engaged students who would open a book such as this one. While they would clearly benefit from reading it, we also hope that the other 90 per cent of students will also read it to help them appreciate more clearly what might be the most important experience of their adult lives. But, for obvious reasons, we do not think that the more severely disengaged students will read this book, unless urged to do so by their parents and teachers. So we ask parents to bring it to the attention of their university-attending children or to use the book to help engage their children in their educational journeys. Regardless of the sources of their disengagement and who or what is at fault, it is the disengaged students who need to be counselled to take the time to examine their lives, where they are going, and why they are at university. This counselling is meant to redirect the ways in which the students in question might spend their youthful energy, and avoid the squandering of educational opportunities, the waste of time and money, and the diminishing of Canada's ability to produce well-rounded, educated, and skilled citizens. That we are so concerned for them to read something that could help them so much speaks to the type of frustrations we as university professors and mentors face. We are dealing ostensibly with bright and capable people, even in the disengaged student, but so many of them remain so unaware of their own strengths and passions that they miss major opportunities for pursuing prudent paths to self-improvement.

Our third audience, in this order of priority, is the academic one. We encourage all of our colleagues – especially those in the classroom 'trenches' – to be open minded about what we have to say about the crisis in the university system. Many are already acutely aware of it, but as we see in chapter 2, for several reasons many are not. There are currently some thirty thousand full-time university professors in Canada, most of whom will find what we have to say supportive of their thoughts and intuitions about their jobs and the students they teach. At the same time, there will be colleagues who disagree with us, either in whole or in part. Some who disagree may not do any educational research themselves, but feel that they still have a comfortable, stress-free niche in the system. This lack of awareness may be because the specific area in which they teach is not as directly affected by the problems of poor preparation, grade inflation, and academic disengagement, or because they are unaware of these issues as a result of their own disengagement and insensitivity to issues that stress their colleagues. Younger professors who were themselves educated in a grade-inflated system and have been giving inflated grades all along will not likely see the problems we see, because they lack an institutional memory. We shall discuss a report from a university professor who returned to teaching in the late 1990s after twenty years in administration, only to find the bulk of his students with poor writing and knowledge skills, but high expectations of the grades they should receive.[16]

Finally, in this book we also speak to those on the other side of the equation – administrators and policymakers – asking that they consider what we have to say, so that we can all continue to improve how we prepare young people for their adult lives. Our aim is not merely to criticize Canada's university system. It is to help improve the system, so that the people passing through it stand a better chance of reaching their potentials, and Canadian society becomes a truly free and democratic society. Only by identifying those areas in need of improvement can we hope to accomplish this goal.

Each chapter in this book is written so that it is essentially self-contained, reintroducing and further developing points made in each of the five chapters. Accordingly, the reader is not required to read this book in its entirety, or sequentially, to benefit from it. For those who would like a self-assessment of our approach and a look at the data on grade inflation in Canada and elsewhere, reading the appendix first will help provide some context and background information.

1 Troubles in Paradise

The Disengaged Student

> Today's college freshmen continue to be academically disengaged ... Students spent less time studying and doing homework, with only 34.9 percent of entering students reporting studying or working on assignments for six or more hours per week in the past year. This marks the lowest figure since this question was first asked in 1987, when 47 percent reported studying six or more hours weekly. Although students are spending less time studying, their high school grades continue to soar with 44.1 percent of freshmen report earning 'A' averages in high school, compared to 42.9 percent last year, and a low of 17.6 percent in 1968. 'The combination of academic disengagement and record grade inflation,' says [Alexander] Astin, 'poses a real challenge for our higher education system, since students are entering college with less inclination to study but with higher academic expectations than ever.

This passage from *The American Freshman*[1] signals the rise of the 'disengaged student' as a new norm among students attending universities in the United States, and, as we shall see, in Canada. This new norm is one of a series of trends undermining parents' hopes that their university-bound children will fully benefit from their higher-educational experiences.

Indeed, life inside the ivory tower has changed dramatically since the present generation of parents was young. It has changed partly because the relationship between the ivory tower and wider society has been transformed, yet those labouring within the university are attempting to focus on the same things they did a generation ago: give priority to abstract intellectual enquiries while performing cutting-edge research. Stated more simply, tenured university professors are first and foremost researchers, especially those at larger universities, and most universities now require a PhD for tenure. Their PhDs are degrees that certify them primarily as researchers, not as teachers. Understandably, then, they are likely motivated by intellectual and scientific engagements with their peers and tend to regard interacting with students as secondary – an attitude reinforced by university administrations that reward outstanding research and publication much more positively and handsomely than outstanding teaching, especially in granting tenure.

While there seems to be growing criticism of this preference among professors, if the job of professor involved the same amount and type of student-focused activity that characterizes high school teaching (as it does in community colleges), one wonders whether the majority of contemporary professors who go to the trouble of earning a PhD and securing tenure would have gone into the profession, or whether they would have sought other jobs involving high-level intellectual and scientific activities. This question merits further investigation, but our feeling is that the professoriate would be less attractive to graduates of research-intensive PhD programmes.

Although some professors are quite prepared to mentor undergraduate students and guide them step by step, they are by no means typical, especially at larger universities. This leaves increasing numbers of undergraduate students who are now pushed into universities in a bind, because taking them under wing and individually leading them through higher education is not the top priority in most universities, especially larger, research-intensive ones. Students at the university level must be self-directed and self-motivated and cannot rely on the system to structure their education to the extent that high schools typically do, and as we shall see, the wider popular culture does not prepare the individual student to take ownership of her or his life's decisions and personal responsibilities. As we argued over ten years ago in *Generation on Hold*,[2] the moratorium on adulthood granted youth has delayed their maturity and increased their reliance on parents, teachers, and other adults to make decisions about their futures.

In addition, students now flooding into universities – the so-called millennial generation – are also different. Compared to past generations, millennials were given higher grades in high school for less effort;[3] as a result, fewer have been seriously challenged to develop their intellects and associated motivations to understand the world in increasingly complex ways. As a result, they are more likely to expect things to be done *for them* by their professors – as if professors were like high school teachers – rather than taking the initiative to do certain things themselves, like reading and thinking about course material in preparation for classes. Consequently, educating all students to their full potential would require far more resources than in past generations, even if that were now a priority. This bind is an underlying theme of this book: the incompatibility of expectations that the wider society holds – and thus the expectations of students and their parents – about what professors should be doing for students, in comparison with what they actually do in the ivory tower.

But let us not be misunderstood here. There are no identifiable bad guys or good guys in the story we are telling; there are simply a number of university faculty members and administrators trying to get by with limited budgets and resources, along with a vastly increased number of students trying to get high grades from them en route to a degree, especially the much-prized postgraduate degree (MBA, MD, MA, MEd, PhD, LLB, etc.). To complicate matters, a significant proportion of those vast numbers of students do not know specifically why they are vying for a given degree or how they will handle one if they do obtain it. What they do know is what has become a conventional wisdom embodied in platitudes repeated by their high school teachers, counsellors, and parents, such as 'Get as much education as you can, and it will pay off for you.' While this advice is true as a statistical average, the situation is far more complex when we look at the variation evident in individual cases, and when we compare those who acquire different levels of education. Indeed, the university experience has numerous demonstrable benefits, as we shall show in chapter 5. However, in the pages to follow, we attempt to convey the complexity of this situation in a way that goes beyond statistical averages and misleading platitudes.

Discerning readers will eventually want to know what alternatives there might be to the situation that has evolved in Canada. One place to begin is a look at how other countries are handling the same issue of integrating large numbers of young people into the 'new economy,' which is anything but easy to enter, except at the most basic level of low-waged, low-skilled jobs. Canada and the United States have similar educational philosophies about the role that (secondary and tertiary) education plays in the transition to the workplace. Both countries are similar in their adoption of a 'soft sorting' strategy, preferring to let young people find their own ways into the job market through trial and error of ostensibly unconstrained choices. This approach is normally justified on the basis of a self-serving logic that invokes liberal democratic sentiments: people should be free to choose their destinies, and their access should not be arbitrarily impeded. This is a laudable ideal, but when put into practice, it presents serious problems for many young people who really *do* need guidance and direction in making life-altering choices. To complicate matters further, a prominent North American belief is that young people in their teens are not capable of making decisions about their future, so they should be encouraged to put important career decisions off until they have more experience. This is precisely what many teens are doing, so much so that we now have a generation of 'twenty-somethings' finally facing choices that previous generations faced in their teens.[4] This is a story that we have closely examined in another recent book.[5]

The alternative to soft sorting is 'hard sorting,' as is done in many other countries, especially in European countries such as Germany. But we are getting ahead of ourselves here. Later we compare these sorting systems (chapter 5), and confront the reality that some type of 'sorting' is inevitable: it will happen one way or the other, and the undergraduate university systems in countries like Canada and the United States are now caught in the middle of conflicting interests regarding how this is to be done.

Higher Expectations, Lower Effort

As noted earlier, there is much that the higher educational systems of the United States and Canada share that make generalizations and comparisons possible and instructive. The quote that began this chapter identifies a crisis in American education that is also being experienced in Canada, although it is likely still more severe in parts of the United States. However, this situation is now upon us in Canada: Canadian high school students have been given increasingly inflated grades, and these students have come to universities with higher expectations about the grades to which they feel entitled (see the appendix for details). This situation has intensified in direct proportion to the increase in enrolments in Canadian universities, as the competition to gain entrance increases. As more and more students with inflated grades, but lower levels of academic interest and ability, have entered Canadian universities year after year, many professors have given in by watering down their courses and inflating grades. Even universities that inflated their grades during the

1970s and 1980s, and thus now take historically high grades for granted as 'normal,' are experiencing unprecedented expectations from recent high school graduates to push grades even higher. The extent to which ground has been yielded to grade inflation varies by university and within universities by department and faculty, but it is one of the new day-to-day realities making life more difficult for everyone involved, and is a chief cause of the 'ivory tower blues.'

To better locate the grade inflation problem, we can begin by noting that the distribution of As and Cs reversed between the 1960s and 1990s on average in American universities, with one quarter of students receiving As in the 1990s, as opposed to only 7 per cent doing so in the 1960s.[6] More recent NSSE studies are finding that some 40 per cent of American university students now report they are routinely awarded As, and an additional 40 per cent are given Bs.[7] Moreover, we can see the continuity of high school grade inflation with university grade inflation in figures provided by the U.S. Census Bureau,[8] where 95 per cent of first-year students now report having been awarded B or A averages in high school. Most striking is the increase in As. In 1970, only 20 per cent earned As in high school (an equivalent percentage reported C average in 1970), but by 2003 the figure more than doubled to 47 per cent.[9]

With so many As and Bs assigned, what about the C? The C was traditionally defined as the reference point for 'average/satisfactory' in the British system, as it still is in many other systems, including the European Credit Transfer System (ECTS; see the appendix for details). Indeed, during the 1960s, some 50 per cent of students were assigned C+s or less in the United States and Canada in most educational institutions. Increasingly, however, Bs have come to signify 'satisfactory' and Cs are viewed as a punishment, creating a plethora of problems that we shall discuss shortly. Some students even complain about Bs and attempt to settle for nothing less than an A.[10]

The data clearly show that Canadian students are either quickly catching up to their American counterparts, or have already done so (see the appendix for details). For example, institutionally based data from all marks submitted in several universities indicate that As and Bs are awarded in the 60 per cent range in lower-level (first and second year) university courses and in the 80 per cent range in many upper-level courses (third and fourth year). And the NSSE studies now being carried out in Canadian universities show that student-reported grades are as high in Canada as in the United States. Moreover, in the 1980s, the average entering grade for Ontario universities was a mid-B; currently it is a low A, and in more prestigious universities like the University of Western Ontario it is a high A.[11] From a statistical point of view, these increasing entry grades can be explained only by grade inflation in high schools. If only 5–10 per cent of high school students were being awarded As, there simply would not be this number of students applying to universities with such high marks. For a discussion of the problems this change is causing Canadian university admissions personnel, we recommend Kevin McQuillan's essay, 'Evaluations, Admissions, and the Quality of Ontario Universities,' written for the Council of Ontario Universities.[12] Professor McQuillan is a former chair of the Sociology Department at Western and currently dean of Social Science at the University of Calgary. We shall report some of his observations a little later.

In spite of this mountain of historical, comparative, and contemporary evidence of grade inflation in Canadian high schools, and now in universities, some observers deny that there are problems, pointing to Canada's performance on the standardized Programme for International Student Assessment (PISA) carried out on fifteen-year-olds by the OECD in thirty-two countries.[13] The PISA assesses reading, mathematics, and science literacy, and Canada scores high in relation to the other countries in all three areas. While Canada's performance looks good at first blush, this research is not without its problems.

First, the range of scores is not as great as the rankings suggest, and rankings can exaggerate a sense of performance adequacy. On reading literacy, for instance, while Canada's score in 2000 was 528 (the second-highest country, with Finland coming in at 543), the OECD average was 488, and the highest possible score was 1000. The United States, with all of its schooling problems, scored 495, just 33 points below Canada.[14] Over a possible range of 1000, 33 points is a very minor figure (a 3.3% difference).

Second, testers readily admit to the potential for errors because results are based on only a random sample of 30,000 students from 1000 schools in Canada, so they 'cannot say with certainly that these scores would have been obtained had all 15-year-old students been tested' (15).[15] Although the error can be estimated statistically, the accuracy of results is still entirely based on the assumption that the randomly selected students actually completed the test, and some of those selected in Canada evidently did not.[16] With such small differences among countries, as we noted, even a minor fiddling of random sampling can affect the rankings and thus enhance the sense that Canadian students are superior to those in other countries. This last point is bolstered by the evidence that when standardized testing has been carried out on entire school populations, as in Ontario, we find surprisingly high rates of failure, especially among students in 'applied' programmes.[17]

And third, if we look at the results for reading literacy, which examined what typical fifteen-year-olds in the Canadian sample could actually comprehend, only 13 per cent scored at the highest level of literacy (Level 5),[18] with most capable of only a moderate literacy, at Level 3 or lower.[19]

Thus, while at first blush Canada may seem to be exemplary internationally on the PISA tests, this assumption is based on rankings of minor differences with dubious validity, and we may simply be looking at relatively mediocre performances in most countries. The possibility that these minor ranking differences may have been exaggerated by those wanting to make the Canadian educational system look better than it is, is supported by the fact that the OECD (the organization overseeing the PISA testing) is critical of Canada's uneven national coordination of standards and an overall 'lack of learning culture.'[20]

Returning to the issue of grades, there have always been grade-driven students. One seminal study of higher education in the 1950s found that students developed creative ways of adapting to grade pressures. In *Making the Grade*,[21] it was found that medical students' focus on a strong grade point average (GPA) overrode an unadulterated thirst for knowledge. However, that study was done in a medical school where less-than-outstanding performances meant dismissal. We are now witnessing vast numbers of disengaged students with GPA perspectives flooding into faculties of Arts, Humanities, and Social Sciences, expecting to get As as they did in high school – with minimal effort. Forget the creative ways of mastering material described in *Making the Grade*; there is often little concern for any sort of mastery among a good number of students. The mark counts and that is it. Unfortunately, when this grade obsession reaches a critical mass among the student body, it diminishes the content of courses and the quality of education for those who really want to learn. At the same time, it reduces the quality of working life for teachers by increasing their job-related stress and workload in dealing with students who have unrealistically high expectations about how well they will do in university-level courses.

A useful voice to add to this analysis comes from a Western professor, Thomas Collins, who spent twenty-one years as an administrator, first as chair of the English Department, then as dean of Arts, and finally as provost and vice-president academic of Western (the second-highest position in the university). These posts took him out of the classroom entirely from the mid-1970s to the mid-1990s. Thus, we have a rare case study in which someone's institutional memory is untainted by the experience of having to adjust his teaching year after year to increasingly unprepared and disengaged students, as appears to be the case for many professors, as we shall see in chapter 2. In a paper written for the Council of Ministers of Education, Collins admitted to some naivety when he returned to the classroom in the mid-1990s, and considerable shock at how standards had slipped in twenty years and how ill-prepared students were for the English courses he taught, especially first-year courses. From his experiences in the trenches during his first year back, he concluded that he could not 'assume even a moderate level of literacy from [these students] ... presumably because they think, or have been led to believe, that they are at least proficient in' English.[22]

Collins blamed this result on poor and inconsistent preparation in secondary schools in reading and writing, poor work habits, and low levels of critical thinking and learning skills. Given the high grades with which these students gained entry into university (Western, in this case), Collins clearly saw the negative consequences of grade inflation that we discuss here. He presented institutional data showing an average 14 per cent grade drop for first year-students, who entered with a 79.5 per cent average as a group, but finished first year at Western with a 65.3 per cent average. Western's standards had not yet changed significantly from the traditional standards about which we write, but high school standards had obviously loosened, giving students terribly false feedback about their abilities, while selling them short by not preparing them for university-level learning.

At the same time, Collins recognized how universities were contributing to grade inflation because, confronted with so many ill-prepared students, he and his colleagues could not grade them by traditional standards, because then they would have failed most of them. Consequently, they patiently corrected papers, but passed on a certain amount of false feedback with higher grades than the work deserved. For example, in his 1997–8 first-year tutorial, out of seventeen students, 'only 4 wrote at an acceptable level of literacy,' by which he means the ability to 'construct basic sentences and paragraphs.'[23] The remaining students struggled but could not move up a learning curve of literacy, so they made the same mistakes in assignment after assignment.

To conduct a reality check on his own experiences, he talked with his colleagues and found that their experience was much the same as his, but they were just accustomed to it as a result of their adjustments over the years. He also looked for other evidence about the decline in standards and student preparation. In one case, Collins gained access to the results of a chemistry test that had been administered each year in Introductory Chemistry from 1978 to 1996. On this test, which contained the same forty questions over this two-decade period, there was a steady decline in average grades from 64 per cent in 1978 to 48 per cent in 1996.[24] One lesson was that if he were to grade his first-year students by the standards he followed in the mid-1970s, he should have been giving Fs instead of Cs to the illiterate students who could not move up a learning curve. So why didn't he or his colleagues fail them? More generally, why weren't universities speaking up more about the lack of high-school preparation among many of the students they were matriculating?

Collins's answer came in part from his inside knowledge as a former administrator. In his words, one reason was that

> Western adopted the invidious internal funding system which rewards Faculties and Departments financially for attracting and retaining additional students in post year-one courses. This system has ostensibly been introduced to encourage interdisciplinary teaching and course development (and strangely so, particularly at a time when students have little or no disciplinary knowledge): its actual effect has been to increase grade inflation across the university.[25]

He and his colleagues discussed this openly and extensively, and in his words, the message was 'Don't mark the students too honestly or we shall have few students in upper years, thus losing funds and probably faculty positions.' He also noted that more difficult upper-year courses, especially those requiring essays, were under-enrolled – avoided by students who 'wisely understand their own deficiencies.'[26] Collins suspected that some version of this funding-induced problem now existed in all universities, but they ignored the need to attack the problem, because remediation programmes would cost large amounts of money.

Credentialism and Grade Inflation

We must repeat that there are no good guys and no bad guys here, even among disengaged students, money-pinched administrators, or soft professors. We believe that two underlying forces have produced this situation that are not the fault of the actors involved: the rise and spread of credentialism and the upward pressure that credentialism puts on qualifying grades. Credentialism encompasses both (a) the belief that preparation for the workplace is best undertaken through formal education and (b) the practice that results, whereby it is virtually impossible to secure a job without some sort of credential. While a case can be made for requiring a bachelor's degree in critical professions like law and medicine – because professions that deal with life-and-death matters require specific learning and knowledge[27] – the logic for this requirement is shaky in many other cases, as in the necessity of having an undergraduate degree to secure an entry-level white-collar job, like bank teller or manager of a small franchised store. We have known for some time that most jobs simply do not require the skills ostensibly acquired through an undergraduate education, yet an increasing number of jobs have required the degree simply for applicants to be considered. Many of these over-credentialed jobs would once have been classified as unskilled, meaning that they could be performed with basic literacy skills and a few weeks of training on the job.[28] Credentialism thus leads to underemployment, as we discuss in detail in chapter 5.

Along with the idea that it is 'good' for professions like law or medicine to require that applicants have a degree, the reasons for the spread of credentialism vary.[29] Many other jobs are now too specialized or too simple to require an apprenticeship system that would provide direct routes to them from, or through, high school. However, after the norm of requiring undergraduate credentials took hold for the professions, the supply of would-be professionals with a bachelor's continued to grow. Then, following the professional model, certain employers simply became accustomed to asking for undergraduate degrees, if only to help them sort through job applications and eliminate enough candidates without the credential to make hiring more manageable. Quite apart from the knowledge acquired while earning the degree, the credential likely said to the potential employer that the applicant had the discipline and determination to see a project through, but with the mass of disengaged students now passing through the system, even this belief may be unfounded in many cases.

While this development on its own may have been relatively harmless – because there are few disadvantages to having university-educated clerks and managers, or even fire-fighters – it has created layers of young workers in competition with each other on the basis of arbitrary credential acquisition. In other words, those who are eliminated from professional and other postgraduate-school recruitment create new layers of competition for each other and for those with lower levels of credentials

Figure 1.1: Percentage of young men and women attending school full-time in Canada 1921–2001

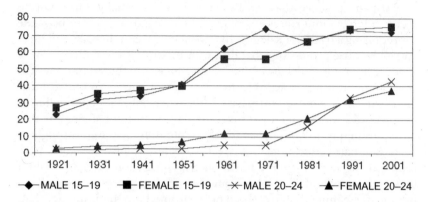

(a 'positional effect' of credentialism, which we shall soon discuss). This practice has spiralled out of control, resulting in 'education inflation': an artificial increase in the number of credentials it takes to secure a good job and a devaluing of lower levels of education that in many cases are sufficient for the skills demanded of many jobs.[30]

We can trace education inflation as a direct function of the rise of credentials, as shown in figure 1.1.[31] The graph shows how educational enrolments among the university-aged population (twenty to twenty-four) have gone through growth spurts and plateaus, initially as a result of university and community college construction in the 1950s and 1960s, then in response to the deteriorating youth labour market, beginning in the late 1970s. In actual numbers, university enrolments have increased exponentially over the past hundred years. In 1900, there were only 6,800 university students in Canada, growing to 23,200 in 1920, and 36,000 in 1940.[32] Enrolments then doubled in each of the next three decades, so that by the 1970s there were about three hundred thousand university students. By 1990, this number doubled again, and by the early 2000s more than tripled, giving us more than 1 million university students today,[33] about 150 times the number a century ago. In contrast, the population of Canada increased by a factor of six (from about 5 million to 30 million).

As more workers with university degrees came onto the job market, employers simply began to take those with the higher credentials, other things being equal. The net result for many graduates is that they are doing essentially the same jobs as did workers of their parents' generation who had a high school diploma. We now find many more young people aspiring to do postgraduate work in an attempt to bypass the bottleneck for those with 'merely' a bachelor's. Those who go on to do postgraduate work for this reason may simply continue with the habits of minimal commitment to their studies, even though they may be quite skilled at going through the motions: they can do well on essays and assignments but do not appreciate the discipline as a 'calling' as previous generations of advanced students might have.[34] Without the intrinsic motivation associated with a vocation, they need to rely on external factors, like a more highly structured programme and more handholding from faculty members – precisely what got them that far in the educational system but exactly what they need to be weaned from if they are to become independently functioning academics or professionals themselves.

In addition, of course, there are the undergraduate students who want to get into professional programmes out of interest, ambition, or parental pressure, but who need at least a bachelor's to qualify. Over half of students who begin undergraduate studies have this as a (sometimes vague) goal.[35] Most of these students will not qualify for entrance into these programmes, and they face significant disappointment after years of post-secondary study and debt accumulation. In spite of hype about the need for an educated workforce, only about 7 per cent of the workforce between the ages of twenty-five and fifty-four have graduate or professional degrees, showing how great the bottleneck is to get into the highest levels of education.[36] We counsel many distraught students from our courses who struggle with the pressure their parents put on them, and they are usually the children of parents who themselves are in one of the professions.

When we put these factors together, we see an additional source of pressure on grades. As more students are forced to use the undergraduate degree as a proving ground for access to postgraduate programmes or to qualify for the white-collar job market, these graduate programmes and job markets simply raise the GPA levels they require for acceptance. The same thing happened in high schools over the past three decades. As more high school students were told that universities were the only viable route to rewarding while-collar careers, they pressured high school teachers to give them higher grades to secure admission to university. As we have already noted, in the past few years, cut-off levels for admission to many universities have risen into the A range. This means that in some universities like Western (the new 'brand' name for this school), virtually all incoming students were A students in high school (the average entering grade to Western was about 87% for the 2004–5 school year).[37] According to *Maclean's* University Rankings '06 issue, 99.7

per cent of first-year students at Western had an 80 per cent or better entering average. A averages were the exception in high schools during the 1960s, not the norm, as some parents and grandparents may recall that when they attended (see the appendix for details). The Ontario Scholars programme rewarded these exceptional students with bursaries of $100 to encourage them to attend university. Now, such programmes are virtually meaningless because so many students can easily hit the mark (40% of high school graduates in Ontario do so).

The sheer number of students now coming to Canadian universities puts pressure on the system, threatening to reduce its legitimacy as a site of true higher education. Although decades of declining funding is clearly an issue, even without increased funding from the government or raised tuitions, Canadian universities *could* handle these numbers if students were better prepared by their high school training, in the skills they bring with them and their willingness to work at their studies. However, there are serious problems in motivation and ability among a sizable proportion of students sent to universities from Canadian high schools. As a result of grade inflation, increasing numbers of students with inadequate learning skills do not feel they need to improve, primarily because they were told for years in high school that they were good or excellent students, when in fact many were not.[38] Most professors can relate stories about indignant students who complain about a low mark, claiming either that they always 'did it this way' and had no problems before, or that they are A or 'honours' students, so there must be a problem with the way the professor grades.

There have always been disengaged students, just as there have always been good students. Lest this sound as if we are claiming that all students are the same, recall from the introduction that we distinguish types of students based on NSSE research: engaged (roughly 10%), partially engaged (roughly 40%), and disengaged (some 40%). The problem is that there are now far more disengaged students in the system, draining resources that could be devoted to engaged students. Whereas the engaged students might have prevailed in the past, the disengaged appear in increasing numbers now, such that professors often comment that they are happy to get even a few 'good students' per class.[39] Confronted with more low-effort, disengaged students year after year, professors reduce course requirements accordingly, and bright students are challenged less.[40] At the same time, many professors find teaching less gratifying and more annoying, as they must now deal with an increasing variety of tactics used by disengaged students to avoid doing the little work now required of them.

Without wanting to sound unnecessarily romantic and nostalgic, we ask parents who went to university themselves in the 1960s and 1970s to think back to what they were required to do in courses to just pass; what grades were assigned for hard work; what sizes their classes were; how they were graded (essays and presentations versus multiple-choice tests); and how much access they had to professors and teaching assistants. They will undoubtedly remember students who were minimally engaged, many of whom were satisfied with what was called the 'gentleman's C.' Those satisfied with the 'gentleman's C' were often from wealthy backgrounds and had no intention of going on to postgraduate degrees because family money, the family business, family contacts, and networks would see to their futures. Most professors apparently did not mind them much either, so long as they did the minimum work and did not play petty political, time-wasting games. Today, few students are satisfied with a C, even though a C technically still means 'average' or 'satisfactory' and allows the person to pass a course.[41]

Giving students Cs can be a problem for the quality of working life for professors because of students' sometimes aggressive or passive-aggressive responses to receiving the grade. Remember, most of these students were routinely given As and Bs in high school, and therefore developed views of themselves as outstanding or 'special,' rather than average.[42] They are likely to say, 'But I worked so hard on that,' when awarded a grade of anything less than an A or B. The truth is likely that they worked hard the night before, cramming to study or pulling an all-nighter both to research and to write an essay that was supposed to involve intensive study, forethought, library time, and at least several weeks of preparation.

Students, professors, counsellors, and administrators now deal with these contradictions and tensions every day, yet few are willing to speak up. Some may simply not have the institutional memory to know that things used to be different; some may fear for their jobs; some may feel it is not their place to say anything; some may not realize that the problems they experience are widespread; some may not like to suggest that there are serious problems with their raison d'être; and others may not want to be branded as cynics. However, because we have the institutional memory to recognize that the status quo is in crisis, we feel we have a responsibility to speak up on these matters, even though some other professors won't, if only because of the heartache and anguish that we see many students going through. This is so for all students, from disengaged through engaged, for all have to cope in some way with this mixed-up system. Accordingly, we also feel it incumbent upon us to report on the social and economic relevance of our own academic research and expe-

rience with this system, which points to the new roles that higher education plays in contemporary society, of which most people – especially
students and parents – are largely unaware.

Credentialism and Academic Disengagement

Motivating people to sit still in schools and engage in regimented,
formal learning has been a perennial problem for educators. Such an
activity seems to be unnatural, and some people have an innate or tem-
peramental difficulty doing it. In fact, attempts to establish the mass
educational system that we now take for granted were fraught with difficulties from the beginning in getting children to show up in the first
place and to continue to show up thereafter. Primary-school enrolments
in the nineteenth century were low and sporadic, and the few schools in
existence found it difficult to get children to attend regularly. Many parents in the agricultural-based society of the time did not support compulsory education, in part because they needed their children's labour to
sustain the material well-being of the family. Even by 1901, although
efforts to implement compulsory education had been underway for two
decades in many provinces, the average daily attendance in primary
schools was only 60 per cent.[43]

Canada eventually established a compulsory educational system to the
age of sixteen, producing six-fold increases in enrolment to that age
between 1900 and 1950,[44] although enrolments would drop when youth
labour was needed, as in the Second World War.[45] As shown in figure 1.1,
by 1950, about 40 per cent of mid- to late teens were attending school
full-time, signalling that the de jure (legal) efforts at compulsory education were producing the de facto (practical) requirement of educational
credentials that we now take for granted for those older than the compulsory age (i.e., although young people are legally required to continue
their educations only to the age of sixteen, most stay in school because of
the practical requirement of gaining credentials for workplace entry).

However, the hollowness of this de facto, pragmatic requirement to
gain credentials undermines teachers' efforts to get their students' full
attention in academic learning and skills development. Most students
feel compelled to stay in school, but there is also a widespread sense that
much of what goes on there is irrelevant to their futures. Certainly, many
students feel that school activities are irrelevant to their immediate lives.
Young people now have many more interesting and pleasurable distractions, against which book learning does not stand a chance except

among a few outstanding students dismissed by the student culture as 'brains' or 'nerds.' Indeed, at the risk of homogenizing all students, mainstream student culture presents itself as a critical mass to secondary-school teachers – and increasingly university professors – in its general disinterest in content and passive resistance to scholastic effort.[46] Many teachers sense this and respond accordingly to these pressures (rather than to the bright students), depending on the culture of the school in which they work.[47] This is one reason why high schools can vary so much in quality: if the administrative culture does not define and defend standards for teachers, students will do so – generally with the principle of least resistance and effort.

Speaking to the increasing distractions that divert students from engaging themselves in academic study and acquiring the basis of a cultural literacy needed for one generation to transmit knowledge to the next, an English professor from Emory University recently wrote in the *Chronicle of Higher Education*, a widely read weekly for American academics and administrators,

[Today's students] aren't less intelligent than their precursors – as IQ scores show – and earlier generations, too, struggled with traditional subjects. But they've taken more courses than previous cohorts, and they have more money and access than ever before. Why hasn't their knowledge level kept pace? In part, because of the new leisure habits of teens and young adults. … the more time young adults devote to activities like sending e-mail messages [and other technology-based leisure activities], the less time they devote to books, the arts, politics, and their studies. Time has proved the formula. In the 1990s the gurus and cheerleaders of technology promised that the horizon of users would expand to take in a global village, and that a digital era would herald a more active, engaged, and knowledgeable citizenry, with young adults leading the way. It hasn't happened. Instead, youth discourse has intensified, its grip on adolescence becoming ever tighter, and the walls between young adults and larger realities have grown higher and thicker.

College professors complain about the result, noting the disaffection of students from their course work and the puny reserves of knowledge they bring into the classroom. But they hesitate to take a stand against mass culture and youth culture, fearful of the 'dinosaur' or 'conservative' tag. The disengagement of students from the liberal-arts curriculum is reaching a critical point, however. And the popular strategy of trying to bridge youth culture and serious study – of, say, using hip-hop to help students understand literary classics … hasn't worked. All too often, the outcome is that important works are dumbed down to trivia, and the leap into serious study never happens. The middle ground between adolescent life and intellectual life is disappearing, leaving professors with ever more stark options.[48]

When there are no standards defined by an administrative overseer – as would be the case when standardized examinations define the knowledge and skills that should be mastered at each level of education – what sets in is the 'disengagement compact,' a term coined by George Kuh, director of the National Survey of Student Engagement (NSSE). This tacit agreement between teachers and students is 'I'll leave you alone if you leave me alone. That is, I won't make you work too hard (read a lot, write a lot) so that I won't have to grade as many papers or explain why you are not performing well.'[49] In this compact, students get higher grades through pestering, or the threat of it, rather than by actually doing the required work or working at a level once required of university students. Not all teachers engage in this compact, but it seems to be spreading, certainly through high schools, and increasingly at universities. This agreement may also be stronger and more widespread in the United States than in Canada, but Canada's higher levels of disengagement in the NSSE research suggest likewise. The disengagement compact has been cited as a symptom of the 'breakdown of social responsibility for learning – on the part of faculty members who allow students to get by with far less than maximal effort, and on the part of students who are not taking full advantage of the resources institutions provide.'[50] This has also been called the 'mutual non-aggression pact.' According to Richard H. Hersh and John Merrow, 'the glue that keeps the pact intact is grade inflation: easy As for merely acceptable work and Bs for mediocre work.'[51]

If they hope to avoid or combat the disengagement, teachers can react by 'getting tough,' but they will bear the consequences personally if they do not have administrative support in a commercialized setting where students are increasingly seen as 'customers,' who, in the logic of commercialism, are always right. Some schools make it clear from the outset that the practice will not be tolerated; others blatantly pander to students' desire to be rewarded for little effort.

How well are teachers and schools doing in 'holding the line?' It appears that the battle is not going well, according to another article in the *Chronicle of Higher Education*. 'Homework? What Homework?' surveys concerns raised on the campuses of some of the best Canadian and

American universities.[52] It is clear that universities in the United States (and in Canada too) ask less of students than they did several decades ago.

The old rule of thumb was that students should spend at least two hours of class preparation for each hour spent in class ('the two-hour rule'). Accordingly, given a normal five-course load and three hours of lecture per week per course, time spent in class and preparing for it should constitute the equivalent of a full-time job. However, as noted in the introduction, recent research from the NSSE indicates that students at most American universities are doing far less work on their courses: only slightly better than 10 per cent of students put in twenty-five hours or more hitting the books to stay on top of their classes. Even the more recent watered down expectation of one hour of preparation for each hour of class is apparently now met by about half the students.[53] The recent *Maclean's* issue on Canadian university students supports this figure. In that issue, 'The Average Student: SWF, 22, Some Debt, Seeks Degree, Job' gives a statistical summary of the typical Canadian university student, who can earn (an inflated grade of) a B to B+ by spending about seventeen hours per week in all aspects of out-of-class course preparation and completion, which translates to the intellectual demands of a BA requiring no more time than a part-time job would.

Surveys of student engagement like the NSSE began only recently, but have already detected the progressive decline just noted, suggesting that there has been an ongoing slide of effort for some time: those doing eleven or more hours per week of class preparation in American universities declined in just two years, from 64 per cent in 2000 to 56 per cent in 2002 (with *preparation* defined as 'studying, reading, writing, rehearsing, and other activities related to [their] academic program').[54]

The NSSE data upon which the percentages in the *Chronicle of Higher Education* article are based were drawn from hundreds of thousands of students from hundreds of American (and increasingly Canadian) schools, so such findings must be taken seriously. Moreover, these findings are supported by another large-scale American survey study, *The American Freshman*, quoted at the beginning of this chapter. Questions from this latter survey on time spent studying during the last year of high school were introduced to the survey in 1987, and this survey has been tracing a decline since. In the late 1980s, about half the students reported spending six or more hours *per week* studying and doing homework, *for all of their courses*. By 2002, this figure was down to one-third.[55] This means that two out of three high school seniors in the United States who made it into university (the cream of the crop?) were studying only about one hour *per week* for each of their courses. A full one in six reported spending less than one hour per week on *all* of his or her courses combined, doubling in fifteen years the percentage reporting doing virtually no work out of class.

Remember, these were the students who made it into American institutions of higher education, and were freshmen at the time of the surveys. This state of affairs raises two disturbing questions: by what standards can one graduate from American high schools and be accepted into an American university, and what are the rest of American high school students doing who do not make it into college or university?[56] Should we in Canada be smug in a belief that Canadian schools are not experiencing the same trends?

In 2004, eight Canadian universities, including the University Western Ontario and the University of Toronto, participated in the NSSE.[57] Results showed that these Canadian universities scored lower than the U.S. national average on all indicators: level of academic challenge, active and collaborative learning, student–faculty interaction, enriching educational experiences, and supportive campus environment.[58] The president of Western explained the poorer Canadian performance by noting the '40-percent difference in per student funding, when compared to the U.S.'[59] Although this funding difference may well contribute to student disengagement in Canada, it does not account for the system-wide problem of low student engagement in *both* Canada and the United States, because American universities have a serious student disengagement problem, even with their better funding. In short, the roots of student disengagement do not lie with funding levels, although poor funding likely exacerbates it (e.g., by creating larger class sizes and greater student–faculty ratios).[60]

Our own published research supports the claim that this is a systemic problem. One longitudinal study following students from the beginning of their first year to the end of their third year in the early 1990s found that students who were bright (having an IQ of 120+) actually became more alienated while at university, and did not find courses challenging or providing sufficient incentives for them to learn to their potentials.[61] Moreover, this research found no correlation between IQ and grades (except in the business school). Apparently, the courses these students took were largely effort-based – rewarding those who actually showed up for class and studied for tests – thereby catering to mediocrity rather the excellence. In such an unstimulating environment, many bright students reported doing the minimum required to get a 'decent' mark, and engaged their efforts elsewhere: reading extensively outside of their courses, working to pay their expenses, or simply having a good time.

Readers may justifiably ask why professors do not simply teach to the bright students and maintain the integrity of their courses (teaching to the 'top half' of the class). Some do, as we have done, but it is usually done at one's own peril because it usually means putting in an inordinate amount of time with students (a) who are unprepared for, or incapable of doing, higher-level work (or what used to be standard university-level work), or (b) who have been conditioned to expect high grades for little effort. At the same time, these professors can develop reputations as being 'unreasonable,' receive poor teaching evaluations, and have to deal with student misbehaviour ranging from passive aggressiveness in classes through to outright aggressiveness when students insist on higher grades or when they fill out course evaluations. In sociology, a lot of students believe they can get by with the 'opinions' they brought with them to university; such students simply refuse to incorporate new information into their assessments and understandings of the world. Change (of opinion) makes them uncomfortable, and those who challenge them to change their views are seen as 'bad' teachers. In the 'feel good' culture of the day, anything that demands change, even of ideas about how the world works, can produce discomfort, which is to be avoided.

As we shall explain in the next chapter, professors are 'in the front line trenches' in the increasingly adversarial environment of the contemporary Canadian university. Those who go against the trend of providing easier courses and giving higher grades can expect a number of unpleasant encounters with students, and sometimes with their parents.[62] At one extreme, the professor as 'lawyer' has to deal with some students who are seasoned grade-mongers and who will pester profs incessantly, sometimes resorting to objectionable and threatening behaviour, ranging from verbal abuse to physical threats (stalking, or in some rare cases in the United States, being shot by disgruntled students). At the other extreme, the professor as 'social worker' has to deal with some students who just do not have the ability to pass their courses, let alone the maturity or emotional stability, and have to be told this for the first time. These are difficult things to handle effectively, and professors are not trained for it. The plain truth is that universities were not originally intended for just anyone who had the grades and the money to gain admission. But with today's grade inflation at high schools and certain accessibility policies to universities, the original intent is changing and producing the consequences we describe.

All signs point to academic disengagement beginning before university as a learned behaviour, probably during high school, but even in primary school.[63] An important study carried out in the United States supports this view, but warrants detailed coverage, lest it appear that all the blame should be placed on high school teachers and administrators. We also invite the reader to gauge the extent to which this is likely characteristic of the Canadian system. American psychologist Laurence Steinberg published the findings of a ten-year study of some twenty thousand American students, drawn from nine high schools, in *Beyond the Classroom: Why School Reform Has Failed and What Parents Need to Do.*[64] It sheds considerable light on the disengagement problem, with Steinberg arguing that its greatest source is not schools per se, but rather parents and peers. On the one hand, he argues, there is apathy among a large segment of parents, one-third of whom have no idea how their children are doing in school. On the other hand, peer culture tends to demean academic success as something for 'brains,' so the highest-achieving students – 10 per cent of the student body – often find themselves marginalized from peer culture. Another 20 per cent report that they do not try to get higher marks because they are afraid of what their friends will think of them. In other words, Steinberg argues that there is little point in trying to reform high schools when so many students feel pressured from their peers to put out little effort, and so many parents do not support their children to engage themselves in school.

Steinberg estimates that about 40 per cent of American high school students are disengaged, meaning that they are simply 'going through the motions' at school.[65] Apparently, these high schools do not weed out disengaged students, but merely pass significant numbers on to universities, as we have seen. Here is how he characterized the situation:

> The stereotyped portrayals of disenfranchised teenagers in the classroom that we have become so accustomed to seeing in film and on television are not, it turns out, exaggerations. True, most students report that they attend classes regularly – only about 10 percent cut classes routinely ... But at the same time, it is clear that when they are in school, a huge proportion of students are physically present but psychologically absent. According to their own reports, between one third and 40 percent of students say that when they are in class, they are neither trying very hard nor paying attention. Two thirds say they have cheated on a test in the past year. Nine out of ten report that they have copied someone else's homework.[66]

Steinberg goes on to note that only about 20 per cent of high school students are actually over their heads intellectually, especially in math and science classes. For the rest, disengagement is 'a response to having too little demanded of them and to the absence of any consequences for failing to meet even minimal requirements.'[67] At first blush, it appears that schools are to blame because of low standards and expectations. However, Steinberg argues that schools are caught in a downward spiral, with a dropping of standards and consequences as a response to student disengagement. When a critical mass of students has a mindset established by an anti-school peer culture and apathetic parents, schools respond by trying to accommodate them in order to avoid widespread dropout.

Roots of Student Disengagement

Although Steinberg does not consider this possibility, the point raised earlier about trying to push everyone through the educational system needs to be reiterated here as the chief cause of systemic student disengagement. A generation ago, these disengaged students would simply have quit, been failed, or been expelled. Schools are now under pressure to prevent dropouts, so they have little choice but to lower standards and expectations when they have large numbers of disinterested or low-ability students. The United States boasts that 90 per cent of young people now earn a high school diploma or the General Education Development certificate (GED) equivalent (by age twenty-six, however), but one has to wonder at what cost to academic standards and at what expense to the education of the more able and motivated students.[68]

To set the context for this general climate of academic disengagement, Steinberg calculates that the average American high school student spends only about 15 per cent of his or her time on academic learning. The typical teen has about 120 waking hours per week, of which 25 hours are taken up with personal care and upkeep and another 60 are devoted to miscellaneous activities like socializing (20–25 hours), a part-time job (15–20 hours), extra-curricular activities (10–15 hours), and television viewing (10–15 hours). While the average school week is about 30–35 hours, only 40 per cent of time in school is actually spent on academic activities and only about 4 to 5 hours per week is spent on homework and independent reading. In reality, then, only about 15 per cent of waking hours are actually spent on academic learning that would foster cognitive-intellectual development and skills acquisition. According to Steinberg, academic disengagement is a prime reason why American students lag behind those in many other countries: the average American teen does about 4 hours of homework per week, while in some countries this is the amount done *per day*.

How does Canada compare to the United States? One study estimated that 55 per cent of grade 12 students in 'advanced' (university-bound) programmes put seven or more hours per week into their homework.[69] This percentage compares favourably with figures reported from the freshman surveys at the time (the late 1980s), in which it was found that about half of American high school seniors put in six or more hours per week on homework, suggesting that there was slightly less disengagement among potentially university-bound Canadian students.

When we look to how much time the 'average' Canadian high school student (i.e., not necessarily the university-bound ones) puts into homework, in comparison with Steinberg's estimate (about four to five hours of time per week on homework), we find from that about half of those in grades 9 through 12 do six hours or less of homework per week.[70] These figures suggest that the typical Canadian high-school student is about the same as the average American student in effort devoted to academic performance.

Mandating such low levels of effort with inflated grades gives the message that students do not need to try harder to improve themselves intellectually, along with the reading, writing, and verbal skills that underpin intellectual acuity. Instead of requiring high school students to exercise independent intellectual effort in digesting material, high schools typically engage in 'spoon-feeding.' The spoon-feeding approach to education (which complements 'helicopter parenting,' discussed in chapter 4) – in which everything is covered in class and students do not have to prepare for classes by reading and thinking about material in advance – is more understandable (but still not condonable) at the high school level where about half the students are of below-average intelligence (by definition, half the population is average or below on a normal curve). However, expectations to be spoon-fed are spreading to universities as more students who have been coddled, regardless of their intelligence, continue their educations at university. While some technological innovations may increase student engagement, others may not. For example, professors who post PowerPoint notes on course websites may simply be contributing to this problem. These forms of spoon-feeding, old and new, contribute significantly to disengagement and are the source of endless aggravation to university professors who attempt to maintain standards. One colleague who was posting her lecture notes on her course website reached her tipping point when students complained that she took the lecture notes off the website too soon – one month after a given lecture!

There are no easy solutions to disengagement and lower standards leading to grade inflation. Any solutions require a widespread understanding of the problem and a determination to address it. However, more students are being *pushed* into Canadian universities today than was the case in their parents' generation. Consequently, the student body, with the exception of fully engaged students, tends to be more extrinsically motivated and instrumental in their approach to their studies. Because they do not see a direct link between their course materials, assignments, tests, and potential jobs, they are less likely to value the intrinsic worth and practical use of their courses, and instead to obsess more about the outcome of courses (grades) than about learning. In other words, partially engaged and disengaged students tend to be motivated more by the promise of high grades rather than the love of learning, and they see their university courses as stepping stones to something in the future, rather than deriving intrinsic satisfaction from the potential learning experiences of the moment. This orientation has been referred to as 'degree purchasing,' and in a recent study of Canadian university students has been found to be related to 'poor study habits, the use of resistance strategies in classrooms, low positive affect, and poor course performance.'[71] 'Resistance strategies' in this research are thought to be a 'form of passive or maladaptive coping method' that involve 'disruptive behaviour or disengagement in the classroom' and getting revenge on teachers through their course evaluations. There is a concern that having large numbers of 'degree purchasers' in a classroom can have a contagious effect on other students and 'poison the attitudes and behaviours of other students.'[72]

With an understanding of the new realities of university life, we can now discuss these new functions of higher education.

The New Functions of Higher Education

Figure 1.1 shows how the current generation of students faces circumstances that are far different from those faced by previous generations, including their parents' baby boom generation. When baby boomers came of age during the 1960s and 1970s, only about two-thirds of fifteen- to nineteen-year-olds were in school (mainly high school), and only a handful of those in their early twenties were in school full time (about

10% of males and 5% of females, including those enrolled in universities *and* community colleges). Thus, in the coming-of-age experience of parents of current students, few went to university and only about two-thirds completed high school. And while the world has changed considerably, one question is whether the university should change to meet the 'new' student, or should the old standards be maintained. Or is there a happy middle ground to be discovered? We consider these options in the chapters to follow.

As already noted, commentaries on the current educational system and its consequences often overlook the fact that those who were not interested in staying in school in past generations – especially males –left school to do something else, like work at agricultural and industrial jobs. Moreover, in contrast to the current generation, those who left could generally find employment that paid a wage that at least kept them out of poverty and at most allowed them to achieve financial independence from their parents. In addition, this employment was more likely to be at the bottom rung of a career ladder, and the gap between youth and adult wages was far less than it is today.[73] Today, starting at the bottom in most jobs is far less likely to lead up any job ladder; increasingly, educational credentials (including multiple post-secondary degrees and certificates) determine career progress. As we see in chapters 3 and 4, the earning power and job prospects of contemporary youth are far less promising than they were for their parents' generation when they were young, especially if they do not obtain a university credential.[74]

This last point is crucial to current arguments that more young people today are going to university because they 'choose' to do so. While undoubtedly true for some students, we argue that many more students would prefer to take secure, well-paying jobs if such jobs were available to them. Given the choice between having a good job now and getting on with their lives, as opposed to postponing their transition to adulthood by going to school year after year while accumulating debts, with little guarantee of a secure future, most would sensibly choose the good job. For those who believe that pursuing a higher education is a 'pure choice' option for all, we challenge them to explain why this 'choice' made by so many young people today was not made by as many of previous generations, especially their parents'. Certainly, some do choose freely to attend universities, especially in the liberal arts programmes, for the sake of pure learning. These are the students who are 'pulled' into the university system. However, there are also many – and probably more – who do so because of pressures that have little to do with learning and that 'push' them into the system, including the social cachet of having a degree.

As we argue, now we are trying to push as many young people as possible through the educational system for as long as possible. This has been the case for high schools for some time and is increasingly the case for universities. Now, many young people are under intense pressure to stay in the higher-educational system, even if they are not interested in school, do not wish to grow intellectually through formal learning, or have no idea about what they should be doing with their time. Those who are not interested in school are less likely to learn at the specified pace and are more likely to fall behind in acquiring skills, creating an ever-worsening situation for them, their teachers, and their classmates as they take up space, waste time, and drag standards down. Now we have a whole new set of problems with which to deal: (a) how to motivate students who are not interested in learning or who do not think that they should be attempting to grow intellectually; (b) how to manage large numbers of students efficiently, yet compassionately; and (c) what to do with those who have been motivated at lower levels by unrealistic rewards (with high grades that do not reflect their abilities) or false promises (with hopes of high-paying careers they will never achieve).

All three problems contribute to the two interrelated phenomena of academic disengagement and grade inflation. However, pushing so many people through high school and into colleges and universities has also altered the basic function of the university.[75] In the past, an important function was largely performed by high schools: sorting people out by abilities and interests, and ostensibly pointing them in the right direction, even if it meant non-educational paths. In the past, universities took a portion of these pre-sorted people and further refined their intellectual abilities and interests, with many climbing to important positions in society. Today, however, universities find themselves trying to do both things at the same time – sort all students by abilities and interests, *and* preparing a subset of them for subsequent careers. These two roles do not work well in unison; instead, the sorting function can often take precedence, requiring two ancillary functions to deal with the over-demand for university credentials from large numbers of unprepared students. These two additional functions are (a) weeding a certain number of students out and (b) 'cooling out' those who have been weeded.

Sorting, Weeding, and Cooling

The emergence of these new functions – sorting, weeding, and cooling – points to the key problem with this increasingly illogical system of education. The root is in the large numbers of 'over-promised' students, who have been told that if they simply stay in school, they will succeed.[76] These students are then passed through high school with minimal preparation for the rigours of advanced, independent learning found in universities of the past, essentially eliminating high school's sorting function. Consequently, instead of taking the time to properly prepare those students with 'university potential' to read, write, speak, and think at that level, teachers often give them inflated grades and a pat on the back, along with the rest who do not have that potential or 'smarts.' The inflated grades of those with university potential may still differentiate them for those who do not have it (although not as well as in the past), but they have been over-rewarded for substandard work in the process. Many of our students confess to this fault and remark how easy – and unchallenging – high school was for them. While they essentially got a free ride, they respect neither their schools nor their teachers for doing so. In short, these practices have a very negative impact on contemporary universities, which must now deal with an oversupply of 'unsorted' students with high expectations and unrealistic estimates of their own abilities.

The result of this development is that universities now assume the same type of sorting, weeding, and cooling functions once carried out principally by high schools. These functions can be summarized as follows:

Sorting involves determining who is certified to go where, optimally done through assessments of ability and interest, and gauging of motivation and effort. High schools now pass on more people who are not sure what they are good at or what they want do, rather than taking the time to help them figure those things out before they proceed to university. One culprit here is the middle-class notion that anything less than a white-collar professional career is a sign of personal failure, a notion that blinds students, teachers, and parents alike to alternatives like the trades.

Weeding involves reducing the sheer numbers of people who want to reach the highest levels, which are mainly professional and business schools that lead to lucrative careers. This may sound like a cruel function, but it is a necessary and inevitable one if only by virtue of the fact that there is simply not enough room at these high levels for all who want access, as we shall illustrate in chapter 5. Several waves of school reform have had the goal of more 'fairly' weeding out people on the basis of ability rather than on parents' wealth, but this has not happened to the extent hoped. Some policymakers have also hoped that educational credentials would expand markets by their sheer presence, but that has not occurred. In fact, most credentials earned in universities can yield only value-added salaries within existing economic organizations like government bureaucracies and corporations. Only business degrees and some applied degrees will actually increase economic productivity, after excluding the credentials a person holds and the place where the work is done.[77]

Finally, *cooling* is the cruellest function of all, but necessary for educational systems to maintain their legitimacy in the eyes of the public. Cooling refers to dealing psychologically with the 'over-promised' students, easing them out of the system by diminishing their expectations, and it is a function especially necessary for students who have been promoted beyond the limits of their abilities and motivations. Cooling is aided by grading curves, which bring high-flying secondary school grads down to earth, beginning with their first midterms (what universities call the 'grade drop,' which is between 15 and 20% at universities like Western).[78] Universities that still grade by this old system bring many erstwhile A students down to a C average, from which they must now climb by increasing their effort and honing their abilities. Those who are unwilling to do this will not survive the university experience, especially those who are 'unteachable' – who have an unrealistically high assessment of themselves and their abilities, and who are therefore indignant when criticized in any way. In the past, when high schools used the same grading curves as universities (where a C meant 'average' and was therefore commonplace, while As were the exception), this was not an issue, because very few students came to universities with the (false) assumption that they were outstanding. Most now apparently do.

Cooling is also carried out by counsellors and administrators who steer ambitions to more realistic goals and by professors who must play the bad guy and tell students that there are 'no more deals' to be made with teachers to get easy grades or to have grades arbitrarily raised. The truth is that cooling is often done for the good of students who should have been told these things long before they went to university. In other words, a certain number of students reached their 'level of incompetence'[79] at an earlier grade, but were not told so because of factors that keep as many people as possible in school. And, of course, cooling is also done to legitimize the university system to the wider society. After all, if individuals are made to blame themselves for their failures, then the system that failed them escapes culpability. However, universities did not willingly take on this function – it has been thrust upon them by the factors already mentioned. Instead, having to cool out large numbers of students constitutes a major distraction from their original missions, especially the pursuit of knowledge for its own sake.

Rather than expending their scarce resources cooling students out, universities should be using these resources to 'warm them up' to reach their full intellectual potentials. However, in the current climate, this is likely to happen for only a minority of students. In the final chapter, we explore the question of how the 'cooling' function can be changed to a 'warming' one.

The Obsession with High Grades: Grade Inflation Up Close

The easiest way to 'warm' students up is to give them higher grades for their efforts. This is precisely what high schools have done in both Canada and the United States, as we have been discussing in other terms. In this section, we explore this practice more thoroughly, showing how it has made life in the ivory tower far more difficult as more and more students have arrived with inflated expectations of the return they will receive for their efforts.

As noted, before the credentialist era, it was customary to peg 'satisfactory' or 'average' with a grade of C. This is clearly no longer the practice in North American high schools, and increasingly in universities, especially in certain programs and in the upper year levels. More and more, the B has become the average grade assigned in many university courses, and in some cases A averages are now awarded. At American Ivy League institutions, the situation is worse. For example, Harvard University awards about half of its students As, twice as many as in the 1960s.[80] We examine in chapter 5 how Princeton University has begun the fight to reverse the trend.

Some people have reacted to these trends by arguing that students are now smarter than in the past, or at least better prepared. But are they? The answer is apparently no, for numerous reasons. One is that grades vary significantly among faculties, with those in the humanities receiving significantly higher grades than those in the sciences, so the 'student-now-smarter' logic would mean that humanities majors are smarter than science majors. A second reason is that standardized indicators like the Scholastic Aptitude Test (SAT), American College Testing (ACT), and GRE have all shown stability or decline.[81]

However, this is the wrong question to ask if we stay with the traditional meaning of letter grades, where a C designates a satisfactory performance reflecting the average for members of each class. Even in a hypothetical class of geniuses, as some might think of Harvard recruits, there is an average, with variation on both sides that reaches to outstanding and substandard geniuses. What would be satisfactory in this class of geniuses might be outstanding in a class of students of normal intelligence, but a C would still designate a satisfactory or average performance among the reference group of geniuses. While geniuses do not likely think of themselves as average, the fact remains that most of them will be average when compared to other geniuses.[82] When high schools tell large numbers of students that they are outstanding, they will have a similar difficulty when they move on to university, where virtually everyone else has been told the same thing. But in this new reference group, there will still be an average, and unless it is pegged at a C, grade compression (the narrowing of the range between good, very good, excellent, and outstanding grades) makes it more difficult to distinguish students who are truly capable of outstanding performances in this reference group, for there is very limited variability between an A– and an A+.

Grade compression, sometimes called grade conflation, thus refers to the granting of too many As and Bs, and too few Ds and Fs, with the result that it becomes increasingly difficult to distinguish 'outstanding' students from merely 'good' students, 'mediocre' students, and so on.[83] The effect is that information is squeezed out of the system, which taken to its logical conclusion means that grades 'will yield no information whatsoever.'[84] Grade inflation differs from monetary inflation because it has a ceiling (100%), whereas monetary inflation can continue to increase indefinitely but keep a relative comparison among original prices.[85] For this reason, some people prefer the term *grade compression* to *grade inflation* to more accurately describe what is happening.

Not all schools have given into the grade-inflation trend, and variation can be found among high schools as well as universities. Universities would routinely need to make corrections for incoming students' grades because of variation in high school grading practices, but such corrections are apparently not a common practice in Canada.[86] When universities do not differentiate among the graduating averages of high schools, students who come from high schools with higher standards are disadvantaged, and weaker students who arrive with inflated grades will likely run into more difficulties adjusting to the higher standards of universities.

Referring to the state of affairs in Canada, our colleague Professor McQuillan (whom we've already cited), notes the following in a working paper for the Council of Ontario Universities:

> While grade inflation and compression are problems that the education system is struggling with in many settings, universities face an additional problem. Local variation in [high school] grading practices casts further doubt

on the reliability and validity of the grades applicants present to the universities. Inconsistent grading practices between and within schools may over-
whelm what little variance remains among students as a result of the
inflation and compression of grades that have occurred. The problem is
acute for applicants to arts and social sciences programs where the variation
in grading practices is further complicated by variation in the set of courses
on which the marks are based.[87]

Meanwhile, in the United States, a controversy is brewing over the
refusal of a growing number of high schools to provide class rankings to
university admissions offices. Over the past five years this trend has developed to the point where 40 per cent of American high schools no longer
provide such rankings, out of a concern that they hurt their second-tier
students. According to Alan Finder, writing for the *New York Times*, 'in a
cat-and-mouse game manoeuvring over admission to prestigious colleges
and universities, thousands of high schools have simply stopped providing that information, concluding it could harm the chances of their very
good, but not best, students.'[88] Some admissions offices respond by cal-
culating their own rankings for these high schools, or relying more on
standardized tests like the SATs. Clearly, university admissions offices do
not trust high school grades on their own, and without rankings or other
information that put a grade in context, the meaning of a grade
becomes unclear and a potentially poor basis for predicting how well the
student might do in university. High schools defend their actions by
pointing out that rankings create artificial distances between otherwise
comparable students. One high school official interviewed by Finder
reported that the last time rankings were handed out, it was one of the
worst days in her working life because she had to deal with dozens of sob-
bing students, adding that 'only one person is happy when you hand out
rank: the person who is No. 1.'[89]

The unevenness of admission policies also has regional implications in
Canada. Only about 20 per cent of those graduating from high schools
in Alberta have As, while over 40 per cent of those graduating Ontario
high schools do so (see the appendix for details).[90] Given that Alberta
high school students outperform students elsewhere in Canada, including Ontario, on international performance tests, there is a concern in
Alberta that their graduates are not competing on a level playing field
when applying for university acceptances, scholarships, and the like.
Accordingly, there has been a call for national grading standards.

At the very least, ignoring inflated high school grades for university admissions simply invites the more disengaged students to continue their bad habits. As we shall see, Canadian universities are also finding it increasingly necessary to provide their own entrance exams and remedial programmes,[91] a practice that has been common in the United States for some time. For example, some 40 per cent of professors recently surveyed in American universities indicated 'that most of the students they teach lack the basic skills for university-level work,' and over half reported that working with these students is stressful.[92] In a survey conducted at Western by the Student Council in the mid-1990s, over 90 per cent of professors disagreed with the statement that 'high school prepares students well for essay writing at university,' and even thought that most students do not have a strong grasp of the rules of grammar or the principles of style.[93]

The fact that American universities have been plagued with this problem for a longer period of time suggests that Canadian universities are on a similar road to more severe problems if we continue pushing students to go on to university without thinking about what they doing. Indeed, Canadian sociologist Scott Davies warns that the 'college for all' mentality that has been common in the United for some time has had the unintended consequence of giving high school students the idea that academic engagement and achievement are unimportant to their higher-educational chances, and that this appears to be happening in Canada as a result of our public relations efforts to encourage widespread post-secondary involvement. Consequently, just as we do, Davies argues that more and more of high school students in Canada who aspire to college or university attendance are ill-prepared for the challenge because they have low levels of academic engagement and interest.[94]

Variation can also be readily observed both within universities and between them, and as we now show between Western and the University of Toronto.

At our own university, Western, grade inflation has differentially affected faculties, and in our own faculty (Social Science), departments vary significantly.[95] Within Western as a whole, grades in first-year and general courses have been up in all the large faculties since the early 1990s, with the reporting faculties showing 10–20 per cent increases in students receiving As and Bs. For example, the Faculty of Arts went from 48.3 per cent As and Bs in first-year courses (and 11% Fs) in 1993–4 to 66.5 per cent (and 6.3% Fs) in 2002–3. Inflation was not as great in honours courses, but the percentage was already at a high ceiling, with figures consistently in the 70 per cent range (though there was a steady creep from 76.7 to 79.4). The Faculty of Science began and ended this same period with lower grades that followed the same pattern. In 1993–4, first-year students were awarded 41.2 per cent As and Bs, with a fairly steady year-by-year increase over the next decade to 58 per cent As and Bs. The percentage of Fs dropped from 15.3 to 9.5. Science honours courses inflated from 60.8 to 68.4 over this period. Thus, we can see the pattern reported in American studies that the arts are more promiscuous in their grading practices, but it is also clear that the sciences at Western are not immune to this looseness.

Within the Social Science Faculty, in the 1993–4 academic year, 36.1 per cent of students in introductory courses were awarded As and Bs, when all social science courses are considered together. By 2002–3, this figure had risen to 56.2 per cent receiving these grades, an average increase of 20 per cent. We see here that the Social Science Faculty was following the traditional grade guidelines until this period, but standards slipped from the early 1990s on, as they appear to have in other Canadian universities like the University of Calgary, and most universities in the United States (see the appendix for details). Honours courses had a similar pattern as found in arts, with As and Bs in the 70 per cent range. In our own department (Sociology), these figures increased from 35.4 per cent of introductory students receiving As and Bs in 1993–4, to a peak of 48.7 in 2002–3, but with considerable variation along the way (a low of 28.6% and a high of 61.8%). This fluctuation may reflect the department's conscious struggle with grade inflation in view of the explicit guidelines it had been following since the mid 1970s (more on these guidelines will be discussed shortly). Honours sociology courses were less generous than those reported for the above faculties, hovering in the low 60 per cent and high 50 per cent range over this period.

Economics is the only department in the Social Science Faculty at Western to have held the line over this period, keeping the percentage of As and Bs below 40 per cent in first-year courses. Interestingly, in a departmental meeting in 2003 whose minutes were posted on the Internet, a concern was discussed about their now anomalous position in relation to the other departments in the Social Science Faculty, with the worry that their lower assigned grades might be discouraging prospective economics majors. Apparently undaunted at the prospect of losing majors, the following motion was passed: 'That the distributions of final grades in Economics 020 sections for the 2003–04 academic year be required to approximate 40% As + Bs, 30% Cs, and 30% Ds with a maximum 45% As + Bs and that the chair will monitor the distributions in the second year courses.'[96]

Sure enough, the Economics Department has continued to hold the line on first-year courses, with a 34.9 per cent figure of As and Bs for 2004–5. However, economics is the most promiscuous of the departments/faculties examined thus far in assigning grades in honours courses, with the percentage receiving As and Bs rising from 77.9 in 1991–2 to 84.8 in 2004–5.

As mentioned, the Sociology Department has followed an explicit set of grade guidelines since the mid-1970s, as have other departments at Western. These guidelines have preserved the institutional memory of the traditional view of grade distributions forming a normal distribution around a C average, which roughly corresponds to the ECTS standards for grade distributions discussed in the appendix, at least for lower-year courses. According to these guidelines, the percentage of As and Bs in introductory sociology courses should lie in the range of 30–40 per cent, with averages to be in the range of 64–67 per cent. For upper-year courses, the percentage of As and Bs can rise to 50 per cent, but the average must remain within 66–70 per cent. Only in advanced honours courses (mainly fourth year) could B averages be awarded (73–77%), with a maximum of 80 per cent As and Bs.

While a wave of grade inflation hit many institutions in the 1990s, no single explanation seems to account for it. Certainly, the pressures from students coming from high schools with inflated grades had some effect. But another factor has already been mentioned, as offered by the former vice-president of Western, who told us that internal funding systems have rewarded departments financially for attracting and retaining students in upper-year courses, and the best way to do that is to give higher grades and ignore inadequacies in student performances.

A similar policy change produced a wave of grade inflation at the master's level at Western. The unofficial guidelines just discussed originally covered master's-level courses, specifying B averages (73–77%), but in the 1990s the Faculty of Graduate Studies imposed a cut-off of 78 per cent for funding to apply to all departments. In other words, if master's students today earn less than a B+ average, their funding will be cut off (teaching assistantships, scholarships, and the like). Needless to say, this makes it very difficult for faculty to grade graduate students according to the traditional guidelines, and we and other faculty have had a number of unpleasant experiences with indignant graduate students who feel 'entitled' to As in all of their awarded grades. They experience anything less as a personal insult.

In addition to this example of intra-university variation in grade inflation, we can also see inter-university variation, in this case showing how the University of Toronto (the U of T) contrasts with Western. The U of T has prided itself on its high standards for years, and in an effort to maintain its reputation as Canada's best university with a world-class ranking, is apparently making efforts to maintain the traditional standards that Western once endorsed.[98] The following is what one U of T professor posted on his course website to confront the problem head on:

> In order to get into the University of Toronto, most of you had to obtain very good marks in high school. In fact, as a group, your average high school mark is likely in the 80 percent (or higher) range. One of the most difficult things that happens to many first year students is that they suddenly find themselves getting marks that are uncomfortably lower than they are used to. Partly these low marks are due to increased difficulty of the classes, but they are also partly due to the University of Toronto's Marking Philosophy.
>
> Given this, I think it is important that we are clear with our students about what our philosophy is, and why we think it is a good one. You may also want to have your parents read this. They are also sometimes shocked by the lower marks, and some of that shock can be reduced by having them also understand our philosophy. In fact, you may even want them to read this *before* you write any midterms so that their expectations for your performance (and your expectations as well) are more appropriate.[99]

This instructor then goes on to explain the marking philosophy, stating that the primary goal of the marking scheme at the U of T is to differentiate between students, for example, the 'really good' and the 'pretty good' students. Referring to the traditional scheme, the instructor continues in plain language to make this point as clear as possible to the widest audience:

> When marking schemes were originally devised, the letter grade of C was meant to reflect average performance. Thus a student who put in the expected amount of work, and learned the material to an average level was expected to receive a C (approximately 65 percent). By placing the average mark at C there is plenty of room for above average students to score in the B range, and for the real stars to show their ability by scoring A range marks. Of course, the flip side of this is that below average students would score in the D range, and those students who did unsatisfactorily poorly are given an F.

In an effort to explain why the U of T does this, the instructor continues by noting that grade inflation has affected many other schools because they have been trying to keep their students 'happy': 'This is an easy thing to let happen. Students are happy when their marks are high, parents are happy when their kids' marks are high, and professors are happy when students and their parents are happy. Thus, by allowing the marks to rise everyone seems happy.'

We can see how a 'customer satisfaction mentality' threatens to creep into higher education, a problem we discuss in the next chapter.[100] This instructor goes on in an attempt to counteract this mentality, noting that grade inflation is not good for all students, even if there is more happiness spread around:

> Say we allow B range marks to now reflect average performance. This now means that we only have the A range for both the above average and the far above average students. This means we can no longer discriminate between above average and really fantastic students. Essentially, we would be punishing the really fantastic students, and these are the very students we should be encouraging.

In an attempt to appease the majority of students who will inevitably receive a C or less, the instructor goes on to write that professors at the U of T are obligated to make the course material sufficiently challenging to produce C averages, but there is 'no shame in getting Cs.' Students are then assured that graduate schools and employers know that 'a B level grade from University of Toronto is equivalent to As at many other schools.'[101]

This instructor should be applauded for taking a stand, as should the U of T. Perhaps it is easier to impose the traditional system there, but at Western it is not. Western too admits high school graduates with high grades, but no amount of cajoling will convince most of the thousands of students we've taught over the recent past that a C is acceptable, particularly because most students coming to Western expect to go on to a post-graduate programme. After years of aspiring to lucrative careers in business, law, medicine, and the like, all but the dullest know that they will not realize that dream with a C average, especially as they see the inflationary spiral continue to the point where a high A average is needed to be considered by even a teacher's college.

We sympathize with those students who have been given unjustifiably high grades in secondary school that feed unrealistic expectations about their future, and their ability to realize lofty goals, only to have them dashed at university. At the same time, there are other students who do not have lofty goals, but just want to get into a career in something they yearn to do, like teaching. We keep in touch with many students, so we have a good idea of their post-university experiences. One student's experiences exemplify the problem of grade inflation in the context of credentialism. This young man has good heart and simply wants to teach children. However, his average was not high enough to meet the cut-offs for teacher's colleges (these cut-offs vary, but are now often in the high 80% range), so he was not even short-listed in any teachers' colleges. Just a generation ago when a high school diploma and a one-year certificate sufficed to qualify for teaching primary school, he would have moved into a fine and rewarding career early in his adult life and do what he yearned to do, instead of taking courses year after year, hoping that a door would open for him. These days, like most others in their twenties, he must repeatedly adjust his plans to think about doing something that he may not be passionate about; he must manoeuvre his way through an often hostile and arbitrary university system; and he will take far longer to settle into a career – with a debt that can be the equivalent to a mini mortgage.

Some observers do not see a problem with grade inflation, saying that we could simply adjust our interpretation of grades accordingly. Certainly, this is the easiest position for university administrators to take, as in Harvard's case where the response was to do nothing about their grade inflation. Others argue that there are serious problems associated with grade inflation. Here are some of them.

One problem has been alluded to: the unfairness when grade inflation is not taken into account in student applications for admissions, scholarships, and the like. People in Alberta have a good case: it apparently has the highest standards in Canada and produces students who are among the best in international comparisons. To achieve this standard, high schools there have not been as guilty of allowing grade inflation to interfere with student engagement. In other words, educators in Alberta have lessened the problem of compressing students with different abilities into the same category, and they provide an example of how clear standards and honest feedback produce clear and superior results. Perhaps what is needed is increasing dialogue between provinces and provincial educational systems.

Comparing schools (or regions) with and without grade inflation helps bring a second problem into focus. Assigning higher grades simply for effort, or to motivate students to try harder, gives students false feedback about their ability. If we give high grades to all who try hard, but who do not improve their mastery of a subject, we are being dishonest and doing a disservice to them and the wider society. Their lack of mastery and learning will eventually show up, whether in comparisons like the Alberta–Ontario example, or if they move on to a higher level of education or manage to land a job actually expecting a highly skilled worker. Consequently, grade inflation is ultimately harmful to students who are given false feedback. Of course, when the disengagement compact becomes institutionalized and more broadly practised, the wider social system suffers.

The only students whom grade inflation seems to help are those at the very low end who either do not care enough to do any work or who do not have the requisite abilities to handle university-level material. However, it helps them only to gain a credential they do not deserve and may not be able to use because prospective employers may see through the façade (these people may join the underemployed, discussed in chapter 5). We are speaking here of students who would fail a course if higher standards were imposed, but who get a D or even a C instead of an F. In addition, there are those marginal students who should get a D in a course, but who get bumped up to a C as a result of the inflationary spiral. What works in their favour is a statistical phenomenon known as 'regression toward the average': their marks are pulled toward class averages, and many of those making their way through the system with little effort or interest, count on it. In addition, not only do they benefit from courses with higher average grades, but they benefit from the grade compression that goes with these inflated averages: just as higher grades become conflated and less distinguishable, so do lower grades (although there are now fewer of the latter). Every year, we deal with several students like this who play the odds to get by with the lowest acceptable marks, short of being rusticated. When they get too close to being expelled, they come begging for a D or a C, claiming that *we* would be the ones making them fail or delaying their graduation. Some readers may still be thinking that these drawbacks are not sufficient to attempt to reverse grade inflation. Pointing out the wider problems associated inflated grades may convince them.

The most obvious wider problem is that inflated grades can mask the failure of schools to actually teach effectively. This appears to be more of a problem in U.S. high schools, where school quality can vary widely because school resources are tied to the local tax base. For example, 'top' students from schools in poor districts may actually only have a performance and mastery level equivalent to poor students in an affluent district. Although this socio-economic variation in high-school quality applies to a lesser extent in Canada, we need to be vigilant about the possibility that our grade inflation, especially in university, is linked with years of underfunding. The 1990s were marked by shrinking budgets and rising grades. Consequently, Canadian universities may simply have been showing the effects of underfunding: assigning lower grades is far more 'expensive' than assigning high ones, and expectations were placed on them to increase the number of students who enrol and stay enrolled. This point may sound counter-intuitive, but low-achieving students (read: customers) require higher maintenance in day-to-day 'hand-holding' (e.g., having obvious things explained to them that are in the course outline), and more time must be spent in justifying their lower grades, with more detailed feedback on essays, or more time spent explaining to them in person why they received a lower mark on exams.

In turn, this failure of schools to deliver the promised product misleads stakeholders in the wider society, especially prospective employers. Being able to play the system to make your way through university may be good training for some jobs that do not require integrity, but it is not beneficial for jobs that require the ability to manage one's time and motivate oneself to complete tasks honestly and responsibly. The attendance and effort of many university students would get them fired if they were in the labour force; in many universities, sporadic attendance and minimal effort often have little or no consequences in grades. It is little wonder that many university graduates report high stress when they eventually do take on a full-time, permanent job.[102]

At the same time, we all know that many students are slipping through our courses with minimal learning and skills mastery, because in the large classes we have to teach, quality control is difficult, some students are willing to cheat,[103] and many have long since learned how to cram enough material when required (a 'just in time' or 'gulp-and-vomit' learning method). But the long-term harm is that the wider society thinks it is getting a higher return on its investment in education than is really so.[104] The wrong signals are sent to employers about the quality of some of our university graduates, and policymakers are misled about the value added by a surplus of university credentials. Put another way, we may not be producing the level and quality of human capital that employers and governments think we are. This simply feeds the inflationary spiral of credential inflation.

Conclusion

Several factors have combined to change the way university teachers teach and students learn. Credentialism has slowly crept into the way we prepare for the world of work, replacing the logic of apprenticeships, on-the-job training, and more coherent ways of entering the labour force. As the value of educational credentials inflated, more and more people were drawn into the educational system just to tread water in the sea of higher education. At the same time, education has become a panacea for dealing with issues in the transition to adulthood, like what to do with idle young people who are not (yet) needed in the workforce. It is now widely believed that everyone should stay in school as long as possible, but little thought is given to the implications of this approach for the schools themselves. To keep teenagers motivated, high schools have inflated grades, so more and more students assume that they have the scholarly potential to go as far as they like in university.

Everything hits the fan when they actually try to make their way through university. While it appears that universities are not effectively weeding out incompetent students, a certain percentage of the most egregious offenders are still being caught by the university grading system, after sailing through the high school grading system with flying colours. Not only are these hitherto 'top' students crushed by the experience of being weeded out, but the university system itself is changed by it. The university system is becoming bogged down by the need to weed out students who should have been told the truth earlier about their poor abilities or given the opportunity to develop their potentials. In short, while universities have always weeded out students, never before have they had to weed out so many who have been misled about their abilities and potentials.

The mandate of the undergraduate degree has in many ways become that of an instrumental filter by which people attempt to qualify for something else or prove something. In the meantime, the old mission of the university to impart knowledge and wisdom and to set the foundation for lifelong intellectual inquiry is given a back seat to other social agendas, demoralizing those who attempt to hold on to the old ideals. This is not the mere opinion of a couple of curmudgeonly professors complaining about 'students these days,' but is supported by evidence from a number of sources, some of which was provided above and more of which is provided in the remainder of this book.

2 The Professor as a Reluctant Gatekeeper

A recent incident mentioned in the introduction illustrates the frustration many professors experience in having to deal with classes over-crowded by students who don't want to be there. In January 2006, a professor at the University of Prince Edward Island made a deal with his over-crowded class in a course on the history of Christianity: those who voluntarily stopped coming to class and doing the course requirements would receive a final grade of 70 per cent in the course (a B-). The only 'assignment' for the voluntary dropouts was to pay their tuition for the course. One in five students took him up on the offer, giving us a unique, objective estimate from a natural experiment of the extent of student disengagement at that university. The professor defended his actions by saying that it was uncomfortable in the class with so many students, and the students who took the offer 'didn't want to be in the class anyway. They weren't going to learn much.' He further asserted that this sort of pact happens all the time, but he was 'just upfront with it.' The administration ordered him to recall the students who accepted the offer, and he was later fired.[1]

This chapter is written to convey an understanding of how some professors now experience their jobs as a result of recent changes in the university system. As David Livingstone and Doug Hart (professors at the Ontario Institute for Education) observe, universities have become the 'gatekeeper to the middle class.'[2] Among other responsibilities, playing this gatekeeping role has become a larger part of the professor's job. While the professor has always been charged with enforcing quality-control, this role has evolved into dealing with ever-increasing numbers of unprepared (unsorted) students who are trying to pass through the gate, as we saw in chapter 1. This function often stymies the quality-control portion of the professor's job, because there are more students who are not concerned with honestly and earnestly meeting the requirements for passing through the gate; instead, a critical mass do the minimum amount of work they can get away with, and still squeeze a 'decent' grade out of their profs.

As already noted, this group may involve all but the fully engaged 10 per cent of students in contemporary universities, and when professors teach hundreds of students each year, it becomes a great drain on their patience, enthusiasm, and job satisfaction. Indeed, it appears that many professors now experience their gatekeeping function as stressful when they have to mediate between the demands of disengaged students and the professional standards associated with teaching at the university level.

Professors have slowly been edged into roles that require them to engage in practices that do not coincide with the scholarly standards that define their disciplines. In many cases, these are the practices and standards that likely drew them to the profession in the first place, although more likely so in the humanistic disciplines than in the technological ones.[3] The humanistic disciplines are found in the Social Sciences and Arts and Humanities faculties, and have traditionally attracted intellectuals and those who aspired to become Renaissance-style scholars. The technological disciplines as found in the natural sciences tend to attract smart people who aspire to become technicians and scientists; although these disciplines certainly do not preclude intellectual forms of scholarship, they are apparently not the norm.

One crucial difference between these disciplines in the contemporary ivory tower is that the humanistic disciplines have burgeoned in good part because they have become a stepping stone to professional degrees or merely a qualifying degree for entry into the white-collar labour force. Some research suggests that the technological disciplines are not as affected by the disengagement trends we discuss here, although the trends are certainly there.[4] Apparently, the humanistic disciplines have not been as rigorous in their application of standards and have developed the reputation as a result of being easy, generally giving higher grades.[5] This reputation is apparently deserved in many cases, as university programmes have attempted to attract larger clienteles, and have therefore developed popular versions of their disciplines that are, in fact, easier to understand than the easiest versions of the natural sciences. Hence, we hear the social sciences disparaged as the 'so-so sciences,' and the natural sciences touted by the expression 'Go hard or go

social science.' However, the humanistic disciplines are no less sophisticated than the technological ones at the more commanding heights at
which professors prefer to function in their professional journals and
conferences.

But herein lies a problem for professors in the humanistic disciplines
that is apparently not as severe for professors in the technological disciplines: they find increasing pressure to teach students at the simpler
level of popular understanding while needing – and preferring – to function at the more sophisticated level. We return to this matter later in this
chapter, and in the concluding chapter, and simply ask readers to keep
this issue in mind as we discuss the job of the professor and the increasing difficulties experienced in transmitting knowledge to undergraduates, and inspiring them to grow intellectually.

How the New Functions Have Affected the Interpersonal Dynamics of Teaching and Learning: Faculty Disengagement

Our focus here is in how university professors have become the 'gatekeepers' of the credential society, regulating the allotment of credentials
among students, who are increasingly treated as customers. The difference between conventional customers, who may be interested in just
buying a pair of shoes, for example, and students in undergraduate programmes is that the latter are put in competition with each other and are
graded relative to each other, ostensibly around some notion of 'average'
(traditionally recorded as a C). Thus, continuing this analogy, if we follow the traditional guidelines laid out in the previous chapter, not everyone can buy a pair of quality shoes (the Fs), and most have to settle for
mediocre shoes (the Ds and Cs). Fewer than half of university 'customers' can get good or outstanding quality 'shoes.' Thus, the competition
for grades in universities is in its traditional form a classic zero-sum
arrangement, but it has two unintended consequences in the university,
especially to the extent that students now think of themselves, and are
treated, as 'customers.'

First, it is little wonder that grades have been inflated to create more
happy customers (as noted in the previous chapter, as many as 80 per
cent of students surveyed are now reporting receiving Bs and As in Canada and the United States; at universities in Canada, the institutional
reporting of As and Bs is 60–70 per cent and rising, depending on the
year level and institution).[6] In its simplest and purest form, a zero-sum
game results in as many winners as losers. However, now virtually all want

to be winners in the sense that they want to qualify for something above and beyond the undergraduate degree. Indeed, students are now typically coached throughout high school to think of themselves as winners, making professors' jobs that much more difficult than in the past, when students came in with lower (though realistic) grades and lower expectations about the return for their performance. Mediocre students especially have these expectations – no one wants to think of himself or herself as average, and most are told that they are 'special'[7] – so professors must break the news to them. Some students have not had to face real challenges in the past, where failures are experienced along with successes, so they will find it especially difficult to face challenges in university, and to deal with the consequences when they are anything but positive. So the stage is set for a confrontational or combative relationship from the very start.

Second, the zero-sum approach to teaching and evaluating students in the credentialing system puts students into competition with each other, increasing the tensions and conflicts between faculty and students, but also among students. This competition is the result of a grading system that assumes a normal distribution around an average, with equal numbers of successes (As and Bs) and failures (Fs and Ds). A different approach to education at all levels would be necessary to help every student in every course reach his or her potential, and there are methods proposed for doing this.[8] This is certainly the direction taken in most professional programmes, which are charged with bringing out the best in all the 'pre-sorted' students accepted into the programme. However, the zero-sum approach is now taken for granted in Canada and the United States (and elsewhere), so year after year teachers are faced with sorting out the winners and losers within a 'soft-sorting system' ('hard-sorting systems' will be discussed in chapter 5).

The soft-sorting systems of Canada and the United States give students false promises about how their educational efforts will pay off. These messages are given in an attempt to keep students in school, and to help universities keep enrolments growing, but they can do more harm than good in the long run. The implicit message is that the educational system leads to good jobs – even fantastic careers in law, medicine, and the professions commonly shown on popular television.[9] But the message is false because fewer than 10 per cent of the workforce hold such jobs, as we saw in the last chapter, yet some 90 per cent of grade 9 students assume that they will go to university en route to such careers.[10] Some have said that the system is 'over-promising' students.[11]

The reality is that not everyone can have a successful, lucrative, and rewarding career; indeed, few people will have one, if we define successful careers by upper-middle-class standards by which one must complete an undergraduate programme and move through a graduate or professional programme to a prestigious career. Still, people will reap some rewards of their educational achievements along the way: those finishing high school will make more money than those who do not; those earning an undergraduate degree will make more money than those who do not, and so forth. So while there are financial benefits to higher educations, the problem is that students are told to set their sights so unrealistically high that they often fail to fully benefit from the educational opportunities made available to them along the way. (We shall discuss the problem of misaligned ambitions in chapter 4.) This soft-sorting approach creates a new set of problems, including the requirement that university professors be the 'bad guys' in telling these over-promised students that they will not realize their dreams.

The role of the gatekeeping professor, and the conflict inherent in the role, can be illustrated using a currency analogy. Grades in courses can be likened to a form of currency; indeed, credentials represent an abstract form of capital.[12] Students vie to receive as much currency as they can in each course, as represented in grades. If, for the sake of argument, we peg 1 per cent to one dollar, the goal of each student is to get as many of the $100 that could theoretically be allotted to him or her (the equivalent of 100%, the maximum obtainable). With the grading-curve logic employed in universities following the traditional model of grading, averages must come out within a certain range, like 66–70. Let us say that someone is teaching a course in which there are eighty students and the final course average is expected to be around 68 per cent. This means that in terms of grade-currency, a teacher has 5440 grades, or dollars, to distribute (68% x 80 students = 5440 grades). What that teacher cannot do is distribute, say 7,200 grades, or dollars, because that would produce an average of 90 per cent, and would put that professor's account in the red.

There are two classical modes of evaluation in education: outcome-based and criterion-referenced.[13] The outcome-based system sets performance indicators that are the same for all students, while the criterion-referenced assigns students positions along a continuum so they are judged relative to each other. The system employed in undergraduate programmes is criterion-referenced, while that employed in professional programmes is more likely to be outcome-based. In order to advance in the outcome-based system, students must essentially reach their potential, as defined at that level of education. In medical schools, this means becoming a competent doctor, so not only would a 90 per cent class average be accepted, it would be expected. After all, we do not want our future surgeons knowing only 68 per cent of the material on, say, anatomy.

In contrast, most undergraduate programmes are based on the criterion-referenced model. Apparently, we *do* find it acceptable for those in the mass education system to only know 68 per cent of the material in, for example, math or sociology courses (suggesting that we do not respect these latter disciplines as much as much as the professions, an attitude that is not lost on students). However, the key difference between the two examples is that the student in the professional programme has already been sorted by ability and interest by the criterion-referenced system that compares students along a continuum, while the run-of-the-mill undergraduate has not been thus sorted. Unfortunately, these two systems have become confused in many people's minds as grades have been inflated and standards have dropped. Earning a grade of 90 does not now guarantee that someone has mastered a discipline at a certain level of difficulty. It simply means that this student is higher on a continuum relative to other students in the class. Teaching students in programmes where the charge is to make them fully conversant with the discipline is closer to the traditional model of the university and is far more gratifying for professors. Furthermore, even though the grades may have been criterion-referenced in the traditional university, the standards were higher, so someone earning a C in that system may actually have known more than someone earning an A in the current system.

Given the results-oriented ethos so engrained in popular culture, where a given set of ends justify the means, learning is not valued as much as passing. So in the competition for grades in the current undergraduate system, more students are trying to get as many of these grades as they can with the least amount of effort, and not with the goal of being fully conversant in an aspect of a discipline represented by a course. Because the quantity of available grades is defined by factors beyond the control of professors and students, students must compete with each other for what are in effect scarce resources. To avoid unpleasant encounters with students over grading, we suspect that most professors would be happy to hand out more grades to match the wishes of all students if it were not for their own sense of professional standards. We have seen how far this approach has been pushed, with anywhere from 60 to 80 per cent As and Bs now being awarded in Canadian and American universities (depending on the school and the source of the estimate). But even the most flexible administrative system does not want this to continue to its logical conclusion, because it would undermine the legitimacy of the under-graduate system as an effective sorter of students.[14]

Grade inflation is the most obvious result of these competitive pressures among students, as many professors have given in and relinquished aspects of their gatekeeping role. However, it is important to note that grade inflation does not end grade obsession among some students. Quite the contrary, it plays to the revolution of rising expectations and feeds grade promiscuity, because now more students want and expect these higher grades. Moreover, the only way to hand out high grades in a system dominated by disengaged students is to lower standards, and simply make it easier for them to get those high grades.

The net result of these pressures is for many profs to withdraw from close engagements with students, even good students. This response can be described as faculty disengagement, the flip side of student disen-gagement. It happens in part because of student focus on the GPA and professors' disdain for grade obsession (versus a pure desire for knowl-edge and learning). This tension, and professors' reaction to it, high-lights the rise of the adversarial relationship between professor and student and the decline of the nurturing, mentoring one.

At the upper end of the grading curve of the criterion-referenced sys-tem, the tension is generally with B students who think they should be receiving As. However, tensions can also rise with A students who do not feel challenged if their professors gear courses for lower-end students (the bottom half of the class) and use assessment methods like multiple-choice tests.[15] At the lower end of the curve, the tension stems from the fact that professors must take some sort of stand, otherwise even a dull-ard would see that the professor is a total pushover with no professional standards. In many cases, the weak students must be told, in one way or another, that they do not have what it takes to make it in a particular course, or in some cases to make it in university at all.

Some students getting grades at the low end can simply pull their socks up, develop the proper motivation, and apply their potential to develop their abilities further. Others, however, are simply in over their heads, and professors find themselves performing an unpleasant task that should have been done earlier: telling them that they do not have what it takes to do well in the subject. Remember that most of these stu-dents were told throughout their high school careers that they were 'very good' (B) to 'excellent' (A). The fact is that most students now flooding into universities are only mediocre and really deserve the C as traditionally defined. Furthermore, significant numbers are below average (D) by traditional standards or incompetent (F) by any standards (recall Professors Collins's experiences described in chapter 1).

The eventual outcome of the professor's gatekeeping role is that a set number of students are finally eliminated from going further in the credential 'game.' The shame is that many should not have advanced as far as they did, or if we really want so many to get so far, we should radically alter the primary and secondary systems to *fully educate each student* to achieve mastery in the required disciplines, using outcome-based systems. As it is, *most* students are set up to eventually reach their 'level of incompetence,' where they cannot be promoted any further because they have not mastered anything.[16] An additional shame is that the system is set up to encourage the lower-end students to blame themselves for this inevitable defeat; this is the cooling out function of higher education. While it may be true that most such students do not have the requisite abilities at their point of departure from the university system, the politics of credentialism is at fault on several grounds, so the fault lies with the system, not with the hapless individual. Credentialism puts high schools in the position of having to give false promises to students, and having to pass large numbers of them off by assigning inflated grades instead of providing honest feedback that would have led those students either to improve their abilities during high school or to quit the system before reaching their level of incompetence in such an ignominious fashion.

With the current gatekeeping arrangements, the system escapes blame, but in cohort after cohort great numbers of over-promised students come to define themselves as inadequate when compared against the upper-middle-class standard of white-collar, professional success to which they have been told to aspire, when they would have been better off pursuing objectives more suited to their potentials and interests. However, the system itself escapes critical scrutiny in good part because professors are put in the frontlines to take the flak from those who are weeded out so late in the game (at the university level). We investigated this flak in a survey we conducted on Western faculty members, and we shall discuss it shortly.

As noted earlier, rather than wanting to be bureaucratic gatekeepers, most professors are likely motivated by intellectual interests in their field and/or a sense of calling to their discipline. However, the evolution of the professor's role to be the keeper of the gate for the uneducated masses has seriously injured the professional integrity of the disciplines that have become popular sorting grounds for undergraduates. To add insult to injury, professors must now absorb whatever blame students deflect from themselves and their school systems. The deflecting of blame is encouraged by the common practice of using course evaluations, in which multiple elements of students' experiences in courses are surveyed. While these evaluations have their positive uses, their negative aspects include the invitation to disgruntled students to take their disaffection out on professors, diverting students from taking an honest look at the whole system and their own role in it, and instead taking the easy way out of blaming their woes on 'bad' professors who would not 'teach them properly.'

The notion of teaching that unsuccessful students likely have in mind is what they experienced in high school, where little was asked of them. Most likely their teachers spoon-fed them material in class (rather than requiring them to prepare by reading material in advance, then discuss its relevance and implications in class). If students do not come to class prepared with a basic understanding garnered from a first reading of the material, it is up to the teachers to spend valuable class time laying this simple foundation of descriptive information, instead of spending time discussing it in more intellectually advanced and engaging ways. People learn by absorbing new material that is slightly beyond their current level of understanding. However, it cannot be too far beyond that level, and that is why reading in preparation for class is important, but if it is just at or even below their current level of understanding, we cannot really call this university-level learning.

Finally, the professor-as-gatekeeper is put in the contradictory role of being evaluated by those who bear the consequences of their gatekeeping. We speak here of course evaluations, which are also implicated in grade inflation. The best predictor of professors' popularity with students is the grades they give: the higher a student's grade in a course, the higher her or his evaluation of the professor will be, net of other factors, and regardless of whether the student truly benefits from the course intellectually.[17] We explore this research in detail in chapter 5. Later in this chapter we relate the findings of our own study of how professors are coping with grade inflation, student disengagement, and other sources of stress associated with their gatekeeping role.

The Growth of Education as a Business

Universities have expanded dramatically in the past half-century, as illustrated in the previous chapter. During this time, changes have also taken place in the wider society, described in books with self-explaining titles such as *The Feel-Good Society,*[18] *The Horizontal Society,*[19] and *Arrested Adulthood.*[20] Books like these describe aspects of a society where the consumer mentality has trumped norms such as respect for authority and basic civility among strangers, and where the 'path of least effort' appears to be the principle governing more and more of people's lives. As consumption has been 'democratized' – people can do 'anything' if they have the money – attitudes toward the 'social contract' have shifted. People increasingly view their dealings with each other as economic exchanges in which the buyer has certain rights and expectations, and 'work' involves minimal effort to get the maximum reward. This view is captured in the popular saying, Don't work hard, work smart! The rights include receiving, or being given, a product with a warranty, and the expectations are that the product will serve them as they want it to, again with minimal effort. As this view of life has crept into the school system, social obligations have tended to be dropped from the traditional equation of rights and responsibilities – that rights come with responsibilities, and are therefore not without certain obligations, like exerting a full effort if one expects full rewards.

Perhaps in response to decreased funding (in Canada) or in the entrepreneurial spirit of rising profit shares (in the United States), universities have increasingly sold themselves to students as businesses that can provide certain services. For example, students are told that they can become some sort of transformed product.[21] Most professors have not played an active role in this academic entrepreneurship. Instead, they have been passively complicit by taking on more and more students each year, perhaps thankful that they have a job that is so highly sought after. We suspect that many professors have not been as conscious of the implications of these changes as they might have been had they paid closer attention to the new place of the university in the political economy of the wider society.

As a result of all of the factors we have discussed thus far, the role of the university has changed over time, and some readers may respond to portions of what we write by arguing that universities should simply accept current realities and adapt to what appear to be new market pressures. We believe that we make a strong case against this view, and provide advice on how to resist market pressures and direct the university system in a more viable direction. As it stands, Canadian universities have already slid in the direction of becoming credential 'markets,' much like large supermarkets where people shop using a list of their needs and wants. Some have suggested the term credential *mill* rather than *market*, but that conveys an image of students as passive products simply being stamped according to set patterns. We think the student is more active than this, and it is this activity that presents part of the problem for contemporary universities. As just argued, some students increasingly act like self-entitled consumers demanding satisfaction.

We base the term *credential mart* on a typology suggesting that universities have evolved over the centuries, from being 'sanctuaries of truth and method' in pre-modern eras, to 'social service stations' and then 'culture marts' in the modern era.[22] While the early universities trained clerics and aristocrats interested in philosophy and science, the social service station university evolved to educate those who would undertake political and public service careers. When the political ranks were filled by a critical mass of the university-educated, the conventional wisdom grew that a university education was essential to those who would run society because it gave them a 'common language and cultural tradition.'[23] Hence, the term *culture mart* to describe the fourth phase of the typology. The culture mart attracted students from the wealthy segments of society who were destined to become the captains of business and industry.

This typology was proposed three decades ago by Canadian sociologist Howard Adelman, before the current trend of university-graduate underemployment, which began in the mid-1970s, when the Canadian public service bloated and could take on few new recruits.[24] At the point where the teaching profession reached its limit in taking on new recruits and the traditional youth labour market could no longer provide entry-level jobs, the university came under increasing pressure to provide a bridge to the while-collar world. Initially, the pressure came from the children of the new middle-class parents who made it into the public service and teaching profession in the 1950s and 1960s. More recently, the pressure has come from working-class parents, as the job opportunities of their children have dwindled into minimum-wage McJobs with little chance of personal or career growth.[25] At the same time, the government has promoted a university education as a panacea for personal, social, and economic ills. This sequence of events brings us to the situation described in chapter 1, where universities have become credential marts.

Together these pressures have landed myriad problems at the doorstep of Canadian universities and in the classrooms of professors. For the remainder of this chapter, we take a look at how professors are handling these pressures.

Life in the Credential Mart

Deskilling of the Professoriate

As the functions of higher education have changed, and professors have reluctantly become gatekeepers in credential marts, many have found themselves with jobs that increasingly resemble those of secondary school teachers. In particular, as the functions of higher education have changed, students have become much more caught up in education as a means to an end, rather than an end in itself. In other words, more and more students approach their university education as a stepping stone to something in the future, rather than viewing it as an end in itself, an opportunity for self-discovery and intellectual development *in the moment*. Accordingly, students are less likely to be motivated to seriously engage the course material, and more likely to simply write down pronouncements from professors for memorization immediately before an exam. Most professors have had the dispiriting experience of giving an impassioned lecture that diverged from the textbook, but could greatly enhance students' appreciation of the relevance of a topic, only to have a student interrupt with the question, 'Is this on the exam?' As this experience is repeated year after year, professors experiencing it tend not to expect anything more of their students, thereby contributing to a downward spiral.[26]

Students who ask such questions do so in all sincerity and apparently do not think there is anything shallow in the act. In our view, they have been conditioned by a system that makes them not so much 'dumb' as 'numb,' in the sense that they do not realize the opportunities and privileges at their immediate disposal. Instead, they are likely thinking about things other than the relevance of the material at hand for their present and future lives. Such students are there mainly in body, not mind, as Steinberg noted in *Beyond the Classroom* discussed in chapter 1. Numbed students are products of a system that has told them to stay in school and everything will work out for them, when in truth they should have taken time to truly evaluate their options and future lives. In the United Kingdom, the 'gap year' between secondary school and university is becoming increasingly common, in part for this reason. Students who never step out of the shelter of the ivory tower to take a look at what life might be like for them when they eventually do so may simply be on 'autopilot' and may not have a useful perspective on their present or future lives that real-world experience would give them, especially the maturity to benefit from what universities fundamentally have to offer.

The consumer mentality among students in a system that mass produces credentials has left many professors underemployed in the sense that their full set of skills is unused in their undergraduate teaching. Many react by focusing more on graduate students and their own research, if those are viable options. However, not all departments have graduate programmes and not all faculty members have lucrative grants supporting research. Moreover, graduate students are increasingly the product of this flawed system, and many are not up to the rigours of graduate school. In any event, professors increasingly find themselves functioning as 'teaching machines' whose role is to pass and graduate as many students as are sent to them along the assembly line, ignoring a large number of substandard performances, as Professor Collins described in chapter 1.

Regardless of the availability of more meaningful activities that utilize their intellectual training and allow them to engage their passions, as we have stressed, year after year professors in Canadian universities[27] face increasingly large numbers of disengaged students in their classes expecting to be highly rewarded for little effort. We remind the reader that these students are not to be blamed for this approach, for they are simply persisting with a high school mentality in their approach to their studies that worked in the past. The problem is historical and systematic more so than it is individual. To make matters worse, many of these students have been taught to adopt a consumer mentality that induces them to expect high grades for merely paying tuition and showing up periodically for class. Among these students, professors will find a critical mass with a level of arrogance that is unjustified by their mediocre approach to intellectual enquiry. This hubris has been nurtured among the last few cohorts of students by what has been called the cult of self-esteem, which we discuss next.

Collectively, these problems have altered the interpersonal dynamics of teaching, from relationships based on mentoring and guidance in the traditional model of the university to relationships that are inherently conflictual and adversarial. The result is that professors are now very much the 'counter clerks' of a big business that requires them not only to keep customers happy about a product that is suspect, but to make them feel good about themselves as 'masters' of this inferior product.

The Cult of Self-esteem and Other Sources of the Sense of Entitlement

Beginning in the 1970s, primary and secondary schools began motivating children and students, not by rewarding them so much for the quality of their academic achievements, as for simply completing tasks. This reward was in the form of psychological boosting – of complimenting the child or student for exerting any effort at all. While previous generations of students might have seen only the best get gold stars (or the symbolic equivalent of an A) for their work, among recent cohorts everyone has been repeatedly awarded gold stars. The idea has been to make all *feel good* about themselves – to have high self-esteem.

Just as encouraging people to go as far as they can in school is a desirable goal in principle, making all feel good about themselves is a laudable ideal. However, in both cases these are realistic goals only if their attainment is deserved. That is, just as the practice of pushing people through school regardless of their motivation and ability has unintended consequences, so too does making people feel good about themselves regardless of their motivation and ability. The most obvious problem with feeding everyone's self-esteem regardless of whether it's deserved is that people come to expect praise and rewards for everything they do – they feel entitled. Less obvious is the possibility that a realistic basis for this self-esteem may not be present in the students' underlying capabilities. Accordingly, when they move on to a higher level where those capabilities are expected, they are now in over their heads and are unable to perform the tasks required.[28] When this happens, students with a false sense of self-esteem can experience all sorts of psychological reactions, most notably anger, anxiety, and depression. It is not coincidental that rates of these psychological problems have been climbing steadily among children, adolescents, and emerging adults in the past few decades during this era of the 'cult of self-esteem.'[29]

At the same time, students with high self-esteem based on false feedback are much more difficult to teach because many cannot take criticism and feedback without assuming that it is personal. Experimental research suggests that such people attempt to preserve their self-esteem, not by altering their behaviour so that it becomes more based in reality, but by attacking the source of the threat.[30] In such cases, a professor may be unjustifiably attacked, either directly through students' offensive behaviour, or indirectly by getting heavily criticized on teaching evaluations. We shall see that interactions with students over grades and teaching evaluations are a significant source of stress for professors, and being unjustifiably criticized by students attempting to protect their self-esteem does not help. Of course, justifiable student criticism can be very useful to professors, but the problem of anonymity on course evaluations makes it difficult for some professors to determine if certain criticisms are justified.

The problem with the feel-good pedagogy of self-esteem is that it leads to neglect of basic pedagogical principles of learning and progressive skill acquisition. In contrast to rewarding everyone regardless of how well the job is done, when a student learns the rudiments and masters the elements of a skill or area of knowledge, that person also acquires a sense of *self-efficacy*.[31] Self-efficacy is a sense that one can accomplish things and that those things are under one's control. Self-efficacy is thus a form of personal agency – an ability to act in the world as a self-determining agent. From this experience follows a realistic sense of self-esteem, and this sense of self-esteem is reinforced with every efficacious experience. Consequently, the person's self-esteem is built on a foundation that will feed it realistically, without self-deception and illusion.

People with high self-esteem, but low self-efficacy, must rely on continual false feedback from others. At university, where the relations with professors are impersonal and ostensibly objective, it is self-efficacy that will carry students through, not false self-esteem. In fact, a false sense of self-esteem can support a form of hubris that puts people on a path to failure, both in objective performance on academic assignments and in interpersonal dealings with professors. Such people can play the system if they stay in it; in essence they are phonies. Most experienced professors can spot them, and have developed means of dealing with their cajoling, blandishments, and other tricks. Some professors use such tactics among students to increase their own popularity, as we shall see. Others – especially those who attempt to maintain traditional standards – find that they have to deflect such student attempts to garner favour. However, when they do so, they must also meet that student's overinflated ego and bear the consequences of the ensuing struggle for dominance. We explore the problems that these professors encounter below.

The cult of self-esteem is reinforced in high schools by a number of practices. Essentially, the objective is to make all feel 'special'[32] and to not confront the possibility that they might not be intellectually or mentally prepared to master the material in their courses. Grade inflation functions in favour of the former goal of making more people feel 'special' than would otherwise be the case if it were acknowledged that by definition most students are average. The practice of 'social passing' or 'social promotion' achieves the latter goal, by advancing students to the next grade in spite of the fact that they should be failed. This approach is widespread in both the American and Canadian systems. In these cases, students should repeat the grade because they are not prepared to proceed, yet are sent on to the next level. In the long run, this does not do the students a favour, however, because in the face of increasingly complex material, they are placed at a compounded disadvantage over time, and the lack of learning can quickly accumulate into a sense of incompetence and of being doomed to failure. This situation has reached serious proportions in many areas, yet has not been scientifically studied in proportion to its seriousness.[33]

In order to maintain the illusion that all is well in a system that promotes students regardless of their competence, the material and the way it is taught must be dumbed down. This practice exposes the roots of student disengagement and shows how it is encouraged on a massive scale: without negative consequences, many people will pursue a path of least effort. We now turn to an in-depth examination of the long-term effects of social promotion, disengagement, and grade inflation on the job experiences of professors.

Learning to Live with Student Disengagement

Professors differ in how they deal with disengagement among their students and how they cope with it personally. It this section, we describe the downward spiral that is taking place as many profs find themselves ratcheting down requirements in their courses over the years as more and more students arrive in their classes without the motivation to do the amount and quality of academic work once required. This decline might not be occurring, or occurring at its current rate, if it were not for student evaluations of professors, those 'satisfaction surveys' that most universities employ in the name of 'accountability.' In addition, student disengagement appears to be part of a wider disengagement from traditional forms of community, political, and civic activities.[34] This wider disengagement is partly due to an individualization of lifestyles made possible by the spread of popular culture through the sophisticated technological devices and media that are now relatively inexpensive and hence increasingly widespread. Involvement in these popular culture activities has taken time away from more serious forms of intellectual practice and enquiry, as does the increasing necessity (and allure) of working at jobs while studying full-time.

Professors' personal reactions to student disengagement will vary in response to a number of factors: how sensitive they are to their students' wants; how thick-skinned they are when they deal with their students' disaffections; how much they share their feelings with their colleagues; how much they reflect on how well they maintain consistent standards over the years; and very importantly, whether or not they are tenured. While writing this book we conducted a survey among our colleagues in the three largest faculties at Western to assess their perceptions of student disengagement and their reactions to it (arts, social science, and natural science). The remainder of this chapter will present the results of this survey, as they are relevant to the topic at hand: how professors are coping with the new functions of higher education and their role as gatekeepers of an increased number of unsorted students. The results provide a rare look into the feelings and opinions of those in the inner sanctum of the Ivory Tower, but we caution readers that we take these results as suggestive and in need of replication on a large scale to increase confidence in them and to see how they vary in different contexts.[35]

Before discussing these findings, we remind readers that the official statistics available from Western discussed in the previous chapter show significant grade inflation over the past ten to fifteen years. In other words, collectively professors have been giving higher grades in all three faculties we studied, and the C grade no longer designates 'average' or 'satisfactory.' Now, over half of students in courses at all levels earn either an A or a B. In social science, this figure hovers around 60 per cent, in arts and humanities it is just over 70 per cent, and in science it is just under 70 per cent. While some faculty members have maintained traditional standards pegged at C averages over this period, we wanted to assess the extent to which professors are aware of the general increase in grades, even if they maintain the traditional system themselves. We also wanted to study the experiences of those who have attempted to maintain the older grading standards, and how it has affected their experience of their job.

Awareness of the Issues: Sliding Standards

In one set of questions, faculty members were asked to report the average grades they give in their courses. At Western, courses are distinguished by categories that ostensibly reflect increasing difficulty and sophistication that are roughly associated with year level and whether they are general or honours courses. Consequently, we can speak of introductory courses (000 level), general courses (100 level), and honours courses for second, third, and fourth year (200-, 300-, and 400-level courses, respectively). It is clear from the data we received that a B average is now the course grade most commonly awarded, and applies to introductory courses and general courses, where the median grade is a B- (70–73%). The average grades awarded increase through the levels of honours courses, with fewer than one-quarter assigning C averages at the second-year level, and virtually none doing so in third- and fourth-year levels (only one professor reported awarding C+ averages in a third-year course). The median grade is a B for the third-year and a B+ for the fourth year. Forty per cent report giving A averages in their fourth-year courses.

These findings are generally supported by the official figures reported by Western, as already discussed, so we can have greater confidence that these data from our survey are reasonably accurate and representative of practices at Western. This confidence allows us to go one step further. Official figures have an 'institutional memory' and are untainted by errors or recall that faculty members might have. In other words, the official figures capture what has been reported for decades on the basis of what faculty members submitted each year over those decades. There would therefore be no human error associated with the biases of under-reporting in ways that preserve professors' own sense of self-esteem and psychological well-being.

In the survey, we developed a set of questions specially designed for professors who had been at Western for ten years or more, assuming that they would have the institutional memory to recall the pre-inflation practices and to have witnessed changes in their own practices or among their colleagues. In response to the question 'Have you intentionally changed your courses over the past decade or so by making them easier or more difficult?' just over one-third indicated 'no' and two thirds said 'yes.' In the follow-up question about whether they made them more difficult or easier (for those who changed their courses), the vast majority – over 80 per cent – said they made them easier, most typically by reducing amount of material covered, along with reducing the number and difficulty of exams and assignments.

When asked if they knew whether any of their colleagues had changed their courses, about 75 per cent of the sample of those who had been at Western for ten years or more indicated that they did not know. The remaining 25 per cent said 'yes,' and all of those indicating 'yes' thought their colleagues made their courses easier, usually by reducing the amount of material covered, and having less frequent and easier assignments and tests.

From these results, it appears that there is some awareness of the twin problems of grade inflation and the dumbing down of courses that can constitute the default response to student disengagement. For those who are not aware of these things, it is possible that they have simply maintained their standards and not paid attention to what their colleagues have been doing. Professors can certainly be so absorbed in their own work that they are unaware of what is going on, even in their own departments.

To get a more global sense of the perceptions of these twin problems among all who participated in the study, we asked the following question: 'Compared to past years, do you think students have similar expectations regarding the grades they receive for the effort they expend?' The response pattern to what they thought current students tend to expect was

Same grades for the same effort	21.8%
Higher grades for the same effort	25.5%
Same grades for less effort	5.5%
Higher grades for less effort	23.6%
Higher grades for more effort	5.5%
Can't say	18.2%

We can see that only about one-fifth think that nothing has changed recently – perhaps because they have not changed their standards and do not pay attention to their colleagues. Another fifth indicated that they did not know, also explainable for the same reason or perhaps reflecting their own disengagement. The remaining responses – 60 per cent – show a majority awareness of some sort of change: one-quarter thought that students were affected by both aspects of the twin problem (wanting higher grades while putting out less effort) and another quarter thought that students were willing to exert the same effort as in the past, but wanted higher grades for it. Only 5 per cent thought that students wanted higher grades while putting out more effort.

A more targeted question probed experiences with one important aspect of grade inflation: feeling pressure from students to give higher grades than they deserve. This pressure has likely been around for some time and predates the current situation. However, the issue is how extensive it is and what effect it has on professors. In response, some 90 per cent responded that they had felt pressures to give higher-than-deserved grades. This influence is often experienced when students come to office hours pleading and cajoling, or more recently doing so through emails.[36] About one-fifth reported that this pressure happened very often, while the majority (two-thirds) experienced it 'from time to time.' When probed further, about three-quarters reported that they experienced this pressure as stressful, and 40 per cent found that this stress carried over into their personal life, such that it could not be 'left on the job.'

Though largely impressionistic, these data make it clear that most professors are aware of grade inflation, and it appears that as a group they have given in to it (as demonstrated by the official record). It is thus likely that many students have been placated by courses made easier in the work required and the level of difficulty of that work and/or higher grades. Again, as already noted, this change varies by professor, department, faculty, and university, but it is common enough to be easily detected in the official record and in queries made of those in the trenches – university teachers. We can take this inquiry one step further, however, and explore how it affects professors' experience of student abilities and motivation, and how these experiences might have changed in the recent past.

Perceptions of Student Engagement: Institutionalized Indifference

Our survey asked faculty members roughly to categorize their students in order to discover how they rated student abilities: 'Thinking in terms of ability, what percentage of the students you currently teach would you put into each of the following categories: *top-notch, competent, mediocre, unsuited for university?*' These categories correspond to the traditional notion of the criteria for letter grades (A, B, C, D/F), although the question did not mention letter grades. The percentages of students judged to belong in each category were grouped into seven ranges (1–10%, 11–20%, 21–40%, 41–60%, 61–80%, 81–90%, 91–100%) and the ranges were cross-tabulated with the categories for rating students. Thus, if X per cent of professors thought that 10 per cent or fewer of their students were top-notch, the figure in the cell *top-notch* would be X per cent. Results are presented in Table 2.1. For those who think that all university students are brilliant, or that all As awarded in high school and university are meaningful, these results will require some rethinking on their part. The majority of professors (75%) think that only 10 per cent or fewer of

Table 2.1
Percentage of professors who place their students in each category of competence

Percentage of students in each category	Categories of competence			
	Top notch	Competent	Mediocre	Unsuited for university
0–10	75	13	8	72
11–20	23	41	28	17
21–40	2	30	34	8
41–60	–	15	28	2
61–80	–	2	2	–
81–100	–	–	–	–

their students are top-notch. A minority (23%) would put this estimate at 11–20 per cent, suggesting that almost all professors feel that no more than 20 percent of their students are top-notch. Translated into typical classes of forty or eighty students, professors would expect about four or eight students to be outstanding, respectively. At the same time, most professors (62%) think that 20–60 per cent of their students are medio-cre or average, which should translate to a C average in the old system. It is also telling that an equivalent percentage of professors (72%) feel that as many as 10 per cent of their students are unsuited for university.

Strictly speaking, then, on the basis of these results, if grade distribu-tions really indicated ability, the following grade distribution should be found: fewer than 10 per cent As, about 20 per cent Bs, and at least 40 per cent Cs or lower – a distribution compatible with the European Credit Transfer System (see the appendix for details). However, as we have seen, this is no longer the case. Accordingly, it appears that grades exceed pro-fessors' actual appraisal of their students' abilities, and that is exactly what grade inflation is all about. This is the same thing that Professor Col-lins reported doing (above) to keep students taking courses in his depart-ment, as it was before the financial reward system set up by Western.

But what about effort, a reader might ask? Surely that counts. Indeed, those who are average or competent can put in extra effort to achieve above their ability. This is precisely what is involved in working one's way up the 'learning curve,' and essentially what should happen throughout the educational career of *all* students, from primary through secondary to tertiary levels. However, moving up this curve requires motivation and effort, and these are what are lacking among disengaged students. Indeed, this situation is what professors face with an increasing number

Table 2.2
Percentage of professors who place their students in each category of engagement

Percentage of students	Fully engaged	Minimally engaged	Disengaged	Marginal ability
0–10	40	2	26	70
11–20	32	11	40	24
21–40	15	45	25	6
41–60	8	28	9	–
61–80	7	13	–	–
81–100	–	–	–	–

of students: refusal to work up a learning curve. When a critical mass of students does not move up, professors have two choices: (1) fail large numbers of students or (2) make the course easier so that the learning curve is either eliminated or made less steep. The first choice is unacceptable to educational administrators and the second choice is unpalatable to professors attempting to maintain standards. We can see from the evidence of grade inflation which choice wins in most cases.

To gain insight into this issue, we also asked our sample of professors to rate their students' motivation. As table 2.2 shows, we listed the forms of engagement-disengagement that professors might witness, based on the large American studies, like those carried out by the National Survey of Student Engagement (NSSE) and the Cooperative Institutional Research Program (CIRP).

Over one-third of professors think that fewer than 10 per cent of their students are fully engaged, which we defined for them as 'meet all of the expectations you set in your courses.' If we include the next rating category (11–20%), just under three-quarters of professors think that only up to 20 per cent of students are fully engaged. None thought that more than 80 per cent of their students are fully engaged.

The category that seems to represent the modal category of student is 'minimal engagement,' which we defined in the questionnaire as 'engaged to the minimal extent required to get a good mark – i.e., go through the motions.' A full 45 per cent of professors feel that this category applied to 21–40 per cent of their students, and an additional 28 per cent think that it included as many as 60 per cent of their students.

Estimates for the percentage of disengaged students are also interesting. The wording we used for 'disengaged' was 'don't care much about their courses, but likely have the ability.' Most conservatively, about one-quarter of professors feel that up to 10 per cent are disengaged. About 40 percent of professors think it applies to up to one in five students, and an additional quarter think that as many as 40 percent of their students are disengaged. Those who feel that 40 per cent are disengaged are supported by the NSSE studies, while those who feel that 20 per cent are disengaged are supported by the natural experiment at the University of PEI, which we've already discussed, in which a professor had 20 per cent of his class fully disengage for the reward of a B-.

Finally, it appears that all professors encounter students who they think 'struggle to pass their courses, even with considerable effort.' In other words, their ability levels are so low that even when they try hard, they find it difficult to pass. Almost three-quarters of professors think this observation applies to up to 10 per cent of their students, and an additional quarter think it applies to up to 20 per cent of their students. If these appraisals translated into actual grading practices, 10–20 per cent of students would regularly fail courses. At Western, only about 5 per cent fail, according to official records.[37]

These results clearly fly in the face of the beliefs that many people – including parents – hold about the typical university student. We conducted this survey to compare our own perceptions and experiences, which have been reinforced over the years in conversations with colleagues. However, we wanted to move beyond the anecdotal level to the more systematic approach, where the same criteria are applied across cases. We are not surprised by these results, as they conform to both previous research on the topic (discussed in chapter 1) and our own experience. We were concerned that we might be seeing more disengaged students in the social sciences, and popular conceptions of the social sciences as 'easy' would suggest that this might be the case. However, in analysing the data from our survey, we found no differences among faculties on these measures. Professors in the natural sciences apparently witness as much disengagement and pressures to inflate grades as do professors in social sciences and arts and humanities. What we find most interesting is the uneven awareness of this among faculty members in all disciplines, especially given the idea of the 'exact' sciences versus the inexact (social) sciences and humanities. We now turn to the effect that this ignorance is having on those professors.

The Downward Spiral: The New Normal

At certain levels, most professors we surveyed sense that something has changed or that something is wrong. Those with lower levels of awareness may simply be so focused on their own work that they have not taken the time to look around or to take a serious look at the performance levels of many students in their classes. The experiences of two colleagues who have been at Western since the 1960s illustrate this point (however, they were not part of this survey because they are retired). Both taught quantitative and statistically oriented courses for four decades, and actually still have the records of the grades they assigned in those courses throughout the time period. In examining these records, they found that, in spite of the 'hard' quantitative and statistical content of their courses, grades inflated in those courses over that time span. However, they do not recall doing anything intentionally to make the courses easier or to inflate the grades, yet they can't explain how or why they began awarding higher grades. Both are adamant that the higher grades are *not* because students taking the courses are smarter or better prepared, illustrating how pressures to inflate grades can slowly slip unnoticed into professors' grading practices in a 'new normal.'

In our survey, we asked about this awareness of change in a number of ways. After being questioned about their grading practices and their awareness of the practices of their colleagues, professors in our sample were asked,

> In your experience, have the students coming to Western been getting better, the same, or worse since you have been at Western, in
> * Level of academic preparation for your courses
> * Engagement in your courses
> * Maturity in approaching your courses
> * Ability to benefit from your courses
> * Respect for you as a professor
> * Willingness to accept your judgements concerning their grades

The response categories provided for them were 'Can't say,' 'Better,' 'The same,' and 'Worse.' Between 30 and 50 per cent thought that Western students were 'the same,' depending on the question, while between 15 and 30 per cent indicated that they could not say. Students were most likely to be rated as 'the same' on 'respect for you as a professor' (50%) and least likely in 'level of academic preparation for your courses' (30%). Given the inflation in grades that has taken place, one would think that most would have thought students were getting better. However, only between 10 and 20 per cent of professors thought that Western students were better than in the past, depending on the question. Ratings were higher for perceptions that students are getting worse: about

20 per cent thought students were not as academically prepared for, or engaged in, their courses; 25 per cent thought students were less mature; and 22 per cent thought students were less willing to accept their judgements on grades.

We expected that more professors would have a more conscious awareness of a decline in the behaviours represented by the items listed for this question. Instead, many professors may have 'reset' their 'gyroscope' of standards to match a 'new normal' that is reflected in the grade-inflated/low-engagement portrait of university education emerging from the research findings. To assess what standards they might be employing in this 'new normal,' we asked them how much time they expect students to prepare per week for their classes in advance. According to the NSSE already discussed, the academic tradition is the 'two-hour rule.' When asked how much time they expected students to prepare for lectures per week, principally by reading assigned material, only about 20 per cent expected two hours or more. The median response was one hour (30% picked this category). One-quarter expect no preparation or less than one hour for each hour of lecture. Thus, on questions about preparing for class, professors at Western apparently now expect about half the time of the traditional rule, making the results of our questions about preparedness even more striking in terms of how little effort is put out by most students. We also get a sense of how many professors have given in to the disengagement compact by requiring little or no work of their students (apparently up to one-quarter have given in).

For those who hold seminars in their courses, the figures are comparable, but Western has a tradition of limiting seminars to upper-year honours courses. Few courses in social science include both lectures and seminars. Science courses are more likely to include a lab component, but the median expected preparation time for these is less than one hour per week.

Expecting a certain amount of preparation is one thing, but whether students actually do it is another. We asked our sample, 'How many students do you think actually come *fully* prepared for your classes as per your instructions to them?' Table 2.3 shows the distribution of responses. It is readily apparent that no one thinks every student comes prepared. Only about 13 per cent believe that any more 60 per cent of students come to their classes prepared. In fact, only two-thirds of professors think that even 40 per cent are prepared for their classes.

These findings are difficult to reconcile with the view that a university education is rigorous and that most students are on an 'intellectual jour-

Table 2.3
Percentage of professors who think that their students
come to class fully prepared

Percentage of students	Percentage of professors
0–10	13
11–20	28
21–40	24
41–60	15
61–80	11
81–90	2
91–100	–
Can't say	7

ney.' If some professors are not fully aware of the lack of student pre-paredness for their classes, yet they feel pressured to give higher grades than deserved, what personal toll might this be taking on them and their experience of their job?

Job Satisfaction and Job Stress: Being Thick-Skinned

A series of questions was asked to assess how professors experience their dealings with students. One set contained a mix of job satisfaction and job dissatisfaction options to the stem question 'Do you find typical inter-actions with undergraduates to be sources of …?' with five possible rat-ings: never, rarely, occasionally, usually, and always.

Three responses reflect satisfaction with the job of professor associated with dealing with undergraduates. The first, 'gratification as a teacher' drew about 50 per cent of responses in the 'usually' category, but only about 40 per cent of responses in the 'occasionally' category. Accordingly, just over half the professors routinely find the teaching aspect of their jobs gratifying. The second question, 'job satisfaction,' drew a similar response pattern with about 60 per cent routinely ('usually' or 'always') finding their dealings with undergrads a source of job satisfaction. Finally, the third question, 'personal fulfilment,' found fewer than half (45%) reporting undergraduates as routinely a source of this form of job satisfaction. While encouraging, the flip side of these figures means that almost half the professors do not routinely find their dealings with under-graduates a source of job satisfaction.

Still, it is also encouraging that most professors do not find their typical dealings with undergraduates as sources of 'stress,' 'frustration,' or 'annoyance,' as asked in a follow-up question. These problems occurred only 'occasionally' for most (50–60%) or 'rarely' (30–45%). However, when we queried further about specific forms of dealings with undergraduates as a source of stress, about 85 per cent report their dealings with students over grades to be stressful (at least sometimes), some 60 per cent find email to be stressful, and close to 50 per cent report grading written assignments as stressful at least sometimes.

Dealing with students who are disappointed with their grades has undoubtedly always been an unpleasant task, but we suspect that students conditioned by previous grade inflation are much more numerous today and much more difficult to deal with, as is indicated by the responses reported above (that many of those who feel pressured to give higher grades than deserved find the stress carrying over into their personal lives). However, email correspondence with students is definitely new, and it is telling that it is emerging as an additional source of stress. The potential problems with email are numerous, and we recommend that professors simply tell students that they will not communicate by this medium. While this is an unpopular thing to say to a generation raised on emails and instant messaging, it alleviates time-wasting and stressful problems, such as answering frivolous emails asking questions that are answered in course outlines, getting into details about why a certain grade was awarded (which invites endless rounds of communication that some students hope will wear the professor down), and giving students an opportunity to write things that they would not dare say in person because they assume an inappropriate familiarity or are insulting.

We understand that email communications have the potential to foster greater student–faculty interaction, but this is sensible only when a small number of students are involved, particularly at senior levels. This problem has become widespread enough to gain the attention of the *New York Times*, which recently reported that while email 'has made professors much more approachable … many say it has made them too accessible, erasing boundaries that traditionally kept students at a healthy distance.'[38]

From his interviews with faculty members, the *Times* reporter found concern that many students do not use this medium responsibly or maturely, and in fact often undermine their own credibility, the consequence of which can be a poor evaluation of the student by the professor when the time comes for letters of recommendation. One dean he interviewed noted that it is 'a real fine balance to accommodate what they need and at the same time maintain a level of legitimacy as an instructor and someone who is institutionally authorized to make demands on them, and not the other way around.' Untenured professors feel especially pressured to respond to what can be a flood of emails, some of which would not have been sent by a more thoughtful, respectful, and mature person, and cause the professor stress in deciding how, or if, to respond. We agree with the *Times* analysis that 'while once professors may have expected deference, their expertise seems to have become just another service that students, as customers, are buying. So students may have no fear of giving offence, imposing on the professor's time or even of asking a question that may reflect badly on their own judgment.'

Job stress clearly needs to be dealt with by universities and by the individuals experiencing it. All indications are that it is increasing, with female professors experiencing it (far) more than male professors, as do those who assign lower grades in their courses. We suspect that many of those who do not report stress are more 'thick-skinned' than others, but we have also witnessed colleagues who have been worn down over the years, rubbed raw by repeated unpleasant dealings with students. Because unpleasant dealings are almost always over marks, the easiest response for stressed professors is to give higher marks and make their courses easier. This takes us right back to the central topics of this book – grade inflation and disengagement – and shows why the 'disengagement compact' is inevitable unless systemic changes provide relief for the 'reluctant gatekeeper.'

Student Evaluations: Necessary Evils?

Most universities employ evaluations of all courses that professors teach, while some make this optional once tenure is awarded. There is widespread support for them, even among faculty members.[39] However, they are not without their problems, as we already alluded, and examine now in more detail. At Western, these evaluations are routinely administered in the last few weeks of each course and include quantitative responses to sixteen questions, as well as space for unstructured write-in comments. These write-ins are later transcribed and given to professors and chairs of departments, while the quantitative responses are posted on the university website. Until quite recently, the public could see these posted evaluations for themselves, where postings date back nine years, but this site has now been made password-protected, accessible only to Western students and faculty.[40]

One telling feature of these evaluations is the response to the ancillary question of 'expected grade' when students first enrolled in the course. In most cases, upwards of 90 per cent of students indicate that they expected an A or B in the course, especially in the upper years. This figure clearly shows what professors face if they attempt to award non-inflated grades and what cooling out they need to provide if they are not to take the blame themselves for the lower-than-expected grades that most students will receive. Readers can see comparable remarks on the popular website www.ratemyprofessor.com, which boasts millions of ratings of hundreds of thousands of professors around the United States and Canada.

To summarize, the chief complaints found about evaluations of university courses are that they are affected by (1) the grades a professor gives, (2) how affable or charismatic the professor is, and (3) some students' desire to take out their frustration on professors for personal slights or grievances they might have experienced.[41] The problem in associating evaluations with grades is well documented in numerous statistical studies and is cited as a chief source of grade inflation and the decline in standards, as we discussed in chapter 1 and explore in detail in chapter 5. The third problem helps explain the wide variation among evaluations and suggests that evaluations can sometimes tell us more about students than the professors rated. Readers should visit the ratemyprofessors website to see this variation, which ranges from vitriolic to romanticized, often for the same professor. When reading these comments, note which ones are from students in the same course. In scientific terms, this variation indicates that the method is unreliable and would not be accepted as evidence of anything in peer-reviewed scientific journals. It also raises questions about how to define with any consensus what constitutes 'good teaching' at this level.

If these course evaluations are so biased, why are they used? We think this is a good question that deserves careful consideration. For example, some argue that it keeps professors accountable. However, if they are also chief drivers of grade inflation, they work at cross-purposes to accountability, especially if universities do not closely regulate grades and correct inflated ones. Some feel that evaluations provide students with a way of having their say, or of letting professors know when they have done a bad job, as one professor (with a child in university) said in our survey. However, as noted, this form of student feedback is often not constructive, and sometimes vindictive, aggravating the increasingly adversarial teacher–student relationship by further driving a wedge between them. Besides, this line of reasoning suggests that even professors with decades of experience in teaching hundreds of courses over the years need to be closely watched for fear that they will slack off. Not only is that unlikely to happen, there is also evidence that evaluations can prevent professors from challenging students to work harder and think about issues in transformative ways that will help them grow intellectually in self-understanding and understanding about the world.

This concern about students 'having their say' is derived, we argue, from the wider consumer mentality of contemporary society, and encourages the perception that professors should satisfy students' expectations rather than students satisfying professors' expectations. This is a classic example of the tail wagging the dog, for people being evaluated are the stewards of a system in which they have a fiduciary duty over those given the 'right' to pass judgement on them. At the very least, many complain that evaluations are simply measures of status, turning teaching into a popularity contest among professors who take them seriously, whether they are attempting to survive in the profession[42] or to preserve their sense of superiority over other teachers.[43]

Bearing in mind the truism that the kinds of questions one asks determine the kinds of answers one receives, we designed a set of questions to get at these issues and assess what our sample of faculty thought about evaluations in general and as they apply to them. The first question asked, 'Do you think the course evaluations carried out at Western provide an accurate assessment of your teaching competence?' The responses to this question were evenly split, with about one-third reporting 'no,' one-third indicating 'uncertain,' and one-third saying 'yes.' Interestingly, those who said 'yes' were statistically more likely to give higher grades in their courses (especially in second-year and fourth-year courses), to report less stress in their dealings with students, and to be satisfied with the evaluations they receive. Moreover, the finding that only a minority are certain that evaluations of their teaching are accurate should raise flags, especially given that most professors in our sample have each taught hundreds of courses.

A series of probe questions were used to get at what professors thought were the sources of biases. The first asked, 'Do you think the evaluations carried out on your courses at Western are affected by any of the following?' Respondents were given five alternates to rate as 'yes,' 'no,' or 'undecided.' 'How students regard you personally' was seen as most influential, with 90 per cent responding 'yes.' The second most influential factor was 'the level of difficulty of a particular course,' with 80 per cent indicating 'yes.' The final three alternatives, in order of importance, were 'the marks you give in a course' (72%), 'the number of tests and assignments' (53%), and 'the amount of reading involved' (49%). These results show a widespread awareness that one's personality is very influential, as are how difficult the course material is, and what marks are given. Also important, but not as crucial, is the amount of material covered and tested. Accordingly, we suggest that most of the variation in the scores that professors receive are explained by (1) how affable or charismatic they are, (2) how easy their courses are, (3) how high their grades are, (4) how many tests or assignments are part of the course, and (5) how little outside reading they require. In other words, the key to beating this system is to teach to the evaluations: be as nice as possible, teach easy courses, give high grades, use the least possible amount of assessment, and do not require independent work. Of course, all of these options work against the ostensible mission of the university, which is to transfer knowledge and transform the student into a more intellectually and morally accountable person, but these evaluations are easy from a bookkeeping point of view, and can be used as a shield of 'accountability.'

In spite of these obvious problems with evaluations, a surprising number from our sample endorsed them. Over half say that they are satisfied with their own evaluations, even if they have specific complaints about them. Many would like a different evaluation system, especially one that directly assesses the amount of knowledge, understanding, and analytical abilities transferred (e.g., through peer evaluations and standardized exams). However, three-quarters *do not* think they would be better teachers without them, and 90 per cent *do not* find it demeaning to be rated by their students. Yet only one-third think that they actually improve the quality of education at Western. One quarter, however, think that they might be *decreasing* the quality of education. When asked if untenured faculty members might be intimidated by evaluations, a surprising 16 per cent say 'no,' although the majority think they do intimidate them (70%). Finally, when asked if these evaluations should be voluntary, most do not think so (80%), even if applied just to tenured faculty.

We find these quantitative data quite revealing, both of the awareness of the problems with evaluations, and the ambivalence about them as being a necessary evil that the professoriate should endure for the sake of a wider 'good,' like accountability, or 'for the students.' Somehow, these fallacious factors supporting their use have trumped the factors that we know clearly call for us to modify or do away with the standardized student evaluations.

Write-in responses were invited in our questions about course evaluations, and we received revealing testimonials about the stress some experience as a result of them, as well as an awareness of the related issues of
grade inflation and student disengagement. Women in particular voiced
their sense of ambivalence about – and displeasure with – course evaluations, especially the fact that the write-in component is open to abuse.
One female science professor wrote,

> Often, questions are asked that aren't relevant to the course, which makes
> me wonder about the validity of the process; also, the comments are often
> of a personal nature (e.g., comments about my attire or hairstyle or worse!)
> and not relevant to my effectiveness as a teacher. Further, many of these
> comments have been of a misogynist nature and I wonder about a system
> that condones such behaviour. Because the current system is anonymous,
> students are empowered to say whatever they wish and they do! It has gotten
> to the point that I do not even open the envelope when it comes. These per-
> sonal attacks make it very hard to take these evaluations seriously any more.

A female instructor from social science expressed the similar concern
that evaluations are of little use, even if they approve of her teaching:

> Well, even though they are satisfactory evaluations, they don't provide any
> information on how a course can be improved, other than the odd time a
> student will suggest that there is too much material covered, and they'd like
> to see the course be easier, which is not helpful at all. There are few
> resources to get help in improving an evaluation. Also, it seems as if just
> being 'nice' to students is enough to get a good evaluation, and niceness
> has little to do with teaching.

This sentiment was repeated, with one boldly stating, 'I do not believe
that the evaluations are teaching evaluations at all. My evaluations tend to
be (well) above average, but I consider the whole enterprise to be based
on criteria that have nothing to do with the *value* of the course.' This
female social science professor did not find the evaluations demeaning,
so much as 'stupid,' because they allow 'students the opportunity to vent
their own frustration by making wholly inappropriate, personally hurtful,
and usually contradictory remarks in the Comments section.' She wanted
real and useful feedback on her courses, not gratuitous and facile one-lin-
ers from students. She concluded that unfortunately 'it has become a
popularity contest used for evaluations by administrators (who don't care

about content so much as perceptions of a course's acceptability) or students who are looking for easy marks.'

Similarly, a female arts professor thought that it was the students 'trying to get through a course without doing the appropriate level of work that give the unfair course evaluations.' She wondered if there was a method to preclude those with a poor attendance record from evaluating the course.

The general ambivalence we found about the problems with evaluations and the desire to do what is right for students were nicely summed up by the following write-in passage:

> I am ambivalent about course evaluations: I believe they contribute to grade inflation in classes taught by untenured or sessional instructors, and in classes taught by faculty who may want to save their energy for research tasks. However, students deserve to have a voice in their classes, and this process allows them to air their views of the teaching they receive. Trying to find better ways to evaluate teaching would be a worthwhile goal.

A number expressed an awareness of getting 'hammered' or 'torpedoed' by vindictive students. When asked how their teaching would be different if evaluations were not used (by implication, not held over their heads), we received responses such as the following:

> First, the scope and difficulty of the courses would be designed solely on the basis of the inherent structure and requirement of a field, unaffected by concerns over their impact on students' evaluations. Second, academic freedom in both teaching and research is the soul of a university life. Both the instructors and the students will be more motivated and challenged if the evaluations were not used. Third, courses differ so much. More technical courses cannot be evaluated using the same criteria as overview type of courses. Those teaching technical-oriented courses are in a disadvantageous position than overview courses. (Male, Science)

Another simply wrote that he 'would do unqualified justice to the subject matter, regardless of audience response.' Yet another wrote about being dissatisfied with course evaluations because many students 'do not realize what they have learned, while others refuse to learn and blame me.' This professor would 'put more pressure on disengaged students' if no evaluations – or better evaluations – were used. Others indicated that they would take more chances in experimenting with teaching techniques and new assignments, and would be more 'effective in their grading (less grade inflation).'

There was also concern that evaluations are too standardized to match all types of courses, given variations in size and format (lectures of all sizes, seminars, and labs), and therefore some people suffer lower evaluations than would be the case if the assessments were more individualized. Some professors would also have liked to design their own evaluations, so that they could see if their particular teaching objectives were met.

Of course, many professors are aware of how the savvy ones, who are good actors, for example, can play the system. As one wrote, 'It's also quite easy to play the system and get better ratings without genuinely improving the quality of education you give.' Another wrote that he knew of professors who 'pander to the students and give out higher grades before the evaluation.' And still another noted that some instructors 'teach to the evaluations ... by manipulating grades,' which he argued was 'certainly the rational thing to do ... given the merit reward structure' at Western.

We also received comments that reflect how some respondents maintain their defences against discrediting information. One female instructor wrote wisely that although 'evaluations can be a form of "venting" for students who have not been as successful as they believe is their due – "What Peter says about Paul, says more about Peter than Paul."' Still others recognized that although they may think their expectations haven't changed over the years, they have subtly changed their view of students in the way that teenagers are said to change their view of their parents over the years – they seem to get smarter as time goes on. Another wrote that although he found many comments that were absolutely wrong about his courses, he regretted that there was no way to correct the misperceptions. In turn, he wrote that he really hated 'going into the class after they have marked their little bubbles,' but he understood evaluations as 'necessary evils.'

We agree that accountability is a valuable aspect of any public institution. However, current measures of accountability seem to do more harm than good. They reduce teaching to popularity contests and are open to manipulation by both professors and students. Rather than being 'necessarily evils,' course evaluations should be positive experiences for all involved. Research conducted by the National Survey of Student Engagement (NSSE) discussed in chapter 1 points the way to such measures: the degree of engagement in courses (how much they prepare for, and participate in, classes), the extent of deep learning (higher-order, integrative, and reflective), and the extent of transformation the student has experienced intellectually and morally as a result of involvement in the course (desire for more learning and for taking the knowledge into future life and career). This NSSE research also found that students actually enter university 'expecting to be more engaged than they are,' and that they shift their expectations to the level of demand once they get there. This same research also found that a certain percentage will rise to the challenges presented to them.[44] We return to the relationship between course evaluations and grade inflation in chapter 5, where we examine the most comprehensive analysis of research on this problem.

Sharing the Blame

While this chapter was written from the perspective of professors, we would be remiss in not commenting on their role in the problems they face. Although students as a group must acknowledge their role in the problems associated with their educational experiences and the disengagement that has seemingly overtaken the university, they are not the only ones to be blamed. Fingers can also be pointed at parents, administrators, politicians, policymakers, and of course, at professors too. It is far too easy to use students as scapegoats for the crisis of the university. And while not all students are culpable, neither are all professors. Yet there are problems that can be laid at the feet of certain professors and instructors, aided and abetted by university administrators.

As in the majority of other fields where, as a rule, employees or workers are good people, most professors too are good people. Being a good person, however, does not automatically make a professor a good teacher. Professors become professors largely on the basis of researching, writing and defending a dissertation, and publishing in peer-reviewed journals, but not as a result of being educated in pedagogy or teaching methods and techniques. Consequently, some professors are not good teachers, and students are the first to single them out. Of course, what constitutes good teaching varies, and different types of students prefer different types of teachers.

At most Canadian universities, professors' jobs have three components weighted in relation to the amount of time they should spend on them: (1) research and publication (40%), (2) teaching and teaching-related activities (40%), and (3) contributions to the wider community, such as committee work (20%). Although ostensibly equally weighted, research and publication are given preference over teaching at most universities, because those who are successful on the former tend to receive more recognition, quicker promotion, and higher pay increases. The expression 'publish or perish' is well known, but there is no equivalent that says 'teach or perish.' Further, many professors who are awarded research grants will routinely write into their grant proposals a request to 'buy off time' (i.e., be released from teaching one or more courses). This flight from teaching exacerbates the problem at hand.

Successful grant recipients who buy off time are usually replaced by part-time and sessional instructors in the classroom. In fact, so common is the practice that most departments and academic units have a semi-permanent, part-time, and sessional team of instructors to service the departments and units whose successful grantees buy off their teaching time. Because university teaching needs to be fertilized by research, it is widely believed that if teachers are to be effective, they must complement their teaching by research. They must be active readers and even publishers, if they are to communicate new ideas and insights to their students. However, when the university makes a part-time commitment to such an instructor, who is not formally required to do research and publish, and when the latter is made to teach four to six courses in order to make financial ends meet, it is likely that such a teacher will make less than a full-time commitment to the students in each course. This is not to say that part-time teachers are not competent as a group, but that they are often exploited and forced to spread their efforts thinly over a large number of courses in fields that they could not possibly keep up with professionally.

Aside from the problems associated with the flight from the classroom, poor university teaching has several sources associated with lower levels of faculty engagement in undergraduate teaching: tenured professors who are simply unprepared pedagogically for teaching as a vocation; tenured professors whose tenure protects them from dismissal and who put in less than conscientious effort in the classroom; recently minted but not-yet-tenured professors, who are new to teaching and its many challenges; and the growing numbers of itinerant, non-tenured, part-time instructors, who are forced to move from department to department for $8,000 to $10,000 per course. Of relevance here is that while the university receives a substantial break on salaries by hiring part-time instructors, the students do not; they pay the same tuition for a course as they would have had the course been taught by a seasoned professor who is an expert in the field. After all, the focus of university is ostensibly on gaining access to knowledge, and a seasoned professor is more likely to possess that knowledge than is someone whose knowledge of a field is simply based on reading of textbooks assigned to students (usually done one week ahead of students, if teaching the course for the first time). But again, it is also the case that some of these seasoned professors are not effective teachers for all types of students, and different students will learn more from different teachers.[45]

In fact, years of scholarly research show that good students, with high ability, can do well in a course, regardless of the quality of teaching. However, weaker students are much more dependent on the quality of teaching for their performance in a course. For example, professors prefer to teach in abstractions, while students prefer more concrete material, and the weaker the student, the more concrete the preference. In addition, students prefer to 'co-construct' with their teachers, to feel that they are learning along with the teachers, rather than feel that the teacher already knows 'everything' about an area.[46] Good students are more likely to relate to professors' more abstract thinking and therefore can keep up with, and possibly add to, professors' line of thought when dealing with complex topics.

This differential ability to learn and engage complex material means, however, that as a greater number of weaker students come into a system, the onus is on the system to find ways to teach them more effectively, but the trick is to do so without compromising standards. Efforts are underway to do just this, although it is thought that when universities grow beyond 15,000 students, as the director of the NSSE, George Kuh, notes, 'At some point, systems such as safety nets, early warning systems, and special support programs may not be able to ameliorate the deleterious effects of large size without taking a significant toll on faculty and staff.'[47]

Kuh is the foremost expert on student engagement and recently published findings on exemplary American universities (out of the hundreds that have used the NSSE) that scored high on measures of student engagement and graduation rates and therefore 'added value' to the student experience.[48] Kuh's intensive study of these twenty institutions provides insights and models for schools that are attempting to improve low levels of student engagement and low graduate rates. He calls these exemplary schools Documenting Effective Educational Practice (DEEP) institutions. He stresses that student engagement is a double-sided coin. On the one hand, if students are to be successful, they must put in the necessary time and effort, writing more papers, reading more, and discussing academic material with their peers and profs more. But on the other hand, institutions must allocate resources and provide incentives for students to put in the time and effort to reach a certain standard. As noted in the last section, Kuh's research indicates that when the bar is raised, most students will strive to reach it, and that in many schools first-year students are actually surprised at how low the bar is, so they begin early to exert less effort than they otherwise would have had the expectations and challenges been higher. Of course, requiring more effort of students requires more efforts of faculty, and this requires a combination of more resources (like more faculty, so classes are smaller) and more engagement among faculty in their courses (like requiring more writing, reading, and participation).

Kuh concludes from his research that DEEP schools share six features that foster student engagement and persistence:

- A 'living' mission and 'lived' education philosophy
- An shakeable focus on student learning
- Environments adapted for educational enrichment
- Clearly marked pathways to student success
- An improvement-oriented ethos
- Shared responsibility for educational quality and student success[49]

These six features are all complex in their own right, and institutions must be careful to ensure that they are fully and properly implemented. For example, while a school may have an espoused mission statement, it will also have an enacted one – what it actually does and how it serves students. Some schools give lip service to their 'official' undergraduate mission, and actually devote most of their attention to the research productivity of their faculty members. The DEEP schools minimize the gap between their espoused and enacted missions.

While Kuh's research into institutions is important, individual faculty members must develop their own strategies if they are to engage students. Again, we can consult Kuh's research, reiterating the three components of deep learning he assesses in his studies of student engagement:

- Higher-order learning, which requires students to utilize higher levels of mental activity than those required for rote memorization
- Integrative learning, which requires integrating acquired knowledge, skills, and competencies into a meaningful whole

- Reflective learning, which asks students to explore their experiences of learning to better understand how they learn[50]

These components of deep learning all require that faculty members develop ways to potentially engage *all* students in a class, having them 'connect the dots' of course material individually and collectively, and move up a learning curve in writing, reading, and speaking. Of course, the larger the class, the more difficult this is to do, and the more disengaged students there are enrolled in a class, the more a professor must engage in a Sisyphusian task of getting those students to prepare for all classes, attend all classes, and participate in class discussions and other activities. Techniques to help faculty members do so are being developed, some with the aid of interactive technologies ('clickers' that each student uses to respond to items in the professor's PowerPoint presentation), and others with the collection of 'best practices' from professors who have made strides in counteracting student disengagement and the anonymity inherent in large classes.[51]

Conclusion: Higher Education as a Big Business

Whatever beliefs and hopes we want to maintain about higher education and its role for the future of society, the economy, and for its graduates, we have to admit that the system is not without its problems. Even the most adamant defender must recognize that the system can be seen in more than one light, and is not a panacea for our economic problems, social ills, and individual destinies. The contradictory and stressful situations in which many professors now find themselves epitomize these problems. In fact, ignoring the problems professors face and taking a Pollyanna view is exactly the wrong thing to do if we want to fix the system and provide university educations that truly develop human talent and potential.

Fixing the university system must begin with the systems upon which it is built. In particular, we need to begin with the secondary system that has nurtured widespread disengagement and rampant grade inflation in its attempt to soft-sort students, while at the same time avoid excessive dropout. However, in many regions of Canada, the dropout rate is still high, in spite of this supposedly more benign system of soft-sorting. We clearly need a system that suits students with all ability levels and motivations, such that those with non-intellectual potentials and motivations have viable options at the secondary level other than a faint hope of becoming a doctor, lawyer, or professor. For them, skills training *during the high school years* needs to be provided so that they find secondary school involvement meaningful to their lives. All interested and properly motivated students should then be provided viable options at the post-secondary level, whether it involves the trades, community college, or university. Students with meaningful experiences at the secondary level should be more likely to make sensible choices for a post-secondary education, if that is their desire at that time. Some will want to wait until they are emotionally prepared; indeed, they should not be pushed into something for which they are not ready. A system that provides such options will in the end be more kind and realistic to students, as well as more productive for society. However, simply ignoring these problems and passing as many as possible onto universities, and expecting professors to teach effectively under such circumstances, is unrealistic, and no manner of public relations spin by governments or university administrators will change that fact. We return to this problem in the final chapter of this book when we consider policy.

3 The Student as a Reluctant Intellectual

Many of today's university students have been funnelled into higher education as a result of policies based on the belief that a university education is superior to all other forms of job preparation. This belief stigmatizes other forms of learning and training as well as occupations that do not have a university credential as a requirement. This is unfortunate for that majority of young people who will not go to university, because they prefer to do other things, cannot afford it, or do not make the grade in high school. However, it is also unfortunate for those young people who are pushed into a situation for which they are unprepared academically or emotionally. It is with these students that this chapter is primarily concerned – the young person who is reluctant to undertake an intellectual journey, but who is thrust into an arena of intellectuals (professors) and would-be intellectuals (students). These students are overlooked in the one-sided, good-news stories about a university education.

The following analogy can help us understand how these students might experience university. Imagine if circumstances were different and we had developed an occupational system where one had to graduate from an art school instead of a liberal arts university to qualify for white-collar jobs. Instead of intellectual criteria, we would all be judged on our artistic abilities. Imagine how you would feel if you were pushed into an art school and had no interest in art and little or no artistic ability. Beyond this, imagine your reaction if your future depended on your ability to satisfy the demands of high-level artists and pass their tests. Would you be resentful, lost, wanting to cut corners, or looking for some other way to play the system and get a credential that is likely irrelevant to what you want to do with your life? Welcome to the world of the reluctant intellectual – the disengaged student.

If readers find our depiction of these circumstances gloomy or cynical it is because we are trying to impress on them some of the gritty realities of the world in which these students live, and how others are affected by these circumstances. As we noted in the introduction, the public-relations type, good-news stories about the many good students in the system who benefit greatly from their university education and go on to enjoy lucrative and rewarding careers are the only stories the public hears about university students and graduates. The public does not need to hear more of these stories, and dwelling on them leads us to ignore the fact that a debate is needed about what to do to fix the educational system. We are telling a different story about the blues that people experience as a result of the current crisis of higher education, and telling this story makes us appear more one-sided than is the case, especially to those who are in denial, who may have unwittingly involved themselves in the disengagement compact, or who believe that there is no crisis in the system. We can live with that and we hope readers can handle a more nuanced and complex story that is not all good news.

The Hazardous Passage to Adulthood

Families today face a complicated situation when it comes to their children leaving home and assuming adult independence. As we have noted, baby boomers did it early and found entry into the labour market and/or post-secondary system relatively easy. In fact, baby boomers were a historical anomaly, aided by the unprecedented prosperity of the mid-twentieth century. It was in their early adulthoods that many baby boomers experienced financial difficulties, riding the roller coaster of recessions in the 1980s and 1990s. However, it is the legacy of these recessions that is making it more difficult for their children to get a foothold in adulthood, whether through direct entry into the labour force or through the post-secondary system of education. We have published extensively on this matter elsewhere, most recently in *Critical Youth Studies: A Canadian Focus*.[1]

There is currently a proliferation of theories about the 'hows,' 'whys,' and 'whats' of the transition to adulthood, as implied earlier in reference to the names given to the current cohort coming of age. Our approach has been to emphasize the deteriorating material (financial) conditions facing cohort after cohort since the collapse of the youth labour market in the late 1970s and early 1980s that left young people with fewer routes to financial independence. Because economic prospects for young people in their late teens and early twenties were poorer, more and more young people were put in the position of having to 'remain younger longer.' In other words, they have found themselves having to live with their parents longer, depending more than past generations on their parents' good graces for financial support, and to stay in school longer, winding their way through a curriculum that many of them feel is imposed on them against their will by unsympathetic adults.[2] The vast majority of the youth population experience this through the secondary system, and about 60 per cent do so in the post-secondary system.[3] This financial insecurity has been exacerbated by a greater onus put on the young person to make a range of life-altering choices, a phenomenon that has been referred to as the 'tyranny of choice' and can be the source of considerable unhappiness and misfortune.[4]

Other approaches have looked not so much at the cause of the current situation as the consequences of it. The most popular approach in the media, and therefore among the public, is what can be called the 'coddling model' characterizing the millennial generation. This approach looks at ways in which young people have been 'infantilized' or kept immature by their parents and schools, and therefore are ill-prepared to take the steps to emotional and financial independence. Whether financial dependence causes emotional dependence, or whether the reverse is the case, is not necessarily well articulated in these approaches, but it is perhaps useful to parents to learn about one of the popular formulations of the coddling model, developed by the well-known pediatrician Mel Levine, in his recent *Ready or Not, Here Life Comes*.[5] In our view, his approach helps us better understand the more severely disengaged student, but not the more engaged students. He openly admits that his characterization of young people does not include the entire generation, so we shall present his views in some detail. For if what he says is true, that is all the more reason for us all to be concerned about disengagement and its long-term consequences.

According to Levine, there is a pandemic among young Americans of 'work unreadiness': 'Swarms of start-up adults, mostly in their 20s, lack the traction needed to engage the work side of their lives. Some can't make up their mind where to go and what to do, while others find themselves stranded along a career trail about which they are grievously naïve and for which they lack broad preparation.'[6]

In researching his book, Levine interviewed young people and their employers. Many young people apparently cannot focus on their work in their first jobs, even after obtaining undergraduate and graduate degrees. Their employers complain that they do not have a long-term perspective and are driven to satisfy immediate gratifications. Especially after receiving so much education, this translates into an aversion for the routine and drudgery that accompany most jobs, and an unwillingness to recognize that they are the new ones in the workplace and need to pay their dues. Moreover, the prolonged education also appears to lead them not to identify with the adult world. Thus, according to Levine, the school-to-work transition is unusually hazardous for many in this cohort, especially those making poor adjustments without the sense that they are out of touch with workplace expectations (like showing initiative or fitting into the rank and file of authority).

Levine attributes this pandemic of maladjustment in this generation to several sources, including parents and the educational system, but also to the matrix of unique influences that have conditioned the upbringing of this cohort. Most influential is that as they were growing up, they were heavily oriented to their peers, and set apart from adult society. Consequently, many failed to develop adult role models and instead role-modelled each other. This produced a generationally high level of 'other-directedness,' where the need for peer acceptance is paramount. Marketers capitalized on this in their adolescence and introduced intense pressures for each young person to be 'cool' within a commercialized and materialistic youth culture. Thus, Levine charges, most young people want to be popular, admired, and 'special,' but all of these are precarious forms of ego-inflation.[7] Many of these young people are now entering universities as a matter of course accompanying the middle-class coming-of-age that is common in contemporary Western societies. However, their childhood and adolescence can be a hard act to follow, to the extent that they 'have grown up in an era that infiltrates them with unfettered pleasure, heavy layers of overprotection, and heaps of questionably justified positive feedback.'[8]

Life at university often prolongs this dependence on peer approval, as some young people continue to be segregated from adult society; in turn, adult society is seen by them as an annoyance in the way of personal gratification and glorification. Levine argues, in line with other characterizations of the millennium generation, that this cohort has been over-structured by their parents and schools, making it difficult for many of them to really become the independent agents they fancy themselves to be. As a result, initiative and originality can be problems, making it difficult for them to learn, and for professors to teach them, at the university level. In addition, the excessive structure of test taking, in the absence of analytic essays and verbal presentations, leaves many in this generation ill-prepared for advanced study requiring more than rote memory. Without these skills, many students are more likely to prefer professors who entertain them by being funny while not requiring much work from them. This leaves them ill-fitted for later jobs that are not entertaining and that require higher cognitive skills. So far, he seems to be describing the disengaged segment of students rather well. Levine summarizes the kernel of the problem as follows:

> Not uncommonly, start-up adults believe that everything they engage in is supposed to generate praise and fun, as opposed to being interesting and valuable. The quest for effusive verbal feedback has been the prime motivator throughout their lives, as they have sought approval from teachers, and coaches. Unbridled and sometimes unearned praise may, in fact, fuel the pressure for grade inflation.[9]

Many university students are now diagnosed with learning disorders, but Levine thinks that the most common 'disorder' is 'incomplete comprehension' that comes from a life-long reliance of rote memory to the exclusion of an understanding of underlying principles that would allow problem-solving independent of ready-made, multiple-choice answers. Many real jobs involve problem-solving where no one will come to the rescue to provide the answer, or where one of four choices cannot be picked to address every problem. Again, the culprit is too much pre-set structure in the learning environment, a problem that also emerges when it comes to self-management. Levine sees many university students as too disorganized to prioritize and integrate tasks with multiple components, like writing essays. Yet again, we can see the disengaged student in his formulations.

Clearly, this characterization does not apply to all students, and Levine is quick to point out that many students handle university and the transition to work just fine. The issue is now the number of students who do not do so, and he believes this number has grown to the point that action must be taken. Our own research, and that of others presented in the preceding chapters, supports his contention that more students are having difficulty engaging in their studies in a way that rises to the standards that once prevailed in universities, and that grade inflation is central to this problem. He also suggests several solutions with which we concur in dealing with the 'new student,' as mentioned in the previous chapter. For example, career counselling and placement services need to be beefed up to take advantage of what we know about the problem and what we can use to help young people understand themselves. This includes individualized counselling and vocational-aptitude tests. Levine also calls for a curriculum that better helps students understand themselves (such as how their identity is formed) and reduce their naivety about the world they will enter. These efforts can be embedded in existing courses, or provided in specially designated courses. As sociology professors with a critical approach to the discipline, we already do so in our courses, but elsewhere have called for an 'education for choice,' where students are taught both about the mechanics of effective choice-making and the consequences of different types of choices.[10]

Levine further recommends that university curriculum be re-calibrated to reflect a preparation for the challenges of the life to come, and to stop its slide toward a high school catering to the paths of least effort to earn high grades. This would include assignments whose completion parallels how tasks are carried out in the workplace, for example, by collaborative project-management. He also calls for professors to vary their teaching methods in ways that reach floundering students, but to do so in a way that does not exacerbate the problem. Overall, he calls for the university 'to avoid hitching itself to that pleasure-packed bandwagon.' If it does not, students prone to disengagement will increasingly view the academic aspect of the experience as 'a credentialing process to put up with while they are having a ball for four years.'[11] We could not agree more, and we are sure that parents do as well. In the final chapter, we look at ways in which universities can change the direction they are taking to accommodate disengaged students who are simply along for the ride.

The Millennial Generation

The crisis in Canadian universities of which we speak did not begin with this generation, or cohort. Rather, it developed slowly as grades inflated in high schools and the youth job market shrank, steering more and more people to stay in universities. Indeed, as we have seen, inflated grades were used in high schools to prevent dropouts, and in universities to fill upper-year courses in a fiscal competition among departments and faculties. We can trace the rise of grade inflation and the increase in disengagement to the 1970s, and see how it influenced early cohorts of late baby boomers, and then so-called Generation Xers. Let us be clear, then, that we are not blaming the situation we are describing on some sort of character defect of the current generation of students. These students are responding to structural influences beyond their control, structural influences that we ourselves have been observing over the past several decades. However, the situation has worsened dramatically since at least the early 1990s, and especially over the present decade, prompting us to write this book and encourage a public debate about what to do about the problem. At the same time, there are aspects of this generation that we must understand if we are to deal effectively with the problem, so we describe some of the thinking about what is unique to this generation.

The current cohort passing through universities has been dubbed various names like the millennial generation, Generation Y, echo boomers, and comers, but the term *millennial generation* seems to have stuck most with the media and the public.[12] Whatever the name, this cohort was born roughly in the early 1980s and later. Neil Howe and Bill Strauss, the two marketing consultants who coined the term, designate 1982 as the most significant date because that is the birth year of those who turned nineteen in the year 2000. It is not crucial what the starting date for this cohort is; rather, the experiences they share in common is, because these experiences shape their values and attitudes as they come of age and how they approach the transition to adulthood.

The following description summarizes characterizations of the millennial generation that follow the assumption that this generation has been more coddled than others – treated with extreme care and attention – and may make some of them more prone to academic disengagement than others.

Among other things, what this generation as a whole is thought to have in common is growing up with advanced technologies: computers – including the Internet, email, and instant messaging – TVs in their bedrooms, cell phones, and miniature music electronics (post-Walkman devices like iPod and MP3 players). They also grew up in the shadow of their parents' baby boomer generation, which involves a unique mix of permissiveness and anxiety, like fears about their personal safety – symbolized by car seats, bicycle helmets, stranger-proofing – and strong pressures to stay in school – bolstered by grade inflation and social promotion. The net result of these technological and parental influences is a generation that has been wired to a virtual world-at-large, especially through their peers, but who have been protected from realities in their immediate lives.

Within this contradiction of exposure to the harshness of the 'virtual,' but protection from the consequences of the 'real,' this generation is believed to be heavily connected with parents who fear that something will upset or hurt them; hyper-social peers through electronic technology; conflict-ridden schools that bend over backwards to keep them attending; and pervasive mass-marketed consumer culture where marketers have taken advantage of their being 'wired' to receive messages from multiple media. This is the most marketed-to generation ever, the generation that has been the object of most parental fear about their safety, and in many ways the generation that has had the easiest passage through the primary and secondary educational systems.

We present this characterization not to put young people down or to over-simplify them, but to help us understand how they might experience the current transition to – and passage through – university. If this characterization has even some truth-value, it helps explain why so many are having such difficulty with university: why so many expect such high grades for little effort and why disengagement is so widespread. If the above characterization has any merit, we can understand how many have been poorly prepared for the potential university experience: a rigorous, no-excuses, intellectual journey that requires them to bear down and focus on their studies to the exclusion of the multitude of influences that saturate them through the media and technologies with which they are wired.

As sociologists we recognize the difficulties inherent in using generational analyses. First and foremost is the tendency to over-generalize, but this is a pitfall of any analysis that uses a large population as a unit of analysis. To illustrate this problem, after elections we are often told that the 'Canadian voter' has spoken and wants something (change, renewal, more of the same, etc.). While these sorts of statements may be true at the unit of analysis of 'the voter,' in reality the statement simplifies matters. At a different level of analysis – that of types of voters – the fact will be that only a certain percentage of voters elected a party to power. Then, if we go to another level of analysis – the entire population – we shall find that a minority of the population actually favour the party elected into power (as low as 20–25%). So, while the most general statement about the Canadian voter has some truth-value, it must be understood at that level and not to represent the entire Canadian population.

In speaking of entire generations, we encounter similar issues, for while we might generalize about the millennial generation or baby boomers, at more specific levels, there are different types of people in each generation, and within these types certain characteristics will be shared only by degree. It is for this reason that when speaking of university students from the millennial generation, we qualify which type of students we are discussing, and the empirically validated typology of engagement discussed throughout this book is the most expedient for our purposes. Accordingly, we continue to use the distinction between fully engaged (some 10%), partially engaged (about 40%), and disengaged (approximately 40–50%) when speaking about students in those cases where we do not want to be misunderstood as over-generalizing.

The Gamut of Student Engagement

As professors with over fifty years of combined university-level teaching experience, we have had our fair share of the rewards that come from interacting with bright, motivated, and dedicated students. Such students can make one's day, one's year, and indeed one's career. These fully engaged students are a joy to teach and learn from, just as they are a source of concern as we worry about alienating them in classes, especially in those courses with a marked unevenness between the 'top' and the 'bottom' halves of student preparedness. The bright students who should be at the 'top' of classes are not only the ones who are informed or who are quick to process new information, but rather the ones who are open-minded, and who come prepared to be challenged and to learn. They accomplish this in preparing for class by doing assigned readings, thinking about them in depth in advance of class, and formulating their own ideas about the salient points in them. Only when enough students do this in advance of class can higher learning involve dialogue and challenge, and move beyond rote learning and the mere exchange of opinions.

Over the years we both have had students who went on to gain academic distinctions, to win gold medals, to complete master's and doctoral degrees, to graduate from law, medicine, and MBA programmes, and to occupy prestigious positions in the economic, political, social, and educational hierarchies as highly valued and productive citizens. These are the students about whom we do not seem to talk enough – the ones who are to be found every year, in every cohort, and in every class, and who readily convince us that our decisions to become professors were wise ones. At every turn, they reward our commitment to teaching. Our sentiments are well stated by a professor from the University of Virginia, who wrote the following about one of his own outstanding students: 'He's endlessly curious, has read a small library's worth, seen every movie, and knows all about showbiz and entertainment ... When I talk with one of his other teachers, we run on about the general splendours of his work and presence.'[13]

Singing the praises of outstanding students is a relative matter, however, and makes the most sense when they are compared with those students who are not outstanding or who are even downright poor because of their lack of engagement. University teaching and student evaluation is a comparative enterprise: the outstanding are such only to the extent that others are not. Our aim in the remainder of this chapter, then, to is develop a profile of the latter with a view to explaining critically, why, instead of making their professors proud, an increasing number of university students do quite the opposite – frustrating them by not even trying or by putting out a half-hearted effort. And while this is not meant to beat up on the weak students or to place all the blame for their weakness on them, they must assume a fair measure of the responsibility. Thus, while the professor from the University of Virginia spoke so glowingly of his student, he laments the absence of fire and passion in many other students. They inspire little admiration and appear to inhabit a world that is uninterested in genius, a world whose 'sad denizens drift from coffee bar to Prozac dispensary.'[14] He further laments that 'many of them have imbibed their sense of self from consumer culture in general and from the tube in particular. They're the progeny of 100 cable channels and omnipresent Blockbuster outlets.'[15] Here, we can see how some of the blame for the crisis of the contemporary university needs to placed on the wider, feel-good, materialistic, consumerist society discussed in the previous chapter.

Unlike earlier generations that had to put out the effort to read to acquire information, the current generation is one that with little effort can 'click on' for information. Practice and experience in reading and writing, and the analytic skills they impart, are today eclipsed by the seductive technology of personal computers, video games, iPod and MP3 players, text messaging on cell phones, movies on DVDs, and similar pursuits that do not expand one's vocabulary, do not teach punctuation or grammar, do not stimulate the imagination, and do not cultivate an appreciation for intellectual culture among young people today. In this respect, the professor from the University of Virginia has found that, on the whole, 'listening to one another, students sometimes change their opinions. But what they generally can't do is acquire a new vocabulary, a new perspective, that will cast issues in a fresh light.'[16]

As we shall discuss later, this may be part of the reason why so many students passing through universities today find themselves at odds with the traditional conception of the university as a place where the analysis of complex ideas requires a preparedness to engage those ideas at increasingly sophisticated levels of philosophical and conceptual abstraction. The here-and-now attitude of concrete and practical rewards that characterizes much of contemporary, hi-tech, popular culture combines with a drive to instant gratification in a society of plenty where most things are treated as disposable. These conditions simply do not suffice to prepare prospective university students for the challenges that professors are capable of providing.

Awareness of this problem is slowly spilling out into the public consciousness. For example, one commentator recently wrote in the *Globe and Mail* that unprepared students 'are an open secret on every university and community college campus in the country. Their presence is an embarrassment to everyone, including themselves. They are the barely literate – students whose skills in reading and writing (and often mathematics) are woeful.'[17] Another *Globe and Mail* commentary reported that the University of Ottawa now has two full-time statisticians whose job it is to flag weak students and offer them remediation services in their areas of need.[18] Meanwhile, at the University of Waterloo, an entrance exam in writing proficiency is administered during the first week of classes. This exam includes a short essay (five paragraphs) that is graded on punctuation, syntax, and grammar – the standard elements that are necessary to be correct before someone can judge the substance of the paper – the thesis, strength of argument, use of theoretical perspectives, and critical analysis of key issues. Apparently, 25 per cent of students fail this simple test. For those parents who believe their children were properly prepared by their high schools, this has to be a chilling statistic, and one that takes us back to the introduction of our book where we identify three hopes parents have for their university-bound children, of which this is the first.

This *Globe and Mail* article goes on to characterize this situation as follows:

> Although professors have long lamented the English and math skills of their students, they are increasingly complaining that too many students – some with top marks – arrive on campus unprepared for the rigours of academia. These students struggle to string together a sentence, let alone a paragraph ... It's a perplexing problem that has become the topic of much debate on university and college campuses. Some officials blame grade inflation at the high school level. Others say that in this primarily visual world, there's little focus on the written word.[19]

One professor at George Brown College in Toronto, who teaches writing skills and has published guides on the topic, estimates that many students arrive there with grade-9 writing skills. He notes that these students are good at emailing and surfing the Internet, 'but when it comes to basic literacy, basic writing skills, they are challenged.'[20]

At the core of this issue is the debate about whether the problem is getting worse – is the trend robust? All indications are that the problem is serious and getting worse, and is not merely the result of universities becoming more severe and professors more crotchety. For instance, although the math and English mediation programmes are not mandatory at the University of Ottawa, in 2004, some 2,500 students enrolled in them, up from only 300 students in 2000. Another difference from the past is that weaker students were more likely those with lower entrance grades, but this is no longer the case. According to an administrator in the University of Waterloo's English proficiency programme, some students with A-pluses in high school English have failed their simple (five-paragraph) English test.[21]

Meanwhile, Simon Fraser University (SFU) introduced new admission requirements (80% for grade 12 English and 70% for math). Those with lower grades can take an English-placement test if they want to press for admission. According to a discussion paper produced by SFU, this move was in response to the complaint that

> a 'significant' number of undergraduate students admitted to SFU are 'poorly equipped' to write at the first-year level or begin the required quantitative courses. The result ... is plagiarism, grade inflation, and a lowering of the levels of lectures and discussions. 'Many faculty members and students have spoken of the demoralizing effect of this problem.' ... One source of this problem is that standards from high school are inconsistent.'[22]

As we have argued, these problems of poor preparation and disengagement paradoxically go to the heart of the matter of grade inflation, which makes it more difficult to separate the weak from the mediocre from the strong. But where do these weak students come from? Is it a facile matter of individuals failing to make judicious choices, as many administrators, teachers, and members of the public at large are so wont to claim? In a social system where good students are praised and rewarded and poor students are ridiculed and frustrated, why would any student choose to do poorly? Surely the existence and growing presence of weak students at our institutions of secondary and post-secondary education merit more critical understanding and explanation, for like it or not, they are an integral part of our society and the integrity and viability of that society are best measured by *both* its most and its least well-educated members. So, we must begin with the question previously posed about why so many poorly prepared students are now found at all levels of higher education, and explore its multiple answers.

Voices of Disengagement

Not wanting to make the mistake of writing about those whom we do not consult, the following section contains the actual words of our students who have spoken out about the causes and sources of their own emotional and intellectual disengagement from the university. In this section, we report on the substance of a number of encounters we have had with students as a routine part of our jobs: in class discussing educational issues, and in office hours fielding students' complaints, compliments, and pleas for compassion. In addition, we have countless discussions out of class and hundreds of email messages. We have kept records of these, both as paraphrases and verbatim, and report the most illustrative of them here. In reporting them, we shall use the term *us* rather than specify which of us observed it. This simplifies the text that would be used and preserves anonymity of the parties involved.

As we have noted, in the current crisis facing the system of higher education, there is enough blame to go around. And students must themselves assume their fair share. In this respect, professors often complain that the consumer culture clashes with the job of the student as traditionally conceived. On average, students are expected by professors to put in a forty-hour week just as if they had a normal job. One difficulty is that many students have full- and part-time jobs in addition to their full-time jobs as students, as we shall see in the next chapter. This means that in terms of time and effort, something has to give, and invariably it is the time allotted to their studies and even their attendance at class. This is why we often hear our students complain that they cannot prepare for their classes by doing assigned readings. Chief among their reasons for not being able to 'pre-read' are summed up in the following comments:

- 'I try to read ahead of time and be prepared for the week ahead, but things like essays and assignments make it hard to keep up with the readings.'
- 'I had a test in another course and had to study for it.'
- 'Professors think you only have one class, so they assign you a ton of work.'

- 'It is too much to do before class. I do it after class.'

Clearly, by not doing the reading prior to the class the student will not derive the full effect of the lecture and any discussion that might be generated (and the more students prepare, the better the class discussion can be), and this is often a sore point with professors, who see it as a time-management problem on the part of students. Professors who teach smaller, seminar classes are particularly galled if most of the students show up without having done the reading for the class. The pregnant silences are most uncomfortable, if not embarrassing, and faced with them, some professors have been known to dismiss the students and walk out of the class. The claim that the reading is 'too much' suggests that there are other things competing for the students' time and attention. As one student asserted boldly, 'Professors are strange beings who don't understand that their students have a life outside of school like friends, lovers, family.'

While some courses may require exorbitant amounts of reading, we find that the amount of reading doesn't matter – a certain number of students will show up unprepared, even if only twenty to thirty pages are assigned per week. In fact, assigning less reading can encourage students to quickly scan it before class, and therefore spend no time thinking about it in advance of class discussions. On the other hand, students who manage their time well do not make such complaints, so serious observers, such as parents paying the bills, are justified in asking just how long it takes a committed student to read thirty pages, and why this would get low priority if the student is serious about the primary task at hand – learning. And why should essays and assignments conflict with class preparation if a student has a well-managed schedule, similar to what might be expected in the workplace? For those students who do not have time to do even to the basic readings of a course, how did their priorities get thus arranged, and why does the system let them away with it?

While it is commonplace for students to miss classes or show up unprepared with the excuse that they had an essay due or an exam that week in another course, we can tell parents and other serious observers that engaged students can easily handle university workloads. We have been told this by students whom we would count as a joy to teach, including older students who return to school after gaining some work experience where consequences count. These older returning students often remark about how easy it is to get high grades if they simply do what is expected of them. Yet even in a climate of low expectations, disengaged students who have piled up a large number of other priorities claim that they cannot handle the load, but they still expect high grades. It is on this ground that professors and students most commonly square off in the adversarial relationship described in the previous chapter. And as much as the university system has grown into a business, the hapless professor is left to bear the consequences felt by these dissatisfied customers.

While it is not difficult to find students with a litany of complaints, there is also a widespread willingness to uncritically accept the university's definition of this situation. For example, when students blame professors for their own poor performance or speak of unresponsive administrators as an obstacle to their success, the system itself is let off the hook. That most students will eventually go to their convocation proudly holding their degrees, in pictures with smiling parents, speaks to the maintenance of the overall legitimacy of the system. But given all of the problems we identify in this book, one must question how the current system prevails. One answer is with the central cultural value of individualism in Western culture, according to which one takes individual praise or individual blame for the consequences of one's actions. Those who believe in individualism are discouraged from pointing fingers at a system that is malfunctioning and are encouraged to adopt a certain sense of resignation about that system. Thus, as students are made to feel they are the architects of their own destinies, one of our students declared to us recently, 'I think students themselves alienate themselves. University gives you all the choices and you decide what you want to do with them. Nobody tells you what to do.'

As for grade inflation, while the majority of students we have spoken with recently were confident that university grades were *not* inflated, it makes sense that when asked how they felt about those who get high grades with minimum effort, the most common answer pointed to the belief that the ones with high grades have *natural* ability or are *naturally* smart.[23] In other words, those who really apply themselves and still get low grades tend to blame themselves for not being naturally smart. This tendency to give naturalistic explanations for social situations also plays into the legitimacy of the current system. And all remains intact so long as students continue to say things like 'I don't consider myself bright at all really. I do find that I was bright enough to get to university, but I have found it very difficult.' Or, 'I have the brightness but not the grades.'

Regardless of their veracity, much of what students have to say is well worth heeding by professors, administrators, and policymakers. Of particular interest is the way their complaints and concerns often address those things about which the university is in deep denial: high tuition costs, crowded classrooms, poor and ill-prepared teachers, and a system of testing and grading in watered-down courses that leave a great deal to be desired. If one wanted to identify a culprit, students themselves speak loudly and eloquently: it is the general high-school system that is singled out as not having prepared them for the university experience. With the exception of those who attended private schools, most complain that 'high school was a joke' and 'it required little effort for good grades.' One student even reported to an entire class during a discussion of their high school experiences that she passed on all her notes to her sister, who was a year younger and a grade lower, and that her sister made it through high school on the basis of these notes.

Once at university, however, some will thrive, while in others an adversarial attitude develops, as one student observes: 'Those students who were babied in high school now come to university in a sea of students where they have to be independent, and no one will lead them by the hand. It is a fight for survival and the fittest will survive.'

Other commonly cited woes deal with forms of student alienation that stem from 'cut-throat competition' among students for high grades, and arrogant professors, who seem to delight in putting down students, and whose lectures consist largely of repeating the material in the textbooks. So one student, angry with disinterested and ill-prepared professors, who lack passion or conviction, suggested that she was forced to teach herself and quipped that she 'might as well just pay the library $6,000 instead of the school.' Such professors, it is felt, lack dedication and give the clear impression they would rather be elsewhere or doing something else. This led one keen student to see university as a game where the professors are in control and the students are mere pawns: 'What I do not appreciate from some professors is the constant reminder of how smart and fabulous they are, how worthless and simple-minded we are, and how some professors go above and beyond to make the university *game* extra difficult.'

We also find a fair amount of disaffection related to restricted course selection in upper years, but by far one of the leading sources of student disgruntlement is the system of grading used at universities.

As might be expected, it is felt that there is too much subjectivity in the grading, and this is especially problematic when several different individual teaching assistants, sometimes with uneven English language skills themselves, are assigned as graders in the same course. Tied to this complaint is multiple-choice testing, which virtually eliminates the most arduous task that professors face: grading written work and making comments that justify the grade given. The multiple-choice test carries with it an air of facticity and objectivity, and students who do not perform well are unlikely to challenge their grade. This produces the charge that 'university does not encourage you to think about what is being taught ... I simply feel testing you on a semester's work in a two-hour exam is solely testing your ability to absorb information as quickly as possible.' Then there is the additional complaint that grading is arbitrarily tied to mandated class averages. Using a variety of computer-assisted techniques, professors can employ item analysis and bell curving to determine exactly where any given class will sit on any given test. Students are aware of this practice and they resent it deeply: 'It pisses me off that class averages are supposed to be about 68 per cent at Western. I should have gone to Brock where they give higher grades.' With a sense of resignation, a fourth-year student noted wryly that 'such tests merely test your ability to take tests,' while another quipped that 'the grading system is used to tell the under-privileged that they do not meet the grade and therefore cannot apply to graduate school.' One who spoke of cramming instead of learning, lamented that after all is said and done, 'I end the semester without having gained/retained a lot of knowledge; you learn a little bit of everything but fully understand nothing.'

Viewed together, these circumstances have bred many cynical and angry students whose complaints are not even on the radar screen of stakeholders, especially parents and policymakers. These students see themselves as caught up in a system that is not tailored to meeting their needs or interests, and that is more given over to making money. Whether or not the understanding is accurate, the mood is summed up by one young woman who charged that 'the university gets money for the first year; they have a good idea of how many students must go into the second year and they cut a lot from first year. We are just dollars to them.' The cynicism and mistrust are deep. One student charged that 'it's a game and you have to learn how to play it,' continuing to assert that there are 'administrators who don't know how the system works and who find loopholes to screw you over to having to come back for a fifth year' to make more money from you. This sense of anger and frustration is captured in students' choice words when we ask them, 'How do you feel about so many other students getting high grades with little effort?' A common reply is simply, 'It pisses me off.'

At the same time, many students sense that university standards are slipping, and the more capable students recognize the jeopardy in which this places them. Thus, one student who believed himself to be bright, felt as though the high-school mentality has taken hold at the university and the quality of intellectual intercourse is correspondingly in decline. He complained, 'They let in too many idiots and have to spend time explaining simple theories and taking attendance.' Then there are some students who recognize that there is grade inflation at the university, but are unperturbed by it. When asked how grade inflation affects them, one the cynical reply was, 'It hasn't. I just slacked off; no inflation; no 80 per cent; no scholarship.'

In many respects, as discussed earlier, these problems of legitimacy can be traced to the transformation of the university from an institution of higher learning into one of big business. As business managers, university administrators see the development of such things as distance education and online courses principally as ways of raising revenue, while being justified by high-sounding claims of making the university education more accessible to more people. It is widely acknowledged that this represents a most mechanical and inferior form of education, and one that, in the estimation of one student, confirms the view that the 'university is run like a big business only concerned with making money.' Another student bemoans that the process is wrapped up in 'too much red tape.' Students frequently complain about getting the runaround from counsellors who 'bullshit you and don't seem to know the rules themselves.' The business aspect of the university is in turn linked to student alienation and the practice of disengagement. As confessed by one undergraduate, 'An undergrad is a low life. To receive a fair ear, one needs to be in a master's or doctoral program.' Other students complain about the stress involved in 'paying for school and trying to get good grades for grad school,' and many of these feel that this stress has negatively affected their health.

The validity of student complaints is supported by many of the analyses of the current system we examined above. Other educational research also supports their claims. For example, large-scale American studies show that stress levels have increased in recent years as students find themselves juggling competing demands on their time. The percentage of first-year students reporting being 'frequently overwhelmed by all I have to do' doubled from 16 per cent in the mid 1980s to 30 per cent in the late 1990s.[24] Young women are apparently experiencing more stress (about 40% report this level, versus 20% of young men), spending more time than young men on student club activities, housework and childcare, volunteer work, and studying. Young men spend more time than young women on exercising, watching TV, partying, and playing video games – all of which can act as stress-reducers.

Student Empowerment

Another place to look for the origins of the current crisis, beyond the strain of underfunding and the turning to the business model for survival, is in the structure and culture of the wider society that houses that system. This means we shall have to look at the culture of the leading political, economic, and social institutions, and how they have shaped the choices and conditioned the attitudes of today's students. One place to begin this search is with the possibility that they are products of a university system that, when faced with declining funding, sought to 'empower' young people and to temper the criticisms of students by teachers – to promise students a more personally pleasing experience than would have been the case in the past where the resources were available to provide all students with intense, deep-learning experiences.

Focusing mainly on the faculties of Arts, Humanities, and Social Sciences, there are a number of related themes or issues that need to be addressed. The first of these is the notion of 'democratization of educational access,' which is intimately tied to the question of political correctness. Starting in the early 1990s, a new politics began to manifest itself on university campuses and soon spread to public spaces in the wider society. It was a politics of empowerment that flowed from the gains occasioned by the campus radicals of the 1960s, and came into its own as many of these radicals became professors, and as the children of those non-conformist baby boomers began to attend university.

The 1960s was a period in which young people were exhorted to question authority and to challenge the traditional ways of their society. Because the rich and comfortable generally benefit from the maintenance of the traditional ways, such challenges came to be seen as attacks against the privileged and all those who harboured elitist understandings of the social order. 'Political correctness' basically claimed that society ought to be reorganized according to the principles of radical equality; that inherited rank and privilege were undemocratic and out of step with the new merit-based society that resulted from the social movements of the 1960s: the women's movement, the civil rights movement, the environmental movement, the anti-war movement, the animal rights movement, and the student movement. It was a lively time when the Cuban Revolution of 1959 and posters featuring its flamboyant leaders (Ché Guevara and Fidel Castro) adorned the walls of students' residences, when the Black Power leaders like Malcolm X and Huey Newton exhorted young people to 'question authority,' when civil rights champi-

ons like Mahatma Gandhi and Martin Luther King Jr. inspired a generation to reject war and violence, and pop icons like John Lennon and Bob
Dylan would sing songs of peace heralding that 'the times they are a-
changin'.' Although ill-defined, what was certain was that the 'change'
pointed in the direction of greater social equality, greater transparency of
political decision making, and greater democratization of access to the
social fruits, all involving a dismantling of 'power relations,' a mantra that
has survived in what is now called 'postmodernism' by some academics.

This is the social ferment out of which the political correctness movement of the 1990s was born, and one of the areas in which it first took
root was on university campuses. Though universities were originally
conceived as elite institutions, democratization of educational access saw
the popular opening up of universities to growing numbers of 'empowered' students, who were fully aware of their rights and not at all shy to
demand them. The contradiction, however, was that while their empowerment was won in the *socially conscious* battles of these movements, the
modern-day student body tends to be *individualist*, in the materialistic
sense of the word, without the egalitarian social conscience of the 1960s.
Supporting this view are large-scale studies clearly showing a dramatic
shift in the priorities of university students, with such values as 'developing a meaningful philosophy of life' and 'being financially very well off'
trading places as important concerns.[25]

Of course, these young individualists did not appear out of nowhere.
They are the products of a social system whose core values are individualism, materialism, and consumerism. And paradoxically, their more
non-conformist and radical baby boomer parents, whether coming from
comfortable or modest families, are today's political, economic, social,
and educational guardians of that social system. But the climate of political correctness does not only comprise empowered students; there are
disempowered teachers, professors, and administrators as well.

The Retreat of Faculty

This, then, is the climate in which many professors square off with many
students (and sometimes with their parents), and rather than taking
unnecessary flak from students or having to put up with the seemingly
endless complaints and challenges, professors often seek to avoid conflict by assigning grades that are not likely to lead to protests on the part
of their students. This brings us back to the disengagement compact discussed in the previous two chapters.

In other words, bowing to pressures of political correctness, to challenges from irate parents, to cautions from nervous administrators, and
to the ploys of some manipulative students who have become democrat-
ically 'empowered,' teachers have been known to take the easy way out:
avoid confrontation and engage in 'social passing' that was once the purview of primary schools (also thereby passing the buck). This aggravates
an already-deteriorating situation and whittles away at the credibility of
the system of higher education and those institutions that it feeds. Consequently, we witness a vicious circle in which professors look to cover
themselves, some students seek to push the envelope for all it is worth,
and administrators are made to engage in a balancing act between the
two. This is why the professor from the University of Virginia, cited earlier, could write knowingly that because 'a controversial teacher can send
students hurrying to the deans and the counsellors, claiming to have
been offended,'[26] most professors are loath to buck the system and opt
instead for 'peace of mind' by placating disengaged students. But the
peace of mind is not guaranteed for, as we saw in the previous chapter,
many professors find dealing with such students a source of stress.

The net result of all this, as discussed, is grade inflation, which has pro-
gressed to the point where, regardless of ability, almost everyone who
enters university today is virtually guaranteed to graduate with a degree if
they simply pay tuition, show up for class periodically, and half-heartedly
sit for the tests and hand in the half-baked assignments in their courses.
And this brings us back to the state of affairs where universities have
become large business enterprises with customers demanding of satisfaction and their money's worth. For the disengaged student, satisfaction
translates to high grades for little effort.

Grade Inflation and the Democratization of Education

Tying education inflation to the new campus culture of democratization
and political correctness, one could identify some major strains with serious implications for the wider society. For while university degrees were
once the sole property of elites, the processes of democratization and
political correctness have witnessed the wide conferring of college and
university credentials on increasingly large numbers of individuals, who
are not necessarily academically or intellectually inclined. And this is
directly tied back into the problem of educational inflation in both its
manifestations: credential inflation and grade inflation.

Although the move toward democratization of access to higher education is a highly positive development, one has to be careful not to con-

fuse equal access with promises that all are equally prepared for the challenge of university, and that all will do equally well or will automatically graduate with equally high grades. In other words, the task is to maintain academic standards and not have them fall prey to some misguided sense of democracy that has resulted in a lowering of standards, and what many are calling a general 'dumbing down' of the curriculum. Aside from the chaos this creates for the educational system and the people affected by it, *faux* educational accessibility does nothing to address occupational accessibility after graduates leave campus with degrees in hand and pictures of their smiling parents at convocation. In other words, while it is laudable to get the disadvantaged to attend universities, it is an insult if the university experience does nothing *for them*. And to do something *for them*, it must do something *to them* – transform them in some way to add value to how they were before attending university. If the outcome is just to collect a piece of paper, the graduates from disadvantaged backgrounds can all meet afterwards to discuss their underemployment and what it is like to live with their parents, while those from advantaged backgrounds proceed as they would have if the entire generation had not been required to jump through this hoop. University of Toronto (OISE) professors Livingstone and Hart refer to this practice as 'meritocracy lite' and doubt that the public would continue to support higher-educational policies if they stopped holding the illusion that the current educational system is a great equalizer.[27]

This was the clear charge made in a provocative piece published in the *Chronicle of Higher Education* titled 'From School to College: We Must End the Conspiracy to Lower Standards.'[28] Speaking specifically about American college and university admissions, the author of the piece could well be addressing the situation in Canada today. He is concerned by the 'decline in entrance requirements and the lowering of academic standards' and the ways in which political correctness has led to the admission of students into 'diluted undergraduate programs'[29] that are not as challenging as they could be. It is felt that, spurred on by political correctness, democratic access has seen weak students going into weak programmes and demanding changes that result in the watering down of the curriculum. The *Economist* also endorsed this view when one critic wrote that 'grade inflation followed the introduction of affirmative action.'[30]

None of this is to imply or suggest, however, that the children of the elites are somehow naturally superior in intelligence. But what it does raise is the serious question of how best to identify and recruit the most motivated and talented students, whether they are of elite or more humble origins. As it stands, the fact that the elites' economic wealth permits them to afford better primary and secondary systems of education for their children, replete with better-trained teachers, better infrastructural resources and facilities, and a generally better learning environment, means that the odds will favour the children of privilege. The onus then lies on the educational authorities to devise a programme that equalizes access but avoids the paternalism associated with dumbing down. Such a programme would have as its key goal the identification of strong and weak students, whether elite or non-elite.

This is an important challenge for administrators and professors alike, for as may be appreciated, the increasingly large numbers of students that have resulted from the democratization of educational access in the 1980s and 1990s have not provoked an equally large or proportionate pattern of public educational spending on the recruitment of qualified professors, on improving library facilities, laboratory equipment, computers, and state-of-the-art classrooms. Add to this the movement of political correctness and what one finds is a highly competitive and politicized system of higher education in which the possibility of failure has been more or less totally removed if the students exerts even a modicum of effort. As one observer laments, 'We all have a sense that grading isn't what it used to be – that in today's academy, the fear of failing has all but disappeared, and that making the dean's list is no longer a pipe dream for students of the meanest capacities.'[31] In sum, then, while this politicization has contributed to greater democracy and more access, it has also led to inflation, declining standards, and student disengagement.

As the competition for scarce jobs becomes keener, education inflation appears to have taken firmer hold of society. In what is often an irrational demand for more credentials, educational institutions have responded by inventing new programmes that have given rise to charges that we are simply creating credential 'marts,' as already discussed. Because high grades are the ticket to graduate schools, professional programmes, and attractive grants, today's students are under great stress, and they experience tremendous pressure from family, friends, professors, and potential employers to qualify for ever higher educational credentials.

Consider, for example, the following. On the first day back from the Christmas break a student came to visit one of us in the office with a deeply sad look on his face as he apologetically confessed, 'Sir, I just wanted to let you know I don't really care about the grade I receive in this course, but as a foreign student if I don't get at least 80 per cent I will be asked to withdraw from my programme.'

The encounter highlighted three matters that are relevant to the recent and current cohorts: (1) the routine assumption that grade inflation is normal and the idea that anything less than an A is tantamount to failure; (2) the apparent inability of the student to realize that he was contradicting himself – 'I don't really care about grades but I do want a good grade'; and (3) the fact that this was a foreign student who had apparently learned the local student culture quite expeditiously. The key point is that as professors have grown increasingly insecure and disempowered, such students have become increasingly bold and manipulative.[32]

Empowered by the political gains of the 1960s campus radicals, some of today's decidedly non-radical students are not averse to demanding that certain materials be included in or excluded from the course curriculum, to requesting that the content, form, and weighting of tests and examinations be changed to suit their needs, to challenging professors to have their work re-graded, or simply to breaking down and crying in professors' offices. Much of this results from the dashing of what two researchers have aptly termed 'grade expectations.'[33] This current state of affairs, whether at the high school, college, or university level, is seen to stem in part from the revolution of political correctness that has empowered students to challenge professors and to shape the university experience according to the politics of the day. As one observer of the educational scene puts it, 'When only young, affluent white men attended college, the white male curriculum went unchallenged. Now every Latino, African American, Asian American, Irish American, woman, gay, and ad-infinitum wants to learn about his or her roots.'[34]

And while there is nothing wrong with learning about one's roots, with learning about the limitations of Eurocentrism and the harsh realities of racism, sexism, homophobia, and the like, such teaching/learning must not be made to replace core curriculum themes and ideas. If the existing curriculum is non-inclusive, the appropriate response is to fix it, to expand it, and make it more inclusive of marginalized themes, societies, and cultures. This is not accomplished by putting in place alternative curricula that segregate students by political ideology or by a politicized ethnic reading of history. If Eurocentrism is wrong in principle, then Afrocentrism, for example, cannot be right, since in no system of logic do two wrongs make a right. At all levels, classrooms should be sites where students are *taught* about politics; they should not *be* about politics.

Empowered by the democratization of education and the revolution of political correctness, students today have won many important rights: a say in hiring decisions, in who teaches what courses, and in the very design and content of their curricula. Whether it is the recruitment of women professors, the inclusion of works written by black historians, the admission of Native voices to politics and literature, or the integration of gay and lesbian perspectives in lecture and reading materials, some students can be quite politically astute, and that is a positive development. On the negative side, however, there are many cases where students are more opportunistic and will attempt 'to define their own workload,' and in those cases where they 'do not receive the grade they need to pass, they often hold the professor and then the administration responsible.'[35] The crisis is also traceable in part to a related educational malaise – to the 'cult of self-esteem' discussed in the previous chapter and the feel-good idea that learning must be seen as fun and enjoyable, or else it is sending the wrong message to the student.

Education as a Commodity

Among others, two general sets of attitudes are common among some of today's university students that work against the traditional mission of a liberal education. As discussed, one set sees the experience as a business transaction in which students are cast as consumers in the education marketplace, with full consumer rights. For these students a degree is a commodity, and attending university amounts to buying a product 'because of the presumption that in return for their money, they ought to receive the degree,' as one American observer puts it.[36] This orientation has been recently quantified and measured among Canadian university students with the concept of 'degree purchasing,'[37] finding that over half of these students reported that statements such as the following were true for them: 'My primary motivation in taking my degree is to get that piece of paper (the diploma) that will give me access to some good jobs.'[38]

Thus, the materialist consumer culture that has gripped the entire society also pervades the university environment, and in the language of commerce, 'since a course is something the students and their parents have paid for, why can't they do with it pretty much as they please?'[39]

The other set of attitudes is found mainly among the 'elite students' from more affluent homes, who see a university education as an 'entitlement' and who enrol in programs and take courses, according to one American observer of the educational scene, 'less for the skills acquired in the classroom than for the social cachet attached to the degree.'[40]

The first group of students 'who take the stance of consumers have an expectation that they are buying a product, namely, a college [or university] degree. If 100 credits are required for that degree, and each credit costs $100, then a college degree costs $10,000.'[41] And this is directly connected with the commodification of education and the idea that, like any other business investment, an investment in education should yield cash returns, or returns that are convertible to cash (jobs). For those students who come from the elite, and whose financial futures are more certain, a university education is more likely regarded as a stage in the life course, and is less directly tied to future job or career aspirations. Indeed, according to this same American observer, for this group, 'college is simply the next in a series of stages leading to membership in a productive society ... college is just what one does, as automatic as sex, marriage, child rearing, and buying a house.'[42]

It is in this climate that the McDonaldization or standardization of education has occurred.[43] As sociologist and social critic George Ritzer has noted, 'McDonald's has succeeded because it offers consumers, workers, and managers efficiency, calculability, predictability, and control.'[44] And what better way to control the process and prove one's success than by developing a formula that, if followed to the letter, will yield the desired results? This is efficient and calculable and will ensure a predictable outcome, all of which makes control that much easier. Once more, however, success defined in this way is not necessarily measured by learning. It is no secret that 'educational standardization dilutes learning by "McDonaldizing" education and encouraging students to plod mindlessly through degree sequences in pursuit of guaranteed vocational rewards,' as one critic remarks.[45] This critic continues by noting that 'it is important to understand exactly how credential standardization is linked to positional advantages in bureaucratic and professional labor markets.' Grades are simply a shortcut to knowing what a student knows; they don't tell us much about the student: 'Credentials reduce uncertainties about candidates' abilities to do known tasks that are associated with these positions.'[46] We thus find ourselves in the difficult position of having to take the kind of uncomfortable consolation that Winston Churchill took when he mused on the limitations of democracy as a system of rule: 'Democracy is the worst form of Government except for all those other forms that have been tried from time to time.'[47] In other words, while grades are not necessarily the best indicators of a student's promise, they are perhaps better and more easily obtained than all other presently available indicators.

Standards and Criteria

By all official counts, Canada scores high in the world on the education of its citizens. To get at the core of the problems we are discussing, however, the idea is not to compare ourselves to most other countries and comfort ourselves with the idea that though in need of change, many others are worse off than we are. Rather, what is needed is a more critical look at available resources with a view to suggesting more effective and efficient approaches to – and strategies for learning the true measure of – educational success. So if other countries are not faring well, that should not be our consolation or the comparison group we use. We should have national standards that we seek to meet, regardless of how poorly the rest of the world is doing. The campaign that began in the 1970s, to support the United Negro's College Fund in the United States, which cautioned that *a mind is a terrible thing to waste,* put the onus on the educational system to get the most out of *all* our young people and students. What has become of that campaign and those like it? Have the governments, federally and provincially, followed through on their commitments to stop the wastage of young minds? A critical look at the educational system today would seem to suggest that this is indeed not the case.

One of the major consequences of education inflation and the credential crisis is to be seen in the irrational, system-wide trend to removing educational 'standards' and replacing them with 'criteria.' Standards are specific to a concrete social environment; they are anchored in a given societal culture and value system. As such, standards reveal a great deal about a wide variety of things that a society and culture hold dear, and also tell much about those things that are eschewed. Criteria, on the other hand, merely tell us how well we are meeting those standards. But in today's educational culture, as standards have become confused with criteria, there is a crisis. At both the secondary and post-secondary levels, there appears to be a blind determination to *satisfy criteria,* which is an illogical undertaking, for one can satisfy only standards not criteria. The distinction is more than semantic, for according to Professor Emeritus Benjamin Singer, 'Attempts to meet criteria rather than satisfy standards are symptoms of a society that mass processes experience, converting it into numbers to facilitate decisions.'[48]

As criteria have come to supplant standards, we find that schools and employers rely more and more on such things as test scores as indicators of competence and as criteria for both graduation and secure employment. It is very much a blind or irrational scramble for what is mistakenly defined as educational success, for living 'in a criterially driven society, we rarely question the criterial systems in place. They are givens, convenient, possessing an air of facticity and finality, and they are difficult to dislodge, particularly when they are at the service of bureaucracies.'[49] This being the case, teachers who want to be successful and who also want their students to succeed, will teach to the test, coaching their students on the specifics of taking and passing the test, regardless of what, if any, learning takes place. And for their part, faced with increased pressure to demonstrate that they have the criteria for success (high grades), resourceful students also exhibit crass instrumental behaviours as they devise creative ways and 'attempts to outwit tests and admission examinations.'[50]

Edubusiness: University as Corporation

As discussed in the last chapter, the university system has evolved over time to justify itself through its products – credentials. From the view inside the ivory tower, professors increasingly see themselves as gatekeepers in credential marts who walk a fine line to preserve the legitimacy of a system that must sort, weed, and cool out students, while at the same time pumping out large numbers of graduates. If we look at the university system more from the outside, in the context of wider society and economy, it is coming to resemble the model of the corporation. As the university has come to resemble a corporation more than an institution of higher learning, professors are viewed more as employees, and students are treated more like clients or customers.

A key feature of the contemporary university is a system governed by corporate management principles. Over time, universities have hired professional managers in favour of administrators with academic backgrounds, who historically governed the university when it was operated more under the model of a sanctuary of truth, as discussed in chapter 2. Without administrators who have risen through the ranks of academia, there is less institutional memory and commitment to the pure ideals of higher learning. This has led to what one critic, Michael Locke, a Western emeritus professor, has labelled derisively as 'edubusiness,' or more succinctly 'edubis.'[51] According to Locke, the promotion of edubusiness erodes the academic objectives of the traditional university and feeds the substitution of business values and ethics for academic values and ethics. In the process, administrators, professors, and students become much more instrumental in their behaviour, and this in turn fuels the drive to acquire more and more credentials, which then exerts more pressures for grade inflation.

At the same time, the problem with grade inflation goes beyond academics and hits at the heart of edubis. We need large numbers of students to pay the bills for a university system that has grown so large and costly. So we admit the unqualified, give them the idea they are university material, and then professors are left with the unpleasant task of giving them the bad news by assigning low grades. The upshot is that even with low grades in watered down courses they graduate with BAs and this ramifies throughout the economy.

The instrumentality that edubis encourages is captured by Linda Sax, director of the national survey *The American Freshman*, who was moved to confess that her own students calculate that if a course component, like class participation, is not worth enough (only 10%), many students will not put out the effort.[52] Many of our own students have confessed to the same thing: seeking out course loads with the least amount of required participation and effort (also called 'shopping for courses'). In the end, the credentialed might be technically trained to complete routine tasks, but they lack the sophistication, imagination, and intellectual rounding that once came with a traditional liberal education and that included advanced literacy and analytic skills. As Locke comments, 'Success is measured by the spread of management or in the salaries achieved by graduates and not in the enrichment of their lives or of the nation.'[53]

As in any business, there are customers, and good business practice suggests that the customers are always right. Therefore, it is not difficult to see how the culture of edubusiness is integral to the culture of commodification, nor is it difficult to see how it matches well with the wider societal culture of individualism, materialism, and consumerism. For above all else, what consumers consume are commodities, and the rendering of education as a commodity has cast the contemporary student in the role of client/customer who shops for courses at the start of each term. Stated differently, educational credentials are mere commodities that are to be purchased and used as the buyer sees fit.

Edubusiness is thus very much at home in the new-look university campus environments that increasingly resemble shopping malls, those new centres of youth recreation and socialization. University campuses now have banks and banking machines, beauty salons, tanning rooms, travel agencies, pharmacies, state-of-the-art gym and exercise facilities, doctors' and chiropractors' offices, computer stores, clothing stores, record stores, and all manner of fast food outlets. To feed the consumer culture, students take on full- and part-time jobs that negatively affect their study time and study habits, which in turn could put them on a collision course with those professors who think that being a student should be the equivalent of a full-time job. As we have seen, however, not all professors are prepared to hold the line; thus, speaking perhaps too generally, our professor from the University of Virginia has stated somewhat wryly that 'at a certain point professors stopped being usefully sensitive and became more like careful retailers who have it as a cardinal point of doctrine never to piss the customers off.'[54]

Finally, we might ask how well edubis is doing at keeping its customers happy when all is said and done – when and if they graduate. Assessment is very tricky because a number of factors are involved. First, there is the actual graduation rates at universities. If at best only about 70–80 per cent of those who attempt university actually graduate from that school, we can assume that a high proportion of those who failed to do so could not be included in the 'happy customer' category. Second, there is the dual problem of actually getting in touch with those who graduate and then getting them to answer customer satisfaction questions. Surveys of graduates are notoriously problematic in terms of response rates, which tend to be about 20 per cent.[55] It is quite possible that only the happier graduates respond, and this would bias the results toward overestimating satisfaction. However, if university graduates are as happy as we are led to believe by the good-news story we hear in the press and from universities, why are so few filling out these surveys?

In any event, the results of these surveys generally show that the level of (any) satisfaction among graduates is only about 70–80 per cent.[56] However, if Canadian universities were really functioning in a free market without government subsidy where there was competition among them to produce good products, this level of satisfaction would signal the probability of imminent bankruptcy. In the business world, the rule of thumb is that customer satisfaction needs to be at least 90 per cent, for each dissatisfied customer not only does not return but is known to tell six other potential customers, each of whom tells six more potential customers, and so on, and soon there are few customers interested in what the business has to offer because of their wariness of its product or service. When there are alternatives, as in a free market, dissatisfied customers simply take their business elsewhere.[57]

At the same time, a 70 per cent satisfaction rate translates to the following estimates of graduate satisfaction of the university student population: at best 50 per cent of those who start would be satisfied with the result of their efforts (i.e., 70% of the 70% who actually complete university); at worst, only about 14 per cent are satisfied (i.e., the 20% of graduates who bother to fill out the surveys). Obviously, the percentage lies somewhere in between, but does not appear to be anywhere near the universal level that the public has been led to believe. To the extent that universities are sheltered from criticism by the public-relations type, good-news mentality of the media and policymakers, we can expect large numbers of dissatisfied customers to go unheeded.[58]

Conclusion: System Failure of Students

When we have asked our students whether they felt that there was a disengagement compact at their university (defined for them as we did in chapter 1), most agree that it exists, and many want to place the blame squarely on the shoulders of professors. One student responded that there is not really such a compact as stated; instead, she remarked that the disengagement compact should be worded 'You don't bother me too much, and I could give a damn what you get in my course. I am here for my research and that is what I will do, you insignificant worm.' Though somewhat extreme, the anger expressed here about the failure of universities to deliver, and of high schools to prepare, is not to be ignored because it is shared to a degree by many students, and as such eventually affects all stakeholders, and not just professors and administrators. Policymakers should also take heed because it is a symptom of what is wrong with the current system. And parents should take heed because this symptomatic anger can interfere with their children's development. It also reveals the fragility of two of the three hopes parents have of their university-bound children discussed in the introduction – that their children will begin university well-prepared by their high school education, and as university students they will fully apply themselves to their courses.

From the students' perspective, the fault lies mainly with those working the system. While this may not be entirely true, those supporting this system need at least to be sensitive to this malaise, and not naively presume that all is well in the ivory tower.

4 Parents as Investors and Managers: The Bank of Mom and Dad (BMD)

This chapter is written with the parents of current or prospective students in mind, to give them some idea what their children are up against, and what they as parents can expect of themselves as the primary financial and emotional support systems of their budding progeny. What we write for them will not be sugar-coated, however, or dumbed down. Instead, we want to convey the facts as we grasp them and give advice as best we can. We believe that parents will benefit from this frank information and the perspective we can provide as professors who, with some fifty years of combined experience, have taught young people who are the age of their children since the late 1970s. Many parents are for the first time dealing with young people aged eighteen to twenty-five, but we are familiar with them in a way that is unique to our profession. Moreover, we have taught several cohorts of students, so have an institutional memory of how things have changed.

Many of our students complain that their parents do not understand what they are going through, especially when it comes to deciding what to do for a career. Accordingly, we write this chapter to help parents gain a sense of their unique place in history, as baby boomers who are parenting a generation raised and coming of age under substantially different conditions – the so-called millennial generation. While we shall rely on certain generalizations about each of these generations, we believe that these generalizations have sufficient applicability to be useful.[1]

Education as an Investment

Higher education is indeed an investment, as we show in dollar terms in the next chapter. The stakes are high for everyone involved, and that is one reason professors are uncomfortable with being caught in the middle.[2] As we shall see in chapter 5, having a university degree rather than only a high school diploma can make an average difference of up to $1 million over a person's working life. For those parents who pay some or all of the cost of the university education, which is easily $50,000 dollars in Canada and $100,000 in the United States in the more expensive universities, it is perfectly understandable that they would want to see their money well spent. We find it paradoxical, therefore, that far less attention appears to be directed to the details of university as an investment, than to investments in stocks, bonds, or real estate.

We argue that parents' attention should not be directed at protecting their children and running interference for them with administrators, counsellors, and professors (as 'helicopter parents' do) so much as equipping them to handle themselves in the academic environment in a realistic, mature, and competent fashion. If they do not, they are simply putting off the need to let their children grow up and learn effective self-management and self-motivation. Giving them 'a leg up' is one thing, but fighting their battles for them is another. Contrary to the trend for the university experience to become an extension of high school and semi-dependency, it still needs to be seen as a preparation for life in adult society and the workplace.

Parents should thus educate themselves about the realities their children face in preparing for, and succeeding in, university. An organization that provides practical information on these matters is College Parents of America.[3] They promote themselves as 'a one-stop shop of information and guidance for parents – from the time they begin preparing for their children to go to college, through the complex admissions process, until their college graduation.' Parents can find resources (e.g., tips for saving money and getting into better schools), discounts on products and services (e.g., test preparation and financial planning), and advocacy (e.g., to control tuition costs and increase tax breaks) with this organization. Given the costs of even applying to schools these days, these discounts may be well worth it. We are not aware of a comparable organization for Canadian parents. The annual membership fee for 2006 was ninety-nine dollars, but as the name of the organization states, membership is available only for Americans.

Setting the Right Goals

Parents will want to arm themselves with as much knowledge as possible about the education their children will get. Some of this information is available from rankings provided by popular Canadian outlets like

Maclean's and the *Globe and Mail* (the United States has comparable ratings systems in magazines like *Newsweek* and *US News and World Report*).
However, these rankings are useful only to a degree, and can be more
misleading than helpful about the university system.[4] For example, one is
hard pressed to find any critical analysis similar to what we provide in this
book about the pitfalls of grade inflation and academic disengagement
(with the exception of the 26 June 2006 issue of *Maclean's*, as we've
already noted and some subsequent issues). In fact, these popularizations
give the impression that everyone lives happily ever after if only they can
find a school that fits them.[5] We shall not go into details about individual
schools in this book. Instead, we offer the following four bits of advice
culled from years of academic research[6] and personal experience.

First, going to university itself – any university – is more important
than going to a particular university. The principle applies in Canada as
well as in the United States, in spite of what one might hear about the
benefits of the Ivy League education, but it applies only if the student
graduates. Going part way through an undergraduate programme will
not help in the majority of cases, except perhaps if a young person is
gifted in a computer field where employers are desperate for leading-
edge programmers. But for the rest of the pack, the bachelor's degree is
all-important. More than a few business employers won't even ask what
the major was or what grades were earned. This is the credential effect,
pure and simple. Of course, if one wants to advance to graduate and professional schools, area of study and grades are all-important, but grades
are not significant predictors of later occupational benefits like salary,
net of the higher salary associated with postgraduate degrees.

Second, what goes in is highly related to what comes out. Students' initial skill level has a great bearing on the skills they will acquire and how
much they change personally by the time they graduate. This is why a
good high-school education is important – certain abilities need to nurtured before attending university. Trying to make up for poor prepara
tion can be overwhelming and is a strong predictor of failure and
dropout from university, as is a lower level of academic engagement in
high school.[7] Thus, those who begin with good capacities for writing and
speaking, for example, have better outcomes because they start at higher
levels. Moreover, they have greater potential for change because they
have already begun to climb learning curves in certain subjects. Those at
the base of a learning curve may not be able even to begin to climb that
curve because they do not grasp the basics, and are therefore more likely
to drop the course and look for courses that either do not have learning
curves or where they have already made a start up the curve.

Third, university can be a mixed experience, providing some students with more challenges and stresses than opportunities for academic and personal growth. Students who can find social support and can integrate into the available programmes tend to feel more positive about university and therefore have buffers to endure the many stressors, so that those stressors do not interfere as much with opportunities for growth and development. Similarly, erstwhile underachievers have a chance to blossom with the right approach in the right environment, thereby making up for past deficits, perhaps stemming from an inadequate high school education. In this case, personal and academic change can be dramatic because students have farther to go to reach their potential.

And fourth, as we have been stressing throughout this book, the effort and involvement students make in the academic environment is all-important. Even the most nurturing environment in the best school cannot make up for a student's apathy and lack of motivation. Similarly, even schools that do not provide nurturing settings have a certain percentage of students who will get much out of their experience there. Our research shows that students who meet their learning environments halfway are more likely to find nurturance and to benefit from their academic experiences.[8] Whether the university experience is 'transformative' (changes the student's skills and outlook), or merely sustaining (keeps the student at the same level in potential and ability to benefit from experience) depends mainly on how open the person is to what a university has to offer.[9]

This is why it is a mistake to push students to attend. Students apathetic about attending, or reluctant to attend, will likely stay that way when they get there.[10] They have the greatest odds of failing and dropping out, and even if they do graduate are more likely to be underemployed and earn less (but admittedly they may still earn more than if they had only high school, because they have the higher credential). Simply stated, most universities will not take students by the hand and force them to become active in their own learning. Certainly learning environments can be important, but students who begin with strong motivations (i.e., are pulled into the experience) will flourish, regardless of the characteristics of the university setting in which they learn or the teaching competence of the professors they have.

Taken together, the overall lesson we can learn from this synthesis of decades of research is that, irrespective of their social class and other background factors, motivated students with the appropriate aptitude, especially those who find an academic environment that supports their involvement, can gain a great deal from attending university if they put sufficient effort into it. The benefits may not be accrued immediately, either occupationally or personally, but the chances are that they will be in the long term.

Nevertheless, we must reiterate our concerns about the context in which higher education now finds itself, where more and more students are arriving without sufficient motivation and requisite abilities. Moreover, a good number are pressured by their parents and pushed by poor job prospects to spend four years doing something they would rather not do (perhaps at a later point in their lives they will be ready, however). To make matters worse, many of these 'pushed' students actually take longer than four years to complete a degree. In the United States, as we have already noted, the size of this group has reached epidemic proportions, with only about one-third of students completing their four-year degrees in four years, the median completion time now being six years (about 60% take this long).[11] This has become such an issue that completion times are being monitored by the Education Trust.[12] We recommend that readers visit this website to see how low completion rates can get at some institutions.[13] Canada has no comparable monitoring mechanism, although some universities do post their seven-year rates, which averages about 73 per cent for universities in Ontario.[14]

As we have argued, the university is now used as a panacea for an economy that does not need the labour of all young people or the level of preparation of about half of those who acquire university degrees. So we professors have been given the task of keeping large numbers of unemployable young people busy – providing a delay from adulthood for them – in hopes that things will work for them when we have given them enough lectures, tests, and essays on topics that are often at best only indirectly related to the work world for which they are preparing.

Estimating Costs

The tuition cost of one year of undergraduate study in Canada during the mid 2000s that is payable to the institution is roughly $4,000 for the general programme in arts, social sciences, and sciences, with a further 20 per cent for ancillary fees, for a total of about $5,000.[15] Additional costs include books, transportation, and room and board, which can range from about $5,000 for those living at home to $11,000 and higher (depending on life style) for those living in residence on campus or independently.[16] Thus, the total costs can range from $10,000 per year for those living at home, to $16,000 for those living independently or in residence (about half of students live away from home).[17] Of course, it is easy to incur cost overruns, so more realistic estimates are $12,000 to $20,000, respectively.

Roughly 40 per cent of full-time Canadian undergrads take out student loans, but their ability to do so is tied to the income of their parents or spouses.[18] Consequently, a certain percentage of students are caught at the cut-off point where they do not qualify for loans, or are dependent upon their parents for a certain portion of the cost. This amounts to a penalty for many of these students, so some countries do not tie loan eligibility to parental or spousal income (e.g., Sweden, as we shall see in the next chapter). At the same time, many parents generally overestimate how much their children are eligible to borrow as well as how much they might receive in grants and bursaries, creating financing problems for these students.[19]

The average amount owed by graduates increased by 76 per cent between 1990 and 2000.[20] Students who take out loans borrow about $5,500 dollars per year and end up owing $20,000 by the time they complete their BA. This is a doubling in debt (controlling for inflation) since 1980.[21] Those who live with their parents while attending have significantly lower debts (about $7,000).

When baby boomers went to university, they could earn enough to cover their tuition through six to seven weeks of summer work, even while earning the minimum wage.[22] Currently, it takes students some nineteen weeks of work to cover their tuition, meaning that not even all of a student's summer wages will cover tuition if the student makes minimum wage.[23]

The most recent research in Canada suggests that many Canadian parents are stepping up to the plate to help their children financially. About 80 per cent of students report getting help from their parents in some form, and the average annual contribution is estimated to be between $3,000 and $5,000.[24] According to a 2002 survey, half of parents with children who were expected to finish high school were saving money, while an additional third intend to do so.[25] The Canadian government introduced a plan in the late 1990s to match educational savings with grants that accumulated with the savings, but apparently only about half of parents are aware of this programme,[26] suggesting that many parents are not fully researching the best way to help their children (not to mention the missed grant money from the government). In fact, the federal government has been shifting its support away from the loan system to the tax system. Between 1990 and 2004, government student assistance based on loans declined from about 65 per cent to 40 per cent, with the remaining difference constituting tax and savings incentives.[27]

Parents most likely to save, and be aware of the government savings/ grant programmes, are from higher income brackets and have higher educations. The median amount of savings in these programmes was $4,000 per account in 2002, but $6,000 if the beneficiary was a teenager.[28] Overall, savings for children have been estimated at between $5,000[29] and $8,600[30] in 2002, with a high average of $14,000 if parents owned their house outright.

Recent surveys also find parents reporting that they are making sacrifices to save for their children's educations. These cutbacks include spending less on themselves, taking on a second job, re-mortgaging their house, and delaying their own retirement. We have many colleagues and associates who are taking the last option, especially those with more than one child in, or planning to attend, university. Other findings are that about 70 per cent of parents provide, or expecting to provide, free room and board, and about one quarter are willing to take out loans themselves to assist their children (among the latter group are parents whose income disqualifies their children for loans, but whose income is really not sufficient to pay the proportion the government expects them to).[31]

While most Canadians have a sense of the general benefits of a post-secondary education, research has uncovered their tendency to overestimate the costs of obtaining one and underestimate its salary benefits. This bias is most severe among low-income Canadians, who tend to think that the costs actually outweigh the benefits.[32] Parents who hold this view may be discouraging their children from developing a life plan that includes a higher education. Indeed, research indicates that most of the information young people acquire about higher education comes from their parents and friends. This tendency is most serious when the young person has university potential, but it is perhaps also a strong factor behind the persistent socio-economic differences in university attendance that governments have been fighting for decades (we shall explore these differences and efforts to address them in the next chapter).

Recent research finds that those from the general public on average think that tuition is $1,000 more than it really is, while those from lower-income backgrounds think it is $3,000 more (similar results have been obtained in the United States). At the same time, most Canadians think that university graduates make only about $5,000 more per year than high school gradates, when the figure is actually five times that amount

(for all university graduates, including those with graduate and professional degrees). Only one in six was even close at estimating the average
salary for university graduates (about $62,000 versus $35,000 for high
school graduates). A full quarter of Canadians apparently think that university grads make *less* than high school grads.

Research also shows that the decision to attend university is not based
entirely on considerations of monetary costs and benefits. In fact, there
appear to be strong emotional or non-cognitive factors at work, especially for low-income students whose parents did not attend university.[33]
'First-generation' students do not have the benefit of parental know-how
when it comes to planning a university education and do not have the
advantage of feeling 'entitled' to that education. As we shall explore in
the next chapter, a number of personal factors appear to discourage low-
income and disadvantaged students from thinking about university as
part of their life plan, especially if it was not in their parents' life experiences. These are personal factors, and a consensus is emerging among
researchers that no manner of financial incentives in the form of loans
and grants can overcome these personal factors to fully equalize access
to a university education.

Baby Boomer Parents and the Experiences of Their Children

Parents of the cohort passing through Canadian universities – largely the
baby boom generation – grew up in a time when their parents were happy
to set them free early in life, and that they did. They left home early –
especially the early boomers born in the late 1940s – mainly to take up
jobs in the burgeoning post-war economy, or to go to one of the new or
expanded universities with the help of a generous loan/grant system. It
did not matter so much if they did not know what they wanted to do,
because it was more possible simply to fall into a job or career, depending
on how things worked out. Even if they stayed living with their parents,
there was less sense of protectiveness: it was common for young people to
hitchhike, even long distances; backpacking around Europe, Australia,
and Southeast Asia was also popular, even for teenagers.

The baby boom generation was the first group of children raised on
television, but TV was generally watched together as a social activity, in
part because there was only one in the house. A hi-fi was a big deal in the
1950s and 1960s, but cheap stereos were an even bigger deal when they
became available in the 1970s. Telephones were shared with other family
members, again because there was probably only one in the house, so

people made plans to get together, not on the fly as can be done with cell phones. Keeping in touch with friends who moved away was expensive by phone, so people wrote letters to stay in touch, and it was a real event to speak with someone long-distance, often doing so in groups and passing the phone around.

For those who were education-focused, grades assigned in high school and university courses were generally accepted at face value, with little questioning or challenging of teachers. As we have seen, only 10 per cent of baby boomers went on to university, so unless this was the goal, grades didn't matter the way they do now with so many young people under pressure to prove themselves through their educational attainment. Accordingly, the B was an achievement, and a C was something to be happy with. Those who got As really stood out. In Ontario, the Ontario Scholar programme was developed to reward those very few who attained A averages. In these and other ways, the baby boomers who persisted educationally were held to higher expectations, so staying in the system meant a full-time commitment. This full-time commitment was also necessary because education was not as technologized as it is now. Technology has made certain aspects of learning easier, and many research and writing activities are less time consuming now, but as some things get easier, they can lose their meaning and appeal because there is less personal attachment to the activities involved.

Consider the matter of essay writing. At universities, essays in the pre-computer era were often accepted in handwriting, or even in rough typewritten form with white-out and editing notations; owning an electric typewriter was a luxury. Research for papers was conducted in libraries by going to the stacks and reading the books and journals in the library. Many readings for courses were put on one- or two-hour reserve, and students had to actually go to the library to read them there, so they had to be read efficiently to give everyone in a course access to them. If a reading was really important, a photocopy could be made, but it was very expensive – the equivalent of almost one dollar per page in 2006[34] – so notes about readings were generally handwritten. In short, essay writing was once a more time- and energy-consuming activity for students. Consequently, students were possibly more likely to feel more 'one with' their research and its product, and thus be more transformed by it.

Today, students with personal computers (PCs) can access most journal articles online from the comfort of their room or home, and save them as PDFs on their computers. Trips to the library are necessary only if books need to be accessed, but many courses now provide reading packs with all the required chapters available for a one-time purchase in the campus bookstore. Essays can now be written using sophisticated word-processing packages available for PCs that correct spelling and grammar as you type and print the essay from among hundreds of fonts and styles. With easy access to electronic versions of journal articles, as well as material available on free Internet sites, text and data can be cut and pasted with ease, raising temptations to plagiarize, especially when students procrastinate on assignments. In short, essay writing has become a mundane process that virtually anyone can perfunctorily perform from the comfort of home. For all but the most engaged student, writing essays can be a detached experience with little meaning and transformative potential beyond meeting another deadline.[35] Educators had hoped that the time-saving nature of these technologies would have left more time for students to deeply engage themselves in their reading and spend more time thinking about essays and assignments, but this has apparently not been the result for most students.

The irony students face today is that it has never been easier to write essays, or to carry out the computations for statistical and other assignments, but fewer of these assignments are now required of students in most courses, as we have seen in chapters 1 and 2. Moreover, where these assignments are still given, more students appear to be encountering problems completing them than when baby boomers were students. The roots here may be both the mundane nature of cutting and pasting an assignment at the last minute and the lack of preparation for engaging oneself in the potentially transformative experience of research and writing.

This brings us back to a major problem with the current university system, built as it is upon the secondary system: students are accustomed to being tested on their retention of material, and few have been given adequate training in writing and speaking, especially in undertaking independent analyses. In this sense, current students have been over-structured in their education, because tests of retention involve a carrot-and-stick approach, conditioning response to the next external stimulus (reward or punishment) rather than cultivating an approach to learning material with critical analysis.

To make matters worse, textbooks are now the most common way of providing material for students in courses at all levels, but even at university, reading comprehension is expected to be at only the grade 10 level. These textbooks tend to be filled with colourful pictures and graphs, with key words highlighted, and running summaries of important points in the margins. Beyond the fact that they seldom present complex material, their layout encourages students to scan them, rather than to carefully read and absorb the material. When baby boomers went to university, there were a few textbooks available, but then mainly in introductory classes. Accordingly, students were more likely to be assigned primary readings, written by leaders in the field. Students had to use their own analytic abilities to comprehend what they were reading, and they were more likely to engage in analysis of these readings in tutorials along with other students and the professor. If everything is pre-digested for students in textbooks and lectures (most recently with PowerPoint presentations that are often posted on course websites), there is little reason for them to actively think about the material, and it is a small wonder that few can think of essay topics that they would be interested in researching and writing about.

In the survey we carried out with Western faculty described in the second chapter, 85 per cent of professors indicated that they use textbooks in their courses. When asked about reactions to these texts they have encountered, over half reported that students have complained that the texts were too difficult, while fewer than 10 per cent encountered students who complained these textbooks were dumbed down. Three-quarters of these professors thought that the texts provided students with sufficient challenge and inspiration, while only one in six found them 'too dumbed down.' Surprisingly, one-quarter had used textbooks even when they were of 'minimal relevance to their lectures.' Given that textbooks notoriously oversimplify material, these responses suggest that few professors pay attention to the texts they make students read. Many textbooks costs upward of $100 and are reissued as new editions every few years as sales drop. These practices smack of a mass processing of students in the edubis (chapter 3) of the credential mart (chapter 2) rather than of sound pedagogical techniques.

We have gone to some length to contrast the experiences of baby boomers and millennials to underscore the possibility that higher education has less personal meaning and transformative potential, now that it is becoming as routine for the millennial generation as high school was for the baby boom generation. Given the expenses involved, parents paying for much of their children's university education need to be attuned to the possibility that their children will not derive the same personal benefit from it that they did if they went to university. We give some advice below about how to deal with this and protect their investments in their children's education.

The Mini-Me and the Helicopter Parent

At a more general level, observers of the contemporary scene argue that parents have been over-protecting their children by micro-managing their lives. An article in *Newsweek* published in 2002 charged that the 'Me Generation is raising the Mini-Me Generation.'[36] The good side is that many parents are very close emotionally to their children, but the bad side is that they may be creating an over-dependence or even a co-dependence with their children. Experts in identity formation argue that parents are not helping their children develop a healthy sense of differentiation from them that helps them explore *their own* interests and aptitudes and develop *their own* capacities to act as autonomous agents. The *Newsweek* article cites reports from university recruiters and counsellors dealing with some parents who are essentially co-authoring applications they get (where essays are required) and participating in job searches when it is time to graduate.

The term *helicopter parent* has recently come into common usage and has been defined as follows:

A helicopter parent is one who pays extremely close attention to their child or children, particularly at educational institutions. They rush to prevent any harm from befalling them or letting them learn from their own mistakes, sometimes even contrary to the children's wishes. They are so named because, like a helicopter, they hover closely overhead, rarely out of reach whether their children need them or not.[37]

This source goes on to explain that the term

gained wide currency when American college administrators began using it in the early 2000s as the Millennial Generation began reaching college age. Their late-wave baby-boomer parents in turn earned notoriety for practices such as calling their children each morning to wake them up for class and complaining to their professors about grades the children had received. Some of these parents had, in fact, chosen the child's college, and hired consultants to help fine-tune the application process.

Further, it argues that the wide use of cell phones is in part behind this phenomenon, calling the mobile phone 'the world's longest umbilical cord.' Parents questioned about these practices claim to be protecting their 'investments' and merely acting as concerned consumers. Citing rising tuitions and other costs, these parents are in a way acting rationally under the circumstances, especially to the extent that university 'is no longer seen as a gateway to adulthood and more as an extension of high school.'[38]

In Defence of the Helicopter Parent

In September 2005, a group of faculty members were chatting over coffee about the new cohort and what, if anything new, we might expect. An associate dean related that he had received a call from an anxious mother of a first-year student, who was to move into residence the following day. The mother explained that her son had never spent time away from home, and without hesitation or trepidation asked whether she would be permitted to put a cot in her son's residence room and spend the first two or three night with him, just until he got settled and comfortable.

While we all laughed incredulously, we all knew what the mother's call represented. It evoked the image of the student produced by overindulgent mothers and fathers. Many baby boomers are determined to avoid the 'mistakes' with their children (mainly social and intellectual neglect) that they believe their parents made with them. Unlike their own parents, who likely did not attend university, many engaged in involved parenting that included reading to the children – some while they were still in the womb – teaching them how to eat healthily, and enrolling them in all sorts of healthy physical activities like Little League sports and dance classes. These are the famous soccer moms and hockey coach dads, who would street-proof their children even as they drove them to games, to the movies, and to school, and who were there even before the final bell rang to pick them up. On the way home, they would interrogate them about all the new things they had learned that day, about new friends they had made, and even about those children they had met who were not 'nice.'

However, the world of current students is different from the world of their parents when they were young: education inflation and credentialism are rampant, good jobs are scarce, rents are high, and the future is less clear, yet staying in the education system until they are well into their twenties is now commonplace. Fortunately, more of today's parents can financially help their children in ways that many of their parents could not. The post-war affluence from the late 1950s to the 1970s and the availability of decent jobs and affordable housing made it possible for many in the baby boom generation to achieve a degree of material comfort and to accumulate retirement savings and pensions that they now want to share with, and bequeath to, their children. Their hope is that as much as they have, their children should have even more, but this good-will turns into anxiety as they look at today's cutthroat economic compe-tition, deskilling, the export of jobs overseas, and the replacement of real jobs with McJobs. So the concerns of over-protective helicopter par-ents become somewhat understandable.

But what is wrong with helicopter parenting? After all, no parents want their children to have a difficult life if it can be avoided. And even if they know that children need to skin their knees a few times, what parents would deliberately push their children down just to prove a point or to hurry maturation along? By being there to pick up their children even before they fall, helicopter parents are doing what comes naturally, and such parents would claim that those who have no children may find this difficult to appreciate. Of course, there is a time in children's lives when they must make that transition to adulthood, and when they might be better served by attending the school of hard knocks. For many com-mentators, that time is university, and they are probably correct. What we recommend, then, is that instead of helicopter parenting at the univer-sity stage, parents do their low flying in the high school years, which is when the bulk of the problems we have identified arise, and at a younger age when helicopter parenting might be more socially understandable.[39]

How Parents Influence and Support Their Children

By warning parents about the problems their children might encounter in university, we are not trying to discourage them from supporting their children who may have the ability and who may wish to attend. To the contrary, we call upon parents to support their children in their educa-tional journey, but to do so from the beginning, from primary school on. However, this support should not involve micro-managing their chil-dren's lives; rather, it should involve (a) ensuring that their children are learning at the rate that the grades they bring home from primary and secondary school indicate and (b) discussing their future education with them realistically, helping them refine their interests and objectives and planning for finances, even if such planning includes alternatives to university.

If their children are not ready to attend, or have other aspirations, pushing them to do so is usually the wrong thing to do. Instead, the best thing for them is to take time off from school and do something else, until they feel that university is then right for them. As we have noted, in the United Kingdom, the 'gap year' this is increasingly common. It may be that they simply need more time to mature. We have received many reports from students who were glad to have taken time away from a formal education so they could get themselves focused. When they do so, they are much more likely to engage themselves in their studies and benefit accordingly. After spending most of their lives in formal institutions, many young people simply don't have a clear handle on their own lives. Indeed, those who are pushed to continue when their hearts are not in it can suffer emotionally, and their studies will most likely suffer. The reality is that students really have just one good shot at their BA. If they truly want to use it to build a career in one of the professions, a poor or mediocre performance will disqualify them, or at least haunt them if they try to improve their performance later. We know many students who did poorly in their first couple of years, but who woke up to the reality of their future in their third year, finding that it was too late and they could not pull their grades up because of the bad habits they had developed (or the skills and knowledge they missed developing). For them, not even stellar performances in their third or fourth years could sufficiently polish their blemished record to get into a professional school or even into graduate school; some then opted for further studies at community college.

Aspirations

It is instructive to examine scientific research into the influence of parents on their children's educational aspirations. The Canada Millennium Scholarship Foundation, under the title *The Price of Knowledge 2004: Access and Student Finance in Canada*, published the best compendium of this and other related research.[40] All evidence points to the fact that almost all parents hope that their children will pursue some form of higher education.[41] The level of parental aspiration for their children's education does vary by socio-economic background, parents' education, and region, but not as much as one might expect. In historical terms, where the experiences of different generations are compared (as in figure 1.1), this level of support for higher education 'is an absolutely fundamental change in Canadian's attitudes to formal education'[42] and reflects a doubling of public support in general for post-secondary among the public between 1970 and the 1990s.[43]

Still, it appears that the level of one's parents' education is the strongest predictor of university attendance, with each year of parental university education increasing the likelihood that one of their children will attend university by about five percentage points.[44] Parents with a higher education can give more appropriate advice and information as well as act as intellectual and emotional role models. Children with more-educated parents are more likely to see higher education as part of who they are – their identity – and to not feel that the university environment is foreign or hostile.

The latest Canadian research shows that holding other factors constant, such as income, if their parents have just a high school education, sons have a 29 per cent likelihood of attending university, and daughters 37 per cent. However, this probability jumps to 53 and 65 per cent, respectively, if their parents have at least some university education.[45] Other factors that affect the probability of pursuing a post-secondary education include working at an outside job for pay while in high school (the association is negative when the hours worked are excessive), grade point average, engagement in high school and extracurricular activities, and gender. Females are more likely to attend, in part because high school males have lower grades, enjoy school less, have less interest in academics, fail more often, and are less likely to have harmonious relations with their teachers.[46] Males also have more opportunities in the unskilled labour market as labourers in construction and factories, and the enticement of these wages, especially when subsidized by free room and board with their parents, provides what many young men see as a desirable alternative to slogging it out in a post-secondary institution while going into debt.

The number-one choice of higher education is university, with some 70 per cent of parents hoping, when their children are young, that they will eventually attend. As we saw in chapter 1, however, only half this percentage of young people will attend, meaning that a lot of aspirations get adjusted, among parents and children alike. Only 2 per cent of parents (with young children) hope their children will eventually follow a trade or undertake some sort of vocational studies. We can see here the effects of years of government policies promoting the university education as the route to the while-collar world, and the unintended consequence of stigmatizing blue-collar work in the process. As we examine in the next chapter, a number of problems in our labour market can be traced to this prejudice, including large numbers of young people floundering in the job market.[47] Much of this floundering can be traced to the fear of being stigmatized as a failure for not getting a degree and/or not working in a while-collar job. The irony is that many skilled blue-collar jobs pay better than entry-level white-collar ones, and that these young people are forgoing considerable short-term earnings as a result of their misdirection.

It is quite understandable that parents would want what is best for their children, but it is apparent that the extreme pressures to attend university mean that a sizeable proportion of young people are misdirected – indirectly by this prejudice, and directly by their parents. Part of the problem stems from the assumption that university can be attended as a matter of course, because it leaves many young people without alternative plans. Those who make this assumption are more likely to have 'misaligned ambitions,' according to an American study reported in *The Ambitious Generation: America's Teenagers, Motivated, but Directionless*. This study found that over half of high school students misjudge how much education is required for their occupational goals, with most of this misalignment caused by overestimating the amount of education they will need to qualify for that specific job.[48] Paradoxically, the strongest predictor of misalignment is parents' level of education: parents with postgraduate degrees were found to be more likely to convey to their children the importance of advanced degrees *regardless* of their children's interests and goals.

Research has also been conducted on how parental aspirations change over time, showing that the number of parents hoping their children will attend university drops as the child gets older, from over three-quarters when children are five years old or less, to less than two-thirds when children are in their teens.[49] The factors that cause some parents to realign their aspirations suggest that some parents are responsive to their child's abilities and wants. The most common reason for parents realizing that university may not be for their children is the fact that their grades are not high enough; the second most frequent reason is a realization that their child would like to have an occupation that does not require a university education. So it does appear that some parents do monitor the reality of the situation more so than other parents. Unfortunately, it appears that these parents are more likely to be from lower socio-economic and educational backgrounds themselves, which helps explain the continuing socio-economic discrepancy in university attendance (discussed in the next chapter).

At the same time, it appears that the aspirations of young people themselves are more resistant to realistic feedback on abilities and potentials. Research suggests that most children form their university aspirations early, not as a rational choice, 'but rather as something they have been socialized to desire from childhood – if not from birth.'[50] Indeed, the percentage of students in their teens who expect to complete a BA steadily hovers between 50 and 60 per cent between grade 6 and grade 12, paralleling the percentage of parents who have these aspirations for their children. That these percentages do not change supports our argument that high schools are no longer sorting and weeding students, but instead are giving many of them false feedback, and setting them up for disappointment as part of 'misdirected trajectories.'[51]

The American study of misaligned ambitions found that high school students who aspired to the highest professional degrees (e.g., doctor or lawyer) were more likely to underestimate the amount of education necessary, as well as to be misinformed about what degrees matched which occupations (e.g., thinking they need a PhD to become a physician).[52] Those with aligned ambitions were more likely to have consciously developed 'a life plan,' which can change 'ambitions from a wish or a dream to an everyday goal,' providing the young person with a valuable orientation toward the future.[53]

Parents can assess their children's life plans by asking them to describe how someone would go from being a high school student to acquire the education and training to secure their desired occupation, including the types of schools that might be attended, the aptitudes and knowledge involved, the exams needed in qualifying, the volunteer experience that might increase the chances of being accepted into programmes, ancillary training that might be an asset, and any job experience that might be preferred of programme applicants. Parents can then help their children develop more accurate knowledge of what it would take to realize these plans. Research shows that young people who can articulate these things will more likely have certain organizational skills and a sense of commitment to a course of action. They are also more likely to be capable of seeing how their lives will unfold within a variety of historical, technological, and economic contexts that affect people's careers. Moreover, this ability to 'abstract' oneself, and treat oneself as an 'object' as seen by others, shows that these young people have an idea of how the adult world works and will consequently be seen as more adult-like themselves as they make their way. And, finally, the knowledge that their actions have meaningful consequences can help reduce the perception that luck is more important than the effort they put into directing their life plans. This knowledge translates into their choosing realistic routes and goals along the way, rather than merely 'hoping' that things will work out in the long run if they just 'get enough education.'[54]

The authors of *The Ambition Generation* summarize the benefits of aligned ambitions as follows:

> Adolescents with aligned ambitions are more likely to use their time and effort strategically. They are more likely to choose challenging activities that are of interest to them, that they are good at, and for which there is a reasonable probability of success. They have high levels of determination to accomplish challenging activities, and they are more likely to persist in their efforts even when the tasks become difficult. Such adolescents will seek assistance from more knowledgeable peers and adults and are likely to dedicate additional time to mastering the activity ... Adolescents who have aligned ambitions are better able to provide explanations for how they spend their time and energy. These explanations are more likely to be judged acceptable by adults since they are oriented to the future rather than the present and focus on ways of joining the adult world.[55]

In our own previous research on this issue, these young people with aligned ambitions can be said to have a greater sense of 'personal agency': they have stronger and more active motivations, and they are able to develop their own personal resources by drawing on the resources offered by others in their lives, like their parents and teachers.[56] This line of research is based on the assumption that students do not enter universities as blank slates. Rather, they have been affected by prior experiences with their families, earlier educational settings, and the workplace (actual or anticipatory). These experiences can be very influential in affecting their motivations for attending universities in the first place, but also their readiness to benefit from what these institutions have to offer. Our research has identified how five motivations for attending university can produce quite different experiences and outcomes. For example, an explicit 'careerist' motivation for attending university (including the desire to develop skills to make more money) predicts the actual salary earned some ten years later.

Other motivations predict whether or not the person will be *under*employed some six years after graduation (i.e., working at a job that does not require the credentials earned). Two of these motivations are associated with being 'pushed' into attending – (a) driven by expectations from their family and friends and (b) attending because they don't know what else to do. The research shows that both of these types of students are more likely to be underemployed six years after graduation. In contrast, two other motivations are associated with being 'pulled' into attending university, and these predict better employment prospects among graduates. The first is a sort of humanitarian motive by which young people want to learn enough so they can have an impact on society, changing it for the better to help others. The second is the motive to improve their own intellect and personality.[57]

The best advice we can give parents, culled from these research findings, is to discuss their children's long-term motives and plans for various courses of action. In doing so, they can help their children focus their goals – whether or not they involve university – and fill in gaps in their knowledge. In doing so, they should also help their children become 'actively involved in their own development,' as developmental psychologists put it, and to see some larger goals in their plans, whether it be improving themselves intellectually, helping others, or simply improving their lot in life. And they should help their children think about these goals, research them, articulate the reason for pursuing them, how they will achieve them, and why they are pursuing them. Although few baby boomers needed a grand plan in order to succeed academically and occupationally because of better economic conditions when they came of age, this is clearly no longer the case, and parents need to realize this as they align their own and their children's aspirations.

Finances: The Bottom Line

One obvious way in which parents can help their children is through financial support. While Canada ranks relatively high in accessibility (fifth out of sixteen of the more prosperous nations compared),[58] it is relatively low in affordability – eleventh out of sixteen.[59] In general, the U.S. and British Commonwealth countries are lowest in affordability, while the more liberal northern European countries rank highest (Sweden and Finland top the list).

However, parents should also educate themselves about the current costs of obtaining a university education, and work out ways in which it can be financed without having their children work during the school year. Almost half of Canadian 'full-time' university students work each year during their studies, with about one in six working more than thirty hours per week and 40 per cent working between eleven and twenty hours, such that the average amount of time spent working is seventeen to eighteen hours per week.[60] This represents almost a doubling of the percentage working during the school year over the past thirty years.[61] In our experience, students who put too many hours into outside jobs encounter the greatest difficulties in their courses, missing classes and having trouble getting assignments in on time. This can produce a form of 'forced disengagement' that is different from the 'emotional' disengagement to which we have been referring in this book. We know of many students' attempts to maintain their emotional engagement in the face of the forced disengagement they experience because of their outside jobs.

The published research shows that the number of hours worked are negatively correlated with time spent studying out of class.[62] For example, 30 per cent of those who do not work spend more than twenty hours per week studying, while only about 7 per cent of those working study more than twenty hours. Conversely, among those working more than twenty hours per week, two-thirds study ten hours or less compared to only one-third among those who do not work. Older studies indicated that grades are negatively affected as the number of hours worked increases. Some more recent studies, however, suggest that grades are not greatly affected by the number of hours worked, although the time to complete the degree is affected, which we comment on next. However, we draw readers' attention to these recent findings that grades are no longer seriously affected for students who work long hours. This suggests that the disengagement compact is widespread. If full engagement were required of everyone, those who exert little effort should stand out in lower grades, unless they also happen to be brighter than those who put in a full effort.[63] Still, the bulk of research findings on this topic, especially in the United States, suggests that working long hours while attending school increases stress, reduces academic achievement, and makes it more likely that the student will miss more classes and drop out.[64]

On the issue of time to complete a degree and the impact of working for pay while studying, the longer it takes to complete a degree (because a lighter course load is usually carried while working for pay), the larger the potential debt, and the greater the opportunity costs of obtaining the degree (opportunity costs refer to the lost income associated with taking the time out of the full-time labour force to attend school). Ironically, this debt accumulated over a longer period may actually nullify some of the monetary benefits of working while attending university.

Moreover, students who take longer to complete their undergraduate studies may be jeopardizing their chances of moving on to postgraduate studies. Admissions are so competitive that anything that compromises students' records can work against them. One factor that can tip the balance of acceptance at the postgraduate level is evidence that applicants are 'well-rounded,' meaning that they have engaged in a variety of pro-social activities. In the undergraduate years, this can involve volunteer activity, membership in clubs and cultural associations, and extra-curricular activities, all of which suffer the more a student works, especially if the hours working top thirty.[65]

If postgraduate work is the goal, everything should be done to help students stay focused on their undergraduate studies and treat their course load as a full-time job that requires lots of overtime. If they are simply after the credential, which is often the case, then the negative consequences of working are not an issue, so long as students pass their courses. Indeed, apparently about one-third of students work primarily for the disposable income to maintain a more comfortable standard of living while at school. On the other hand, about one-third think that they absolutely have to work, or they could not afford to go to university if they did not work. These perceptions should be examined by students and their parents, and discussed to determine their validity.

Whatever the reason for working, more and more Canadian students are treating university studies as a 'part-time activity,' or as two observers characterized the situation in the United States in the mid-1990s, these students 'don't work their way through [university] rather, they work [university] into their lives.'[66] In fact, it is more useful to divide American students into three categories: full-time school (20%), full-time school/part-time work (50 per cent), and part-time school/full-time work (30%).[67] All of those hours spent on a paid job can mean that assigned readings go unread, ideas aren't discussed with classmates, and intellectual interests aren't explored (e.g., by doing extra reading in areas that have sparked interest and curiosity). Unfortunately, these are the activities that may produce the 'sleeper effect' associated with liberal educations, and pay off later in a person's career in unforeseeable ways.[68] Working while studying is also a reason why time-to-completion rates are increasing in the United States. As we have noted, U.S. research shows that now less than half complete the 'four-year degree' in four years; six years is the median time. One American source remarks that for these students, 'the notion of [university] as a place to luxuriate in friendships and lose oneself in philosophic reflection is a relic of a bygone era.'[69] Canadians need to ask themselves whether they want their university system to continue to drift toward the American one, where only a small minority of students give their full attention to their studies and its potential long-term benefits.

Conclusion

Parents need to be aware of the new and unique influences on their children's generation, even if their own children are not as affected by these influences as much as others. However, we encourage parents to take a hard look at the situation and their children's adjustment to it. Not only is there a tendency to think that things like we have described apply only to 'other people's children,' but these things affect all students, even if they don't apply to them. All students are affected by academic disengagement when professors dumb down their courses to accommodate a critical mass of such students flooding into them. The brightest and most prepared students do not get the education and level of challenge they would otherwise receive, and the disengaged students themselves are simply passed on to face serious disappointment later when they hit the job market. Our own research has found that the brightest students actually become more alienated from their studies, more cynical about the entire educational process, and less motivated to achieve, the longer they are in the undergraduate system.[70] Moreover, the most deserving, high-achieving students are hurt by grade inflation to the extent that those who do little serious work get comparable marks. This not only can demoralize them, but it can put their future chances of promotion to graduate and professional schools in jeopardy.

At the same time, parents need to support their children emotionally and financially to see them through this period. As we have seen, there is an increasing student financial need today as governments have shifted their support at the same time that the labour force has treated young people more and more as marginal workers. In effect, both government and business have downloaded expenses onto parents, requiring them to become a 'safety net' during the increasingly precarious transition to adulthood and financial self-sufficiency.[71]

5 Policy Implications: So What Is University Good For? What Is Added beyond Alternatives?

This final chapter is written for all who have an interest in the policy side of higher education: how and why it should be structured, what should be supported in its present form, and what should be changed to improve the system. In order to discuss these things, some repetition of points made through this book is necessary, but we do so by revisiting issues with the collective knowledge garnered from earlier discussion. Accordingly, as with the other chapters in this book, this chapter is written so that it is essentially self-contained and does not require the reader to have read this book sequentially or in its entirety.

Credentialism Revisited: A Brief History

It has never been easy to convince the entire population of Canada about the benefits of education. This was true of grade school in the 1800s, high school in early 1900s, and now university in the early 2000s. Figure 1.1, provided in chapter 1, shows the relatively slow growth in the percentage of young people attending schools in the first half of the twentieth century. As recently as the 1960s, a significant portion simply did not complete high school (largely because it was not a prerequisite for many jobs), and the vast majority did not go on to any form of higher education.[1]

You Can Lead Them to Water, but ...

In earlier times many people simply did not see the value of education beyond the '3 Rs,' especially those from rural areas and the urban working-class. Much of the learning that took place beyond basic literacy was generally seen as irrelevant to the needs of day-to-day life, largely because it was abstract and removed from the practical requirements of making a livelihood and maintaining family relations. In addition, because the possibility of upward social mobility was remote for most people, education was not seen as something to strive for in advancing one's life-prospects.

According to the American sociologist Randall Collins, throughout the centuries, higher education in Europe was the purview of religious clerics whose calling was to preserve knowledge and control its dissemination. In the 1800s, wealthy Americans sought it as a means of helping their children establish networks so that they could maintain their parents' social standing in their adult lives. For young men, it was a way of establishing business and professional contacts; for young women, it was a means of cultivating marriage prospects, while making themselves more interesting companions to those prospects. Others went to university out of sheer interest and intrinsic motivation, often not expecting it to culminate in a career, except perhaps teaching or public service, but neither occupation required it. In the United States, where the entrepreneurial model of higher education evolved, some 1,000 private universities were founded in the 1800s, but 700 failed because they could not attract enough students.[2]

According to Collins, it was this massive bankruptcy of for-profit universities that led to development of the curriculum that we now take for granted in North America, and the view that universities have something to offer beyond pure intellectual refinement. In order to market a university education, it became necessary to offer courses beyond the classics that were seen as more relevant to the modern world and more enjoyable to study. Over the late 1800s and early 1900s, the curriculum expanded to the sciences, social sciences, and humanities courses as part of an elective system that could be studied by non-intellectuals, but at the same time allow academics to pursue their higher-level research.[3] Thus, the modern academic disciplines have had a symbiotic relationship with undergraduate education, making it possible to develop and expand distinct departments in universities as enrolments rose.[4] At the same time, a 'fun' social life was offered, including varsity sports that encouraged a school spirit and acceptance of fraternity and sororities, which had previously been discouraged and existed as secret societies. As a result of these efforts, the image of the university changed from a strictly scholarly model to a 'socializing model' that would provide a common language and cultural tradition for business and political leaders as the 'culture mart' described in chapter 2. This new model apparently worked – by 1920, there were over one thousand colleges in the United States successfully recruiting students.[5] The number of private and public colleges and universities in the United States now totals some 3,400, 1,200 of which grant two-year associate's degrees that can count toward a BA.[6]

Following the Second World War, and during the Cold War, the consensus emerged that countries like Canada and the United States needed to invest in higher education to produce the 'human capital'[7] necessary to develop advanced technologies and technocracies to match those that were emerging from the Soviet Union. Motivated in part by a fear in the spread of communism, the Canadian government (along with other governments, especially in the United States) heavily invested for the next twenty years in the higher educational infrastructure that we now have. This is the system that was laid at the feet of the cohorts born during the 1940s and 1950s. Those students who had the interest and ability could take advantage of a generous grant and loan system, sometimes even if they had not graduated from high school (i.e., by gaining entry with a 'mature student' status).

At first, the increasing number of baccalaureates was quickly absorbed into management and teaching positions, and the public service. However, as mentioned in chapter 2, by the mid-1970s the ranks of the public service and the teaching professions were filled to capacity, as the job market became saturated with university graduates.[8] It was during this time that we first heard about underemployment, the very striking example being the PhD taxi driver. While the doctoral cabbie was likely rare if not apocryphal, this irony was the harbinger of what was to happen over the ensuing three decades. Now, over-educated taxi drivers are commonplace, especially among the ranks of recent immigrants whose credentials are not recognized in Canada. Although enrolment levelled off for a period, as can be seen in figure 1.1, it took off again in the 1980s with annual increases that lasted into the early 1990s. By the time that expansion of Canadian universities paused in the 1990s, the production of baccalaureates had increased nine-fold[9] from the 1950s (while the Canadian population increased by only 50%).[10] Then, apparently stimulated by government enrolment funding in 1998,[11] at the time of writing, there have been six consecutive years of record growth in university enrolment. Between 1998 and 2004 alone, university enrolment increased by 20 per cent, such that there are now some 1 million university students in Canada.[12] This growth has outpaced predictions made in 2002.[13] In fact, as noted at the beginning of this book, among OECD countries, as of 2000 Canada could boast having the greatest proportion of the population with advanced credentials, with 41 per cent having either university degrees (20%) or community college diplomas (21%).[14]

In order for there to be a proportionate payoff for this investment in higher education, there needed to be a proportionate increase in the number of jobs in the labour market requiring them. However, clearly the labour market did not have places for all of these graduates. Before the massive expansions of the university system in the 1950s and 1960s, only a small percentage of jobs could be roughly classed as 'highly skilled,'[15] and as of 2001, only 16 per cent of jobs were thus classified by Statistics Canada, as we pointed out in the introduction.[16] Yet, in 2001, 28 per cent of those aged twenty-five to thirty-four had a BA.[17]

It is easy to see a source of the credential underemployment problem: as much as degrees are highly sought after by young people, the production of university degrees has outstripped the need for them in the workforce.[18] In a market of supply and demand, when the supply of an item exceeds the demand, the value of the item decreases. If we use the example of money, when a country prints more money than there is a demand for, especially if there is no corresponding increase in the production of goods, that country experiences inflation – the money is worth less, and it costs more to buy the same item. Inflation is particularly bad if the country does not have sufficient resources to back that currency. This is precisely what we have done with higher-educational credentials: we have produced more than the demand required, and these credentials are now worth less. Moreover, it appears that the baccalaureate credential is printed in spite of fewer resources to back it, especially as a result of financial cutbacks. That is, it is worth even less as standards have declined to accommodate disengaged students and as courses have been watered down and grades inflated. It represents less learning and less skill acquisition. In this respect, government policies that uncritically promote a university education to the exclusion of other forms of education or training can actually work against the goal of increased productivity through the production of credential-based human capital.[19]

Put another way, it now requires more credentials to obtain a good number of the same jobs today than it did before so many (grade inflated) credentials were produced. While there are some benefits to this inflationary situation (as we shall see), not only are Canadian taxpayers carrying the bulk of the cost to produce a surplus of BAs, but individual students and their parents are assuming a greater cost as well. In effect, they are running faster on the educational treadmill just to stay in the same place in the occupational structure. In this sense, university credentials have more of a 'positional' quality than a transformative one, to the extent that degrees are used by people to compete for occupational status, rather than to develop productive skills.

This status competition has serious consequences for young people from less affluent families because the ante has been raised in the credential game. Less-affluent students thus have a more difficult time staying in the status-competition game, often having to settle for less opportunity than what their abilities and interests would otherwise dictate. In this way, wealth continues to reproduce itself along family-background lines (social class) in spite of attempts during the twentieth century to democratize society by creating a meritocratic educational system. We would venture to say that if high schools actually nurtured abilities in all of their students – and did not use inflated grades to appease their more affluent students – the malaise we describe in this book would be a far lesser problem. Universities would have a better foundation for recruiting students on the basis of merit, drawing from the full talent pool of society. As it is, a significant proportion of the human capital of the nation goes untapped and un-nurtured, as the wealthy use their advantage to ensure that their children benefit most from what the economy has to offer.

Some defend this hyper-credential system by pointing out that university graduates make more money than high school graduates.[20] While this is clearly the case, this reasoning ignores the possibility that quite a few of the jobs currently occupied by university graduates were once filled by high school graduates, or even high school leavers. It also ignores the fact that those who once occupied those jobs with less education now have to spend more money to get that education (an opportunity cost) or take a lower-level job. Before the hyper-credential system, those who were motivated and keen could find their way into the types of managerial and service positions in which numerous university graduates now find themselves, and no one thought the worse of it. However, now those equivalent managerial and service positions are reserved for university graduates, even though the skills involved have changed little (with the exception of computer skills, which are now generic and certainly not integral to what is taught in undergraduate courses). For example, jobs like 'manager of Blockbuster video store' are apparently now listed as requiring a university education by the U.S. Bureau of Labor Statistics,[21] and diplomas are now offered in Canada to qualify people for such positions (as we shall discuss shortly). It is this type of job-education matching that is behind government predictions that 45 per cent of jobs in the future will require sixteen years of education that we noted in the introduction. Such predictions can become self-fulfilling prophecies, signalling people to get more credentials, thereby actually producing more credentialed applicants from which employers can choose.

Others criticize this system for introducing frivolous obstacles to enhance the prestige of certain occupations, and therefore the fees they can charge. An article published in *Canadian Business* in the mid-1990s laid out a case against the juggernaut of credentialism, arguing, 'Our quest for credentials has created a monster.'[22] The authors take issue with the increasing credentialization of the teaching profession, especially at the primary level, which has grown from the requirement of a grade 12 diploma and one year of teacher's college in the 1960s, to a BA plus two years of teacher's college just thirty years later. The authors of the article find this to be particularly hypocritical when those changing the rules were not required to have these degrees to get where they are. More and more of what used to learned as part of working in a job has been shifted to educational institutions, while at the same time constructing an obstacle – or weeding mechanisms – for job applicants. Even jobs like firefighting are increasingly using and/or requiring post-secondary credentials, as are those like travel agent and hairdresser.

In turn, some schools have responded by offering programmes for these jobs. Ryerson University offers a number of them that are cited in the *Canadian Business* article as suspect in terms of the need to credentialize them. The authors of that article took issue with Ryerson offering a Certificate in Public Relations and another in Early Childhood Music Education. More recently, Ryerson has launched programmes in retail management – for example, clothing stores and record outlets – apparently stimulated by $1 million in donations from each of Wal-Mart, Sears, and Loblaws.[23] While these skills are no doubt useful, it means that fewer people can now move directly into entry-level management positions by climbing an organizational ladder, as was the practice for the previous generation.

Such programme requirements are also making it harder for those already in the workforce to move up a career ladder because they are being cut off by graduates with little workforce experience, or the field they want to move into is being flooded with graduates for whom there is little or no work. The authors of this *Canadian Business* article summarize their complaint this way:

> The Canadian dream has always been founded on the promise of personal mobility – the notion that an individual can seize on new opportunities as they arise. Educational requirements are now tarnishing that dream, lock-

ing people into their current jobs and barring new entrants. Do we really want to construct barriers to mobility, especially when a rapidly changing economy makes it crucial for people to be able to regear themselves for new types of work?[24]

Finally, it becomes apparent that while credentialism has a certain logic that makes it an expedient system for dealing with some labour force demands, youth employment problems, and the like, it has a fatal flaw at the university level – an Achilles heel – that undermines its ability to maintain its own legitimacy. This flaw is grade inflation. For reasons we have discussed, as the educational system increases the rewards allotted to students, grades become compressed at the high end. The more this happens, the less able the system is to differentiate levels of ability and motivation, so its credentialing function loses it legitimacy. Moreover, because grade inflation encourages disengagement, there is less preparation and training of those students compressed at the high level, further compounding the problem. We shall thus take another look at grade inflation and why it is plaguing the system.

Grade Inflation Revisited: Underlying Causes

Given the alarming implications of grade inflation, we must examine its underlying causes if we are to recommend solutions to the problems it creates. We begin by repeating the simple point that we are trying to educate a far greater proportion of the population than in the past, and this effort alone has a number of far-reaching, but unintended, consequences. As we have pushed more people to acquire more formal education, we have mandated high schools to graduate as many people as possible. However, to do so, the public system of mass education has simply dropped standards, not significantly increased the human capital potential of students. One of the strongest predictors of early school leaving is grades. Students who repeatedly receive low grades year after year tend to internalize their low achievement as part of their sense of identity. Just as students can come to define themselves as 'A-students,' others can do so as 'C-' or even 'D-students.' Obviously, someone who continually receives such grades will eventually adjust aspirations accordingly. Given that some 90 per cent of grade 9 students aspire to go to college or university, and fewer than half do, a certain amount of downward aspiration adjustment is inevitable and necessary. But a side effect of this readjustment can be disillusionment with school and the relevance of learning. When we add to this the lower reward now for a high school education, low-achieving students are at risk of dropping out because they do not see much to gained by completing even that level of education.

Most high schools have no control over their curricula, let alone external factors like the credentials now necessary for job entry. Consequently, it would appear to be a rational response on their part to give what rewards they can to entice students to stay in school, and grades are the principal rewards under their control (as are easier and fewer tests and assignments). Giving higher grades for less effort may be sufficient to keep a number of teens from dropping out, but apparently it is not fully effective because the high-school dropout rate is still surprisingly high.[25] However, when higher grades are used to prevent school leaving, reward levels are higher for everyone, with no accompanying increase in standards and expectations. So students who would not have dropped out are also given higher grades without requiring more effort from them. This has an immediate consequence and a long-term one as well.

In the short run, students define themselves as more 'able' or 'knowledgeable' when they really are not. Those who receive As are also getting the message that they are 'excellent,' when they may be only 'good.' This can bolster their self-esteem, but not their abilities or willingness to try harder. Thus, when students who should have received a B for being good at something are mixed with students who are excellent at it (A-students), the effort required of both types of students is diminished. The hitherto A-student can coast to get the same grade given to the less able, but 'good' (B) students. When schools also do this with As and A+s, the same problem occurs: those who are excellent are grouped with the outstanding, so the outstanding can do less for the same grade, and learn less as a result.

At the same time, some among this larger group of A-students come to think that they do not need to do more because they are at the top; they can become know-it-alls, or 'unteachables.' This is one of the more frustrating long-term problems that grade inflation creates for professors: increasing numbers of students coming to universities with A averages, who are not excellent or outstanding in skills, knowledge, or potential for advanced studies. These students are harder to teach in any meaningful way (beyond memorization) because they have less reason to think that they have something to learn; they often maintain a defensive know-it-all attitude, while expecting the high levels of reward for minor to moderate efforts.

This is especially a problem in the arts, humanities, and social sciences, where much of the learning involves ability to develop evidence-based arguments, which can be mistaken for mere 'opinion' by students of lower ability. The traditional goal in these faculties is to teach students to develop *informed* and intellectually defensible arguments. This can be accomplished only by gathering as much knowledge as possible about a subject, and through critical analyses of the available evidence, drawing conclusions about issues and problems. If students come to these courses with the arrogant attitude that their pre-existing opinions are sufficient, they see no need to engage themselves in the intellectual journey that is ostensibly the norm of university life.

If most of the highly rated students do not want to take this intellectual journey, then who will? Few will, obviously. Consequently, without a sufficient number of motivated, bright students to inspire, professors will over time stop trying and will simply give uninspired information-based courses that easily lend themselves to processing the mass number of students now being pushed through their courses. In turn, students will complain about boring lectures, but most will not do the preparation needed for the Socratic methods that make classes really interesting and transformative for students. Most universities are already far along this path of mass processing in information-based courses, and with the enrolment increases predicted (as we have already outlined), this situation will only worsen.

This issue of the proportion of young people we are trying to push into higher education can also be seen in the methods needed to process these numbers, especially in the financial retrenchment that has been imposed on educational systems for the past two decades. Without more teachers and professors, methods of assessment have tended to become more efficient in processing the larger numbers of students, but less effective in nurturing and encouraging higher-order skills like effective essay writing and public speaking, and analytic and critical thinking.[26] At the same time, with many students learning only in large, impersonal lecture courses, there is less possibility for them to derive an affinity for the material, the course, or any aspect of academia. Without this sense of connection, the university education itself is less likely to have an effect on students' identity formation and is more likely to be seen as an obstacle to be traversed by any means necessary, including playing the system, cheating, lying to professors and parents, and the like.

As students have become more accustomed to test-taking as the sole means of assessment, especially in easily graded multiple-choice or short-answer formats, more have become proficient test-takers (as we saw in chapter 2, some professors apparently take advantage of this approach by 'teaching to the test' and therefore improving their course evaluations). Being a good test-taker may require only a good memory for cramming in facts the night before an exam, and have little to do with the skills normally associated with higher learning, as we have mentioned. Consequently, more students are better at test-taking, but not at effective writing, public speaking, or disciplined thinking. With large numbers of proficient test-takers, and little or no other means of assessment, it becomes difficult for university professors to give lower grades, especially when the students come expecting to get the same grades they received in high school.

In response, and in an attempt to minimize the flak they might receive from students, courses are more likely to be effort-based and set up to accommodate the norm by which students expect to do well simply by cramming for exams. Accordingly, marks may not only improve during a course as students adapt to each specific professor's style, but professors adjust their courses to these new types of students. The result is that grades will tend to rise in courses over time, in part because students are likely better test-takers and professors have redesigned their courses to keep this critical mass of proficient test-takers happy. Grades then rise, but in response to a narrow set of skills (short-term memory needed for cramming and deductive reasoning associated with multiple-choice tests). As a result, our university graduates are less likely to have higher-order skills and reasoning abilities. This problem will only worsen if graduate and professional schools continue to use high grade-point cut-offs to screen applications to their programmes. We have heard many such complaints about the graduates from our teacher's colleges: those who get into teacher's colleges on the basis of their high test-based grades often lack the social skills, and even writing skills, that are essential to being effective primary and secondary school teachers. Some cite this as a contributor to the problem universities now face: many past university graduates now teaching in our primary and secondary schools were not given the requisite writing skills themselves and are therefore poorly prepared to inculcate them in their own students, or to recognize substandard abilities in them, and so pass them on to universities as qualified.

The prestigious American *Chronicle of Higher Education* is replete with articles, commentaries, and letters repeating the alarm about grade inflation and its consequences, and these have been appearing more frequently over the past decade. We could write a whole book on what has been published there but need to limit ourselves to providing readers with a sample of the topics and titles of recent items. Although these articles specifically describe the American scene, we have seen that Canadian universities either have comparable problems (e.g., large numbers of entering students in need of remediation), or are not too far behind (e.g., in grade inflation), and both countries give highly inflated grades by historical and comparative standards (see the appendix for details).

Some American professors have begun taking legal action. One math professor is suing a school because he claims to have been fired for refusing to inflate grades.[27] His case is based on the assertion that the school wants as few failures as possible and a set number of high grades, regardless of class performance. In another action, the American Association of University Professors placed a school on its list of 'censured administrations' for firing two (untenured) professors for not following a policy requiring 60 per cent of a grade awarded each student in first-year courses to be based on effort.[28] The South Carolina school admits that it accepts a large number of unprepared students and the policy is ostensibly to give them time to adjust. In effect, it means that students can get an F on merit, but an 'A for effort,' allowing them to pass the course. Exactly what constitutes 'effort' is left to the discretion of the professors, but apparently failing students is not.

Meanwhile, there has been an ongoing brouhaha for several years over grade inflation in American Ivy League schools. As noted in several chapters, Harvard University has garnered the most attention, with over 90 per cent of students graduating 'with honours,' up from only one-in-three students some fifty years ago. One Harvard professor has his own personal adjustment to grade inflation there (where over 50% of students get As, up from about 30% twenty years ago).[29] He now assigns two grades to students: one for the registrar giving the 'official' (inflated) mark, and one for the students giving 'a realistic, useful assessment of how well they did and where they stand in relation to others.'[30] His article in the *Chronicle of Higher Education* is an excellent primer on what is wrong with grade inflation, including grade compression, the loss of the sense of excellence versus mediocrity, the decline of faculty morale, and the roots of grade inflation in the self-esteem movement.

This professor of government has taught at Harvard since 1962 and has witnessed the rise in grades and the pressures from students to give them. However, he experienced this change as distasteful, noting that 'there is something inappropriate – almost sick – in the spectacle of mature adults showering young people with unbelievable praise. We are flattering our students in our eagerness to get their good opinion.'[31] His colleagues told him to just think of a B+ as a C, as average, but he cannot get beyond the pandering of professors in search of the approval of their students, especially on teaching evaluations. This pandering reflects a loss of authority that he believes harms students: 'Professors who give easy grades gain fleeting popularity, salted with disdain. In later years, students will forget those professors; they will remember the one who posed a challenge.'[32]

Harvard's decision after several years of debating the issue of inflated grades was to do nothing, but Princeton University has launched a campaign to reduce the percentage of As to 35 per cent.[33] One prime target is what they call the 'mercy A minus,' a term whose meaning is self-evident. Prior to the 2004–5 academic year, the first year of the campaign, the percentage of As reached between 50 and 60, depending on the faculty. At the end of that year, As dropped by 5 to 10 per cent, signifying that further efforts were needed in the campaign. The following is posted on Princeton's website, showing the university's resolve to confront the problem:

> Beginning with fall term 2004–05, grades awarded at Princeton University reflect new institutional grading expectations for undergraduate courses and independent work. These expectations result from the determination of the Princeton faculty to address locally the persistent national problem of grade inflation. This statement explains the new expectations so that the academic records of Princeton students can be properly understood both in their own context and in relation to the records of students in other institutions where grading practices are different from those we have adopted.[34]

This official proclamation continues to state that As will be awarded for no more than 35 per cent of undergraduate grades, and no more than 55 per cent of the grades in junior and senior independent work. It also notes that these guidelines are more in keeping with past practices before the early 1990s, and distinguish Princeton's grade distribution from other Ivy League schools. This website also provides specific definitions for each grade level:

> As the Princeton transcript explains in greater detail, the University faculty has agreed that grades in the A range signify work that is exceptional (A+), outstanding (A), or excellent (A-). Grades in the B range signify work that is very good (B+), good (B), or more than adequate (B-). Grades in the C range signify work that is acceptable in varying degrees. The new policy sets expectations for academic departments and programs rather than individ-

ual faculty members. It does not mean that only 35 percent of students in each course will receive a grade in the A range, nor does it mean that a student who does A range work will receive anything other than an A range grade. What it does mean is that if faculty make rigorous evaluative judgments about the quality of student work, we expect that over time, on average, across the University, about 35 percent of undergraduate students will be doing course work of the highest quality, and 55 percent will be doing independent work of the highest quality.[35]

Note that Princeton is only attempting to lower the percentage of As to 35 per cent. Some Canadian universities, such as the University of Toronto, are apparently attempting to keep *both* As and Bs to approximately that limit, although mainly at lower-level courses. Still, Princeton is setting the right example and we believe that all universities should adopt such a policy and make it public. Doing so will alert students to the call for them to perform at a certain standard if they expect a high grade. It will also protect professors who attempt to maintain standards and stands as a warning to those professors who have been getting an easy ride by engaging in the 'disengagement compact.' We also call on high schools to follow suit. Unless they are part of the solution to grade inflation, they will remain part of root problem by passing on poorly prepared students who have been given unrealistically high grades.

The Science of Grade Inflation and the Route to Reform

Throughout this book, we have discussed grade inflation and related problems from a variety of perspectives, using evidence we have compiled from a variety of sources. This section reviews a recent book on the topic that extends our analysis: *Grade Inflation: A Crisis in College Education*,[36] written by Valen Johnson, a professor of biostatistics at the University of Michigan. Johnson was sufficiently alarmed by what has been happening in American universities to take time from his research interests in statistical theory to write that book. As a statistician, Johnson gives us some additional insights into this difficult problem.

Johnson begins by noting the grade inflation scandals at American Ivy League schools in the late 1990s and concerns about grade compression or grade conflation. Before that time, he argues, an A+ was not awarded at most universities. Instead, it was used mainly at primary schools. At universities, an A sufficed to signify an outstanding performance. Increasingly, however, the A+ has been called upon to differentiate gradations of supposedly superior performances, along with the A-. This happened as the C lost its legitimacy as the standard for average work, replaced by the B and B+. Part of the problem, he argues, is that the Ivy League schools developed the mentality that the 'average' student was to be found at other, inferior, schools. At less prestigious schools, grades then became used as a way of motivating students to try harder and stay in the system. Lower grades came to be viewed as punitive at the level of higher education. At the same time, the 'postmodern view' gained ascendance among many faculty members: standards are relative and students' knowledge needs to be accepted as comparable to that of professors'. When professors believe in relativism, a position more likely in the arts and humanities, they become less confident in their judgements of student's work, and more likely to reward student performance based solely on students' pre-formed opinions or their 'voice,' even if it is one of poor grammar and style.

Johnson argues that these sources and justifications of grade inflation are at the root of disparities in grading practices that have serious consequences for faculty members, because students gravitate to courses that give higher grades and they subsequently give better evaluations of the professors teaching those courses. We saw some of these consequences in chapter 2, where we examined responses from some faculty members at Western. As Johnson notes,

> Stringent graders, by virtue of their lower course enrolments and lower course evaluations, are less likely to receive tenure, salary increases, and promotions. Professors know this and respond by raising their grades to meet student expectations. Grade inflation ensues when stringently grading professors chase their more leniently grading colleagues toward the beginning of the alphabet. It is exacerbated when students differentially choose courses with the winners, since there are then more students taking courses with instructors who assign 'above average' grades. Finally, with traditional incentives for students to achieve eliminated, academic standards fall.[37]

In a sense, all of this should be self-evident, or as the Harvard professor with the dual grading system remarked, 'Educators should instinctively understand why grade inflation is a problem.'[38] However, this is clearly not the case, otherwise Johnson would not have written his book and we would not be writing this one. Johnson argues that grade inflation is accepted because of five myths, which he systematically examines throughout his book:

1. Student grades do not bias student evaluations of teaching.
2. Student evaluations of teaching provide reliable measures of instructional effectiveness.
3. High course grades imply high levels of student achievement.
4. Student course-selection decisions are unaffected by expected grading practices.
5. Grades assigned in unregulated academic environments have a consistent and objective meaning across classes, departments, and institutions.[39]

Johnson examines the evidence available from observational through correlational to experimental studies, covering some seventy years of research, the sum of which shows that each myth is just that – an unsupported belief. Professors assigning lower grades tend to get lower teaching evaluations and vice versa;[40] in fact, experimental evidence confirms that grading practices actually '*cause* biases in student evaluations of teaching.'[41] Students will tend to take courses where the anticipated grade is higher than other courses;[42] indeed, student evaluations are 'not reliable indicators of teaching effectiveness and account for only a small proportion of the variance in student learning.'[43] As for what the evidence says about the other myths, courses with higher grade-distributions do not produce students with greater achievement; courses with higher standards have lower enrolments; and grading practices differ considerably between disciplines and instructors.[44] One of Johnson's chief concerns is with the lower enrolments in science and mathematics courses, where grading is more stringent. He believes that there would be a shift toward more students studying and majoring in these areas if grading practices were more comparable, especially because research shows that the humanities faculties over-reward students in relation to science faculties.

Johnson has remedies for the problems created by grade inflation. Chief on his list of problems are unjust evaluations of *both* students and professors. Unjust evaluations of students are unfair to outstanding students whose merit is cloaked by grade compression, and unjust evaluations of teachers are unfair to outstanding teachers of difficult material who get low scores from students who refuse to rise to the occasion. In addition, he is concerned about student avoidance of courses from which they would derive the most benefit. These reforms need to begin by opening up institutional discussions of grading practices within each university. From the highest level of administration through to the student body, discussion of the problems of grade inflation needs to be open and everyone needs to be informed of them. Incoming faculty especially need to be told of current practices, and information should be shared among faculties where there might be differences. As our study in chapter 2 suggests, most faculty members do not know what their colleagues do and each faculty member seems to try to function as an autonomous unit, as if unaffected by what others are doing. Moreover, our study shows a wide variation in how faculty define what their grades mean, especially the notion of 'average' (ranging from a C to a B+, and varying by the year-level of a course). The efforts of Princeton University, which we have just discussed, can act as a model here.

Johnson also recommends institutional constraints on grade distributions, imposing standards similar to the norm that used to prevail in many schools (as discussed in chapter 1, and in the appendix). He recognizes, however, that there will be much resistance from faculty members, especially those who are rewarded by current practices. As a statistician he is able to suggest adjustment formulas that administrations can use in modifying the grades handed to them. They allow professors to continue to grade the way they do, but introduce a dual system that adjusts grades to a pre-set average. Some formulas can even take into account the GPA of students enrolling in a course, thereby not penalizing higher-achieving students with the 'grading curve.' Johnson further recommends the use of formulaic adjustments by institutions because his research finds that some faculty members try to work around imposed constraints if the awarding of final grades is left in their hands.

A simpler method of adjustment would be simply to exclude teaching evaluations from considerations of professors' merit and performance scores. Of course, this move would be resisted from many quarters, as our research reported in chapter 2 indicates. More palatable, but also requiring institutional intervention, would be to correlate each professor's grade distribution in a course with his or her evaluations. In this method, some proportion of the professor's rating would be ignored at the higher or lower level. For example, if guidelines specify that no more that 20 per cent of grades are to be As, and a professor awards 30 per cent As, then the best 10 per cent of evaluations would be eliminated from his or her official teaching scores for that course. Conversely, the lowest percentage of evaluations could be eliminated in proportion to, say, the number of Ds and Fs awarded.

The long-term effect of these formulaic adjustments would be to bring high graders in line with institutional definitions of grades, because they would have to explain to their students why the grades appearing on their transcripts are lower than the grades they awarded during the course. In addition, there would be no monetary or ego-based incentive for giving surplus high grades. Formulaic adjustments could also be used in recruiting students in universities that want to promote themselves by their high standards (rather than easy degrees), as Princeton is currently doing.

Of course, we could also use other educational systems as a model, as in the case where standardized final or exit exams are given (e.g., the United Kingdom and China), or where students must demonstrate a certain level of proficiency, as with bar exams in the legal profession. This would turn the disengagement compact on its head, motivating teacher and student alike to do their best in all aspects of courses. Professors could be rewarded on the basis of the performance of their students on these exams, and students would be motivated to help professors teach courses to their capacity and derive rewards from doing so when they take the exams.

Finally, we could also heed calls to include assessments such as those used in the NSSE that measure how much is required of students and how high the bar has been set for them. These evaluations would not be so much about satisfaction and popularity as how challenged students were to read, write, and engage themselves in the material and how the course transformed their 'critical thinking, problem solving, effective communication, and responsible citizenship.'[45]

Whatever the solution we might seek, we should heed Johnson's call for reform, which would begin with an acknowledgment of the problem. In his words, 'To right the boat, two things must happen: More principled student grading practices must be adopted, and faculty assessment must be more closely linked to student achievement.'[46]

The first and easiest step that we recommend is for all universities to post their grade distributions on easily accessible links on their websites. Currently, in Ontario, universities are required to post their graduation rates, graduate employment rates, and student loan default rates,[47] so grade distributions could be posted on these pages (as could NSSE results). These postings should have full disclosure for each of the preceding ten years, as well as information for every five years dating back to the 1960s, or to the founding of newer schools.

We commend the move to have all Ontario universities participate in the NSSE each year as part of an accountability framework to be developed with the provincial government. In fact, in early 2006, all eighteen

Ontario universities, and over thirty universities across Canada administered the NSSE survey. We hope that all these universities will post their
results on their websites with easy access to *all the data*, including students' reporting of the grades they are receiving. Of the eight universities participating in 2004, we found that only two published the full data
(Queen's and Waterloo). Several others published partial data, sometimes reflecting only the areas in which they performed better than
other G10 schools, but that is not satisfactory. Disclosure should be full at
all these public institutions, but there appears to have been a cloak of
secrecy in this case, perhaps because of the embarrassment over not
emerging better than our American colleagues. If these 2006 and subsequent results are published, we shall be in a better position to draw conclusions about grade inflation across Canada, and the debate we are
calling for will have benchmarks on which arguments can be based and
compared.

The University Graduate Revisited: What Is Added beyond Other Trajectories to the Workplace and Adulthood?

Assuming we have convinced readers that university is not for everyone,
especially those who are not ready or who have been pushed into attending, but it still holds promise for those who approach it for its intrinsic
qualities, what else can we say about what students can expect in return
for their tuition dollars and time invested?[48]

Educational researchers have asked this question repeatedly since the
expansion of the university system beginning in the 1950s. While
researchers now have a good idea of the answer, those who are most scientifically rigorous admit that certain questions remain inconclusively
answered because of the difficulties in doing controlled experimental
research in real-life settings.[49] In addition to the standard necessary
experimental controls, a crucial one is almost impossible to implement:
comparing those who attend university with entirely equivalent people
who do not attend.[50]

The methodological problem is that those who attend have more in
common with each other than they do with those who do not attend. For
example, those who attend universities are on average smarter and from
wealthier families. To conclusively attribute the success of smart people
from wealthy backgrounds in whole or in part to university would require
comparing them with an equivalent sample of smart people from wealthy
backgrounds who do not go to university. Since the majority of these peo-

ple go to university, we would have somehow to convince a sufficiently large number not to do so for the sake of our research – an unlikely scenario. But even in the 1950s and 1960s when there were still large numbers of such people not going to university, the logistics of rounding them up were extremely complicated and difficult to carry out, so it was never done. Accordingly, no researcher ever conducted a perfectly designed study of university outcomes that conclusively answered the question about the ultimate benefit of a university education.[51]

We mention this because a number of macroeconomic studies show that university graduates make more money and have more successful careers than non-graduates.[52] While undoubtedly true, one problem with this logic is that, were it not for credentialism, these same people might have been equally successful: smart, keen people from wealthy backgrounds have always done well without a university education in developing their own 'human capital' (marketable skills). Their achievement could have been the result of their ability, but also of a variety of other reasons, such as their knowledge of (upper) middle-class culture – known sociologically as 'cultural capital' – or their (upper) middle-class connection in the work world – known sociologically as 'social capital.' Thus, the 'ability' involved may not be raw intelligence so much as skills inextricably connected with cultural and social capital.[53]

Another problem with this logic is that many of the jobs calling for a university education from applicants require the same skills as they did before university credentials became so common. As we have discussed, employers may simply be capitalizing on the supply of more highly educated applicants, assuming that someone with a university degree is smarter and keener than someone without one. In fact, few researchers who have seriously examined this possibility deny that it is a highly operative factor in hiring practices. The explanation is called 'signalling theory.'[54]

Careful researchers also keep several other problems in mind before drawing conclusions. In addition to the self-fulfilling problem of credentialism, the period during which university is usually attended (age eighteen to twenty-four) is a time in life when much change can take place in people with or without attending university. These are called 'maturation effects' by researchers and are difficult to distinguish from the effects that might be attributable to university experiences. In other words, some of the same developmental effects not associated with the pure acquisition of knowledge might have been brought about by four years of travel or four years of working at a challenging job. In addition, people have different abilities when they begin university. Those with greater abilities may change because of those abilities, and not necessarily because of their experiences in university: they may have changed regardless of whether they were travelling, working, or going to school.

Still, and bearing these research problems in mind, spending four or more years anywhere must do something to change the person. Indeed, research does show that there are some predictable effects that result from spending this time in university. After examining 2,600 studies conducted during the 1970s and 1980s, educational researchers Ernest Pascarella and Patrick Terenzini concluded in *How College Affects Students* that

> students not only make statistically significant gains in factual knowledge and in a range of general cognitive and intellectual skills; they also change on a broad array of value, attitudinal, psychosocial, and moral dimensions … changes in intellectual skills [tend] to be larger in magnitude than changes in other areas, but … the change that occurs during the [university] years does not appear to be concentrated in a few isolated areas. Rather, the research portrays the [university] student as changing in an integrated way, with change in any one area appearing to be part of a mutually reinforcing network or pattern of change in other areas.[55]

While such changes appear dramatic, Pascarella and Terenzini caution that the studies showing them have not safeguarded against all the methodological problems associated with sorting out the direct effects of the university experience. The few studies that are more rigorous make more modest claims about the impact of university, generally showing that 'hard intellectual' as opposed to 'soft personality' development more often takes place, with the strongest evidence pointing to verbal and quantitative skills, critical thinking, and the use of principled reasoning in judging moral issues. However, the magnitude of these effects is not great, with the degree of change being at best about 10 to 15 per cent on a given scale.[56]

In the softer personality and attitude areas, evidence of any effect is mixed. Factors like liberalism, self-concept, personal adjustment, and psychological well-being show change levels similar to those of intellectual factors. This is good news for those who see university education as an opportunity to broaden their, or their children's, intellectual and psychological horizons – to become less parochial. For this reason alone, some parents from rural and small-town settings would like to see their children attend university and gain a better sense of the world, a goal that we wholeheartedly support so long as they take the opportunity seriously and engage themselves deeply in their studies. However, there is little demonstrable effect of university attendance on deep-seated personality factors like identity development, interpersonal relationships, and maturity. This may be because some deep-seated personal characteristics are resistant to change during this period or simply that these factors are not targeted in any systematic way at most universities (whereas the intellectual attributes are directly targeted), so expectations of substantial changes in personality may be unrealistic.

Many readers would be happy even if university affects only the graduate's material quality of life. Here the answer is clearer, although still confounded with the self-fulfilling credentialism effect. As already noted, university graduates, on average, have higher earnings than those with less education (including an incomplete university degree), but they also have more stable employment, more career mobility, and higher career attainment. Unfortunately, we do not know with complete certainty whether there is something added in the university experience that is absolutely unavailable elsewhere, whether less-able and less-motivated people are simply weeded out, or a combination of both.

There is little doubt, however, that, as Pascarella and Terenzini point out, the BA is 'the single most important educational rung on the socioeconomic attainment ladder.' They refer to a 'socioeconomic positioning effect' that produces subsequent benefits by giving graduates 'material and nonmaterial resources and opportunities'[57] with which to further their occupational position and personal development. Moreover, the jobs they have access to are more conducive to subsequent forms of psychosocial and cognitive development as well as career mobility. However, this is clearly a 'credential effect,' referring to the subsequent positional benefits of possession of a credential, independent of what underlies the credential, like knowledge and skills. In fact, we submit that a good number of students have a sense of this credential effect, which explains why they believe they do not need to put much effort into gaining that credential. The most obvious credential effect is monetary, as we shall soon see, and this is likely what motivates disengaged students to stay in school.[58] It also makes other forms of higher education, like vocational programmes, less attractive, even though graduates of these programmes are essential to the economy.

Lest readers get the idea that a totally skeptical position can be taken on the merits of a good liberal arts education – when students actually apply themselves – the knowledge, skills, and personality development acquired during the university years may have 'sleeper' or indirect effects in the sense that long-term occupational and lifestyle outcomes are enhanced in ways that are difficult to calculate. In a recent study of the long-term employment rates and salaries of Canadian graduates, the authors conclude that in comparison with applied-program graduates, those

> graduating from programs in the humanities and social sciences had considerably more difficulty with the school-to-work transition ... But once that transition was made, the generic nature of the skills they acquired appeared to stand them in good stead – because of these skills they have a greater longevity and ... [aptitude for] continued lifelong learning in the face of labour market changes.[59]

The possibility of sleeper effect is interesting, but again it is impossible to tell whether there was something about the curriculum that did it (as opposed to a maturation effect), whether the most egregiously disengaged or academically weaker students were simply weeded out, or a combination of both.

Show Me the Numbers: What Science Says about the High End of Benefits of Higher Education

Monetary Rates of Return

Policymakers have recognized the economic benefits of a university education for some time, and have attempted to make the general public aware of these benefits. For example, bachelor's degrees can grant an advantage over a high school diploma of 20–40 per cent higher annual earnings,[60] and rates of private return for Canadian university graduates has been estimated at 22 per cent for women and 14 per cent for men.[61] These rates can actually outpace other forms of investments, like equities, bonds, and real estate.[62] Moreover, the lifetime earning advantage of a university degree, even for underemployed university graduates, is substantially higher than for high school graduates – in the magnitude of between $500,000 and $1 million lifetime benefit in earnings, net of the direct and indirect costs of obtaining that education.[63]

In short, completing a university education is on average a wise investment, although this investment works out better for some than for others. Some university graduates will make less than higher-paid secondary school graduates, and some secondary school graduates will make more than lower-paid university graduates. An estimate from the United States is that about one in four university graduates earns less than the average high-school graduate and about one in four high school graduates makes more than the average university graduate.[64] However, to the extent that university can be mainly four to six years of fun, followed by years of higher salary, there is quite an incentive for people to forego other forms of post-secondary education like apprenticeships, a possibility that smacks of unfairness to those who do not take the university route to the labour force.

A social rate of return can also be calculated for each university graduate: the eventual return to the government coffers in taxes from workers with higher incomes, net of the costs of training them. This is estimated to be about 10 per cent per university graduate.[65] Of course, if Canadian society were as non-credentialist as in earlier generations, many of those without university credentials in business and government would be making higher wages and paying more tax anyway.[66]

Armed with this knowledge of the rate of return, Canadian policymakers have increasingly downloaded the cost of tuition to university students, restricted the funding that might have hired more professors, and held back the increasing faculty–student ratio.[67] Funding to universities has decreased steadily since the 1980s, with per student government funding to universities declining by some 30 per cent,[68] resulting in a doubling of tuition levels.[69] Canadian universities now count on student tuition for about one-third of their operating budgets, aided in part by a doubling to trebling in the number of students paying tuition since then.[70] Rising tuitions have contributed to student debt, which as noted in the previous chapter has tripled over the past twenty years, to an average of some $20,000 for university graduates who have taken on loans.[71]

The impact of these policies is not self-evident, and at first blush one might conclude that they have had the effect of reducing the appeal of the university education. However, as we have seen, university enrolments continue to grow at unprecedented rates. As we also saw in chapters 1 and 2, however, it is not likely a love of learning that has driven this increase, but the desire to avoid the poor labour market for those without a degree. This is the positional feature of the university degree that points to the often neglected side of the credentialism – the declining job prospects for those at lower levels of education.

Thus, while those with higher credentials do in fact experience an advantage over the less educated in workplace opportunities (higher salaries and less unemployment), it appears that much of this advantage is at the expense of those not fortunate enough to gain higher credentials. For example, between 1980 and 2000, while (inflation-adjusted) average incomes of young Canadians with a BA remained about the same, the incomes of high school graduates dropped 10 to 15 per cent.[72] Similarly, during this same period, the real earnings of young American baccalaureates increased by 5 per cent, while the earnings of high school graduates fell by 20 per cent.[73] When all those who do not use the higher educational route to the workplace are considered, their incomes dropped by between 20 per cent (for females) and 30 per cent (for males). This segment of the youth population has been dubbed the 'forgotten half' because they are often not included in research and policy efforts directed at young people.[74] Referring to this often overlooked side of credentialism, one American source argues that 'it should be kept in mind that the "rise" in the college premium was almost entirely driven by the *collapse* in the earnings of high-school graduates and dropouts ... This is what caused the doubling of the college premium.'[75]

Herein lies a paradox faced by the current generation, or what we have referred to as the 'credentialism paradox': credentialed skills often have little to do with the work that is eventually preformed, but without the credentials, one's employability and earning power are seriously jeopardized.[76] One consequence is that those with higher levels of education are taking lower-skilled jobs that used to be performed by those with lower skills. This leaves those with lower skills with fewer job opportunities and lower wages as a part of a 'downward cascading effect' that is unrecognized by promoters of post-secondary education as a panacea for the problems faced by young people today.[77]

This downward cascading effect has also been described as a result of 'over-schooling' that creates a 'labour queue.'

A significant body of research indicates that education credentials have devalued during the twentieth century. This devaluation was largely caused by 'over-schooling,' i.e. a vast expansion in educational attainment that was not equaled by an upgrading of the labour market ... This process has implications for individual strategies of educational investment, especially if one prescribes to labour queue theory, which sees education as a relative good for which employers compete for employees with the highest credentials in order to reduce the costs of job training ... In an over-qualified labour market, employers will fill the 'highest' jobs with those who have the 'highest' qualifications. Since over-schooling means that there are too many workers who are highly educated, some of these workers are necessarily allocated to 'mid-level' jobs. This process is repeated for those with mid-level qualifications, where, since there are not enough mid-level jobs, many are forced to compete for low-level jobs. It follows logically that this pattern has its most serious effects on the labour market opportunities of those with lower levels of education, thus widening the gap between educational levels in their occupational returns ... If people wish to avoid downward mobility – as is implied by the mechanism of relative risk aversion – they need to achieve a higher level of education if its value decreases.[78]

Critics of the position that we and others advocate on the relationship between post-secondary education and the youth labour market point to macroeconomic analyses, such as those produced in the late 1990s by an economist at the University of British Columbia, Robert C. Allen.[79] This unpublished paper gets a surprising amount of attention in policy circles, in good part we think because it says what a lot of people want to hear about the good-news side of a university education: graduates make more money and are more employable, including those from the humanities and social sciences. We do not dispute this point, as readers will note from what we have stressed, and we commend Allen for attempting to counter the view that liberal arts programmes should be cut in favour of vocational ones. However, this aspect of our argument applies to all young people, not just successful graduates. Not only does Professor Allen underestimate underemployment among graduates,[80] which we revisit next, but he does not take into account the downward cascading effect just noted. Besides, the macroeconomic position is insensitive to the issues of grade inflation and disengagement, which are the primary focus of this book.

In considering policy initiatives to help young people with their integration into the labour force, then, we must be concerned with the experiences of *all* young people, not just the more fortunate half that makes it into post-secondary education. Considering the current realities facing young people in the labour force, it is little wonder that there is a 'rush on credentials.'

Looking beyond Statistical Averages: What Science Says about the Low End of the Benefits of University Education

Underemployment Revisited

As we have noted, in the 1960s, the higher educational system was expanded dramatically with the building of many new colleges and universities. The assumption driving this expansion was that the skills transmitted through higher education in the form of human capital – skills that translate into income – would meet the needs of an advanced industrial economy and generate economic wealth for the individual graduate and for society as a whole.

This human capital theory assumption has been borne out at lower levels of education (with the acquisition of basic literacy and numeracy) and in the more applied areas of higher education, but is faulty as a full explanation of educational outcomes.[81] In particular, the higher-educational skills imparted by the liberal arts education are largely passive in the sense that they need an existing occupational context in which to be used – they do not on their own create new jobs or economic activity. For example, while a general knowledge of the sciences or the arts garnered from an undergraduate degree may be useful in certain occupations, outside those contexts they do not generate income on their own. This logic has been called a 'field of dreams' approach – 'build it and they will come.'[82] As we have seen, they are coming; however, other problems emerge when they leave.

As already noted, problems with expansion of the university system became evident as early as the mid-1970s. Although 'good jobs' were still available in business and professional services, an increasing number of graduates found only 'bad jobs' in consumer services.[83] As the supply of graduates grew, a buyer's market in favour of employers resulted in most sectors. In this situation, employers could take those with the highest credentials, even for lower-skilled jobs, so many of those with higher degrees increasingly found themselves taking jobs that did not require any or all of their skills. Consequently, there was a downward cascading effect whereby those without higher degrees faced increasingly stiffer competition for jobs, leaving them with fewer and poorer-paying jobs in the labour queue.[84]

Government reports traced the growing credential underemployment throughout the 1980s and 1990s, finding that up to half of Canadian university (under) graduates were in jobs two years after graduation not requiring a university degree.[85] This proportion of underemployed graduates declines to about one-third after five years, but appears not to improve much beyond that.[86] For example, a recent Statistics Canada survey found that, among all workers aged twenty to twenty-nine, in 2000, about one-third felt they were overqualified,[87] a finding confirmed by another Statistics Canada report using a different methodology.[88] When the full age range of the workforce is included, one-quarter of those with post-secondary educations felt they were overqualified for their job.

While these government-sponsored studies used a methodology based on subjective judgements of underemployment, it is possible to assess this issue with more objective measures, as we did in a recent book.[89] Using published data from the 2000 census, we noted that in the 1990s, some 600,000 jobs requiring university credentials were created in the Canadian workforce (the demand). While this was good news for those who got those jobs, some 1.2 million university degrees also came onto the labour market (the supply). This means that there were *two* new university graduates for every *one* job created requiring them. Hence, using an objective supply-demand estimate, the 50 per cent underemployment rate for university graduates derived with other methods appears to be reliable.

Many of those who graduate with a BA clearly do not face an easy task in moving into the workforce – certainly not as easy as many government and media pronouncements imply about the importance of a higher education. For example, it appears that up to half of university graduates need at least fifteen months to find a full-time job that lasts more than six months.[90] Faced with this prospect, it is understandable many would take unskilled jobs, even jobs requiring only high school diplomas.[91] Indeed, research reported by Statistics Canada on graduates from the 1980s and early 1990s clearly shows the downward cascading effect of overqualification, with the following proportion of post-secondary graduates overqualified by two or more credential levels (e.g., a bachelor's graduate taking a vocational job, or a master's graduate taking a job actually designated for a community college graduate): '31% to 43% for college graduates, 19% to 29% of bachelor's graduates, 8% to 17% of master's graduates, and 9% to 21% of doctoral graduates.'[92] Thus, while this is clearly bad news for graduates who invested in higher degrees than they can use, it is also bad news for those with lower levels of education who had their prospective jobs taken by these overqualified graduates who were ahead in the labour queue.

The most recent research reported by Statistics Canada found that 'the number of university-educated workers who were overqualified for their job was nearly one-third higher in 2001 than in 1993.'[93] In this case, the criterion for overqualification was a university graduate taking a job for at least one month that required at most a high school education, and 30 per cent had done so during the 1990s. Broken down by age, almost half of those under thirty years of age experienced this form of overqualification.

It is also understandable why so many of those faced with disappointments in securing a job to match their credentials would choose to obtain more credentials, if only to stand out from the mass with 'just a BA.' Now, over half of university graduates with BAs re-enrol in subsequent educational programmes.[94] This includes the 7 per cent who obtain a community college diploma within five years of gaining their BAs, their rationale apparently being that they are looking for something that is 'practical.'[95] We see here another aspect of the positional problem of credentialism, where some people have lost the gamble to improve their occupational status by getting a BA without having an educational plan for why they are doing so, and not acquiring the human capital skills that would secure them a position of higher status.

In sum, in economic language, with an oversupply of higher degrees, workplace demand for graduates decreased. Over time, university graduates had less to bargain with in the sense that their credentials lost market value. This inflation in credentials was fuelled in the 1980s when university enrolments in Canada increased by some 40 per cent. In the 1990s, the number of university graduates in the workforce increased some 50 per cent, from about 2.5 million to over 3.5 million (out of a total workforce of 14.5 million).[96] As we write, and as noted, enrolments continue to grow at an unprecedented rate, with actual growth outstripping predictions.

The Accessibility Issue

In spite of decades of government attempts to make the university education more accessible to those from lower socio-economic backgrounds, university attendance is still affected by family income, even with the dramatic increases in enrolment that we have discussed. After the expansion of the system in the 1960s, children from high-income families were are 2.5 times as likely to participate in university as those from low-income families. Still, some progress has been made in recruiting from the less advantaged segments of the population, and the largest group among these recent recruits has been young women from middle-income families. There was a narrowing of the family-income gap in the late 1990s, with the participation rate of those in the lowest income quartile (i.e., the poorest quarter of the population) rising to 19 per cent (versus 40% for those in the highest quartile), up from only 10 per cent in the early 1980s.[97]

Parents' education is perhaps more influential than income, although the two predictors are obviously linked. Young Canadians are more than twice as likely to go to university if their parents did so, as opposed to having parents who simply completed high school. They are three to four times more likely to attend than those with parents who did not complete high school.[98]

Part of the problem is that two government policies have apparently been working at cross-purposes. On the one hand, there has been the policy to increase accessibility, so that the most able students would be the ones attending universities. On the other hand, there have been the dramatic increases in tuition rates, raising concerns that attempts to get brighter children from lower socio-economic backgrounds into universities are being compromised. However, the research shows that there is a complex relationship between economic background and propensity to attend university, both in Canada and in other countries.[99] Some Canadian research indicates that young people from lower-income families do not cite financial barriers as more of a disincentive than do those from more affluent families. Indeed, the fact that more economically disadvantaged young people are going to university at the very time that tuitions have increased dramatically suggests that finances are not the serious issue that policymakers have thought they were.[100] However, it is likely that parents are picking up more of this financial burden for students of all backgrounds, and dropout appears to be related to unmet financial needs, so those with less affluent parents may be at a disadvantage in the long run.[101] Moreover, students report that they could finish their degrees more quickly if they did not have to work during the school year, and more young people from lower income backgrounds work during their undergraduate years, slowing their progress and affecting their performance.[102]

Just why more of those from disadvantaged backgrounds do not aspire to attend, actually attend, or persist once they attend, university is currently unclear from the available research.[103] Some research is showing that identity-based 'personal factors' are more important than financial ones for those from certain backgrounds, as in the case of Aboriginal students.[104] Without having parents who attended, as in the case of 'first-generation' students, universities can seem foreign, impersonal, or forbidding, and not an easy place where one can 'belong' or find 'comfort zones.'[105] Without parental guidance or role-modelling, there can also be a number of misunderstandings about what is involved. For example, as noted in chapter 4, most people actually overestimate the short-term costs of university in relation to the long-term benefits (by a factor of five), even those from affluent backgrounds with university-educated parents.[106] However, those from lower-income families have the most serious misperceptions. On average, those from economically disadvantaged backgrounds tend to think the costs outweigh the benefits, in thinking that tuition is higher than it really is, but also in seriously underestimating the income advantage of university graduates over high school graduates.

This misperception is even more striking when one considers that people from disadvantaged origins have more to gain from getting a university education than do people from more advantaged backgrounds, because their earning potential is lower without a higher education. In other words, poorer people have a lower denominator of expected lifetime income, so they have further to rise as a result of gaining the advantage accrued from more education. For example, black women in the United States have the greatest private rate of return because the jobs they can get without a university education are so poorly paid.[107] It would appear, then, that policy efforts need to be directed more at correcting misperceptions among the disadvantaged as well as to learning more about their personal reasons for not attending or persisting in university.

While we should clearly be trying to get the most able and motivated young people to attend university, what is missed in these calculations is the larger force of credentialism where many young people are pushed to go to university when they would have been happy to move into the labour force and take a decent job, as was the case in the past.

The Relative Merits of Soft and Hard Sorting Systems: Dealing with Accessibility

Societies inevitably sort their citizens into statuses and roles. In modern democracies, people like to think that they sort themselves into these statuses and roles. While there is clearly more individual discretion in people's life-chances in these democracies, the amount of control people have over certain aspects of their lives is also overestimated. For example, people tend to mistake the freedom to consume commodities with an overall freedom from obstacles stemming from discrimination in the realms of social class, racial status, and the like.[108] Moreover, societies tend to have hierarchical structures, many of which are pyramid in shape.

This logic can be used to illustrate to the interplay of educational and occupational hierarchies – as one moves from the lower to the higher levels, the number of positions systematically decrease. For instance, the bulk of the population completes a primary education, most complete a secondary one, less than half now complete an undergraduate or community college programme, a small percentage complete a master's degree or equivalent, and very few earn doctorates. Similarly, we find corporations roughly structured like pyramids with CEOs at the apex, supported by a small number of directors, who are in turn supported by layers of management down to the lower level. These layers of management have a pyramid shape that sits on a base of employees that increase in numbers as we move to the lower levels.

The reality of these structures shows the flaws in the logic of encouraging the bulk of the population to aspire to the highest levels, as we do when we tell everyone that the university route to the labour force is the only one that will prove their worth. As noted earlier in this book, some 90 per cent of those beginning secondary school aspire to move into these higher levels, in good part because they have been told by their school, parents, and government to do so. When we tell everyone to aspire to these heights, we in effect create an *inverted* pyramid, where those with high aspirations are at what was the base, while those with low aspirations are at what was the apex. Figure 5.1 illustrates how these two pyramids look when superimposed, and it shows how the current system sets up a large number students for eventual underemployment if they follow through on their aspirations, or at the minimum for the disappointment of aspirations discussed in chapter 2 when they are weeded and cooled out of the education system.[109]

A more benign and rational system would minimize disappointments and misdirected trajectories into the labour force, while at the same time maximizing all students' potentials from the beginning. The 'soft' sorting system that we support – even venerate – in Canada and the United States is neither benign nor rational in these respects. Other societies employ 'hard' sorting systems that put people in educational tracks early that lead to relatively predetermined career destinations. This type of intervention is unpalatable to many North Americans who have grown up in the soft system and who have been taught to value the more extreme forms of individualism, supported by tales of rags to riches successes and to think in terms of sayings like 'the cream always rises to the top.' They also tend to think that young people in the harder sorting systems are ruthlessly sorted on the basis of stringent and unfair exams that forever after determine their life-chances and socio-economic destination.[110] Or, they think only of the German apprenticeship system, with the image that most children are 'condemned' to be plumbers or electricians, an image that is based on an inappropriate demeaning of the trades.[111] However, a variety of systems simply provide more structure for young people for their entire education-to-work transition, and if we

Figure 5.1: The distribution of educational aspirations plotted against the structure of the workforce

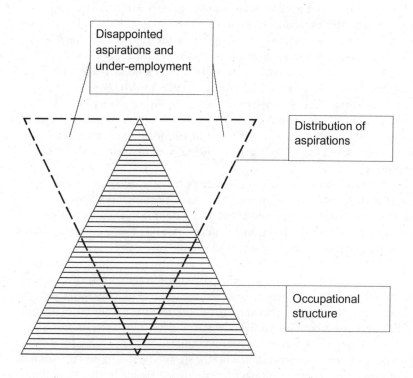

look at the experiences of those systems, there are some lessons to be learned. These lessons promise some relief to those in North America who are tired of hearing excuses for a system that is contradiction-ridden and in crisis, as the analysis in this book suggests.

The best of these more structured sorting systems can be found in Europe and have been monitored by the OECD for some time. In a recent report sponsored by the OECD, a listing of 'what works' in education-to-work policies from various countries was provided. [112] At the level of secondary education, this involves strong efforts to keep *everyone* in school by providing them with a varied curriculum that is meaningful to local economic activities and opportunities, as well as providing intellectual stimulation for those who would go on to some form of post-secondary education. These efforts are supported by safety nets that help minimize the number of students who would leave school only to face unemployment. Schools can contribute with proactive and individualized counselling and guidance to match students with courses and programmes that suit their interests and motivations, giving special attention to weaker students. Some countries, like Sweden, give students a study allowance while they are in secondary school (until age nineteen),[113] which rewards their persistence and discourages them from taking on part-time jobs while in school. This monetary incentive keeps them more engaged in their schoolwork by providing the discretionary income that young people in other countries take on part-time jobs to earn.[114] Those who do leave school early are tracked at the local level, and plans are made to get them back into the educational system and/or labour force as soon as possible.

In conjunction with these educational policies, which take a local focus first and then look to the more global and post-secondary influences, 'youth friendly' labour markets assist young people in their transitions by providing ample on-the-job training in companies. These countries (like Germany and Switzerland) attempt to minimize the prevalence of a dual (youth vs. adult) labour market, sometimes with active employment policies (wage subsidies to employers) that encourage the hiring of the young in the same job categories as older workers (like Sweden).

Countries can do all of this *and* provide high-calibre university systems. While there are many fine university systems to draw from for comparison, Sweden's system provides a useful comparison with Canada's. Before discussing its university system, though, it should be noted that vocational programmes in upper secondary school provide basically what Canadians get in community college – courses of study in hospitality, health care, media, child care, etc. But these courses of study are also integrated with the local labour market and industry, including job placement.[115] This minimizes the development of the dual post-secondary system that Canada has allowed. Even in the United States, where there are also community colleges, these culminate in an associate's degree, which counts as sort of a 'half BA,' which can be upgraded. In parts of Canada, we have the strange system where an increasing number of graduates with BAs revert to the community college in an attempt to complete the school-to-work transition, but this puts them in their mid-twenties before doing so.[116]

For those who go on to university in Sweden, no tuition is charged, and they are entitled to a generous loan/grant system. A study-loan assistance programme is available to all, regardless of parental or spousal income, which can be repaid at 4 per cent of subsequent income at a low interest rate. And about one-third of this loan is received as a non-repayable grant that qualifies as pensionable income.

Participation in universities doubled in Sweden during the 1990s, and the expansion continues. Like that of other industrial countries, the goal of the government is to eventually encourage up to half of the youth population to obtain higher degrees – in this case, mainly university degrees.[117] When properly prepared and engaged, there is no reason why this percentage of the youth population cannot participate.

Conclusion: The Idea of the University – Education versus Training

The idea of the university is quite straightforward. It is a place where certain types of knowledge are produced and shared. But unlike other places where knowledge might also be pursued and produced, universities traditionally do so in a systematic and rigorous fashion. Often described as places of 'higher' (as opposed to 'lower') education, universities are ostensibly engaged in the production of knowledge that is more sophisticated or refined than one might get from 'lower' education. Although they are often taken as elite institutions with elitist concerns, the thrust of our argument is different. The notion of 'higher' as it is used here is not meant to convey some misplaced sense of superiority or arrogance that is commonly associated with the wealthy, who have traditionally been the recipients of university education. Rather, we understand 'higher education' to refer to the order of abstraction required for grasping certain types of knowledge.

In their approach to the world, some people are more philosophical and reflective, while others are more practical and hands-on. The former, for example, will want to know *why* things work, while the latter will want to know *how* things work; *why* speaks to analysis and explanation, *how* speaks to description. While all explanation must begin with some description, description alone is never sufficient, so universities deal with both, but they tend to place more emphasis on analysis and explanation.

Therefore, while both explanation and description are important, in unravelling the complexities of knowledge, whether of the physical, social, or spiritual universes, explanation calls for a certain degree of abstract thinking with which the practically oriented can be impatient. And along with that sort of thinking comes the development of a specialized vocabulary that is uniquely suited to the discussion of such diverse and abstract concepts as freedom (politics), gravity (physics), love (imagination), and even belief (religion). Developing the quality of mind that is suited to such pursuits, to deal effectively with abstractions of all sorts, and to look reflexively and objectively at the thinker herself or himself, is the task assigned to university professors.

Thus conceived, higher education is about the sculpting of the human mind and spirit; the cultivation of rounded human beings, and the facilitation of civilized discourse among them. It is about generalization as opposed to specialization – the inclusion of as wide a range of people as possible in a conversation about what matters to human beings and the planet they inhabit. As already noted, that conversation will concern the social world in all of its complexities, the natural and physical world with all of its beauties, and the spiritual world with all of its mysteries. The pursuit of knowledge of the foregoing is synonymous with the pursuit of education, and in that pursuit there is room enough for Shakespeare, Newton, Einstein, Freud, Marx, Jesus, and Mohammed.

This view goes directly counter to that of some students who, when asked what things bother them about the education they are receiving, respond to the effect that their courses are not related to any future goals, yet they have to take them. This can include students who want to go into medicine or business, and refuse to take courses that don't look good on their transcripts because they are seen to be too 'soft' or off-topic. Even if these students do beat the odds to make the cut into their professional school of choice, they may lack a well-rounded intellect that would help them appreciate their discipline later in life; if they do not make the cut, they have squandered the opportunity to develop their intellect and they have little on which to fall back.

This is one reason why we advocate the liberal arts education as part of life-long learning, and suggest that policy and practice encourage all interested people, regardless of age – trades worker and academic alike – to sample this form of educational experience.[118] Increasingly, the liberal arts education is squandered on that portion of the student body – the disengaged – who are impatient to be doing something else, or on partially engaged students who take a 'gulp-and-vomit' or 'just-in-time' learning approach of dubious benefit.

Viewed in this way, higher education is separate from training and vocationalism. For us, higher education speaks to our *democratic* and *egalitarian* concerns and embraces the central philosophical issues at the heart of the human community: the promotion of social justice, the inculcation of a sense of morality and social responsibility, a commitment to the pursuit of social equality, and the recognition of the dignity of all people irrespective of class, race, sex, culture, or country. In the educational process, this is achieved by putting the stock of human knowledge in the service of humanity, especially the least fortunate and least able, and not using it to diminish some and elevate others. Training, on the other hand, is equally important, but speaks to the acquisition of technical knowledge and the details that are specific to a given field. As such, training is more narrow, particular, and instrumentally geared to meeting definable goals and honing personal careers. It is what the would-be engineer learns about structural stress on tall buildings during earthquakes, what the medical student learns about the spread of cancer in a human body, or what the aspiring lawyer learns about precedent.

In an ideal situation, then, we would have a harmony between education and training, and the engineer, doctor, manager, and lawyer will also have some knowledge of or exposure to the arts and literature, to philosophy and politics, and will have cultivated a sense of social justice, morality, and social responsibility to those in the wider community that sustains them all. A liberal education and vocational training do not have to be competing missions, but a liberal education must never be made to take a back seat to vocational training, for without an educated and socially responsible population all the 'training' in the world will make only a limited contribution to the public body and human welfare.

In short, university teaching of the liberal arts is about the dissemination of knowledge and the preparation of well-rounded citizens, and we are concerned that this is in jeopardy as more and more students have been told to use the liberal arts degree as a status symbol to gain access to white-collar occupations. While some of these students clearly benefit and go on to combine their liberal education with some sort of vocational or professional training, as we have argued, it appears that the liberal education side of this equation has increasingly been given short shrift. The fault lies with policies and practices that 'sell' the undergraduate degree as something amorphously 'good' for labour-force entry or as a qualification for professional schools, and is manifested in the growing numbers of disengaged and partially engaged students enrolling in courses that should be demanding a fuller commitment to deep learning. These policies and practices simply encourage large numbers of students to look at some obscure future horizon without appreciating the opportunities at hand in the present to transform and enrich themselves. Giving them 'soft' (inflated) grades in return for their tuition money simply bypasses the philosophy of the liberal education and undermines the fiduciary duty that the university system has had to both preserve and advance civilization.

What we are advocating is the need to preserve and reinvigorate the liberal arts philosophy of education, which is best described as critical, democratic, and egalitarian. It deals with the dynamic tension between the individual and society, and highlights the need for individuals to be made aware of their social responsibilities. Cultivating that *awareness* is synonymous with teaching and education, which is the process by which individuals are encouraged to stand outside of their individual selves – outside of their narrow and personal interests – to see societal goals as superior to their own. We are convinced that a society is only as strong as its least educated citizen, which is why the purpose of education should be to strengthen the community, whether it be the local, provincial, national, or even international community. The disengaged student, who passes though the university system unaffected by these liberal arts ideals, is morally numb and represents a form of self-indulgence that should be unpalatable to all citizens of modern democracies. Passing disengaged students through the university system without somehow transforming them wastes the legacy that has brought civilization to the point where we can provide higher education on such a large scale. No individual, regardless of his or her number of degrees and diplomas, is worth anything if the wider social context that nurtures and sustains him or her is left to ruin.

Education is a right, but like all rights, it comes with important responsibilities. And this is where the *critical* aspect of teaching and education is key. For what we advocate is not a blind endorsement of what might well be any social order, but rather a social order consisting of, and fashioned by, an informed (educated) citizenry, that is able to challenge injustice in any form. In this context, every individual has a social responsibility to the wider social whole of which he or she is a part. Understood in this way, a liberal education ought to enable students to see that wider whole and to put its interests and welfare above narrow, personal, and sectarian interests. We urge all of those involved – students, parents, professors, administrators, and policymakers alike – to discuss and debate the mission of the contemporary university and its potential to provide a high-quality liberal education before that potential is lost to other interests.[119]

We do not offer specific solutions to this and other related problems discussed in this book because those solutions first require that the problem be widely recognized, and this is not currently the case. Moreover, because the causes are multifaceted and have taken a long time to develop, quick fixes are not to be expected. The solutions will also be complex and will apply differently to diverse institutions in various regions. And because the causes ultimately lie with the wider society, the solutions will have to begin there: with the recognition of this potential range of causes, a debate about those causes, and a consensus about their solution. Ironically, the more aware the public is of the issues involved – an awareness that can be nurtured by a liberal education at any level and in any form, even self-taught – the more likely it is that these things will happen.[120]

We leave readers with the recent words of Western's President Paul Davenport, which show that the spirit of the liberal arts education is still alive at the heights of Canada's university administration, even if its practice is in crisis:

> While graduates in the life sciences and physical sciences, and professionals in health, engineering, business, and law are also critical to a modern economy, we must not neglect the central role played by the liberal arts. Many of the key issues facing Canada and other developed countries – the ethics of biotechnology, the management and celebration of cross-cultural differences, the proper scope of government in a mixed economy – are issues of the liberal arts which do not have technological solutions.
>
> While the liberal arts are thus important to the economy, they are equally important to our national discourse on values and policies. As an economist and university president, I believe the rising standards of living associated with the new economy will increase the desire of students to come to investigate the great questions of the liberal arts: Who am I and why am I here? What are beauty, virtue, and justice? How can we build societies that reflect our values of justice and compassion?[121]

Appendix

Methodological Considerations

No book can be everything to everyone, just like no university course is for everyone. In undertaking this book project, we encountered all sorts of opposition and resistance. Some of the resistance is the result of mere differences of opinion, and some rests with appraisals of the academic merits of certain forms of evidence, so we happily lay these out for readers and potential critics who may think that we are not aware of them.

There are four concerns that can be raised about our claims that the Canadian university system is in crisis, and the evidence we cite as the basis for our arguments.

The first pertains to our use of American research alongside Canadian research. While we acknowledge that Canada's post-secondary educational system has much that is unique and enviable, there is also a great deal of overlap with that of the United States. In fact, in comparison to university systems in other parts of the world, Canadian universities have far more similarities than differences with American universities. This point is not surprising, given the close social, cultural, economic, historical, geographic, and ethnic compositions of the two countries. Because the development and evolution of American educational institutions are quite similar to Canada's, it is only to be assumed that their problems will also mirror Canada's. So in principle there is nothing wrong with cautious and informed generalization between the two countries on matters related to their institutions of higher education.

One obvious point of difference between the two countries is the fact that in the United States many universities are private and not reliant on government financial support (ironically, the best of these private schools are having greater difficulties with the problems we write about, as discussed in chapters 1 and 5). This makes Canadian universities most similar to state universities in the United States. Some Canadians believe that their own universities are on the whole better than the average American state university, but there is little evidence for this view. For one, Canadian universities, especially those in Ontario, have suffered years of cutbacks – some 30 per cent over the past couple of decades.[1] Such cutbacks are not to be found in most U.S. state universities. This decline in funding is one of the reasons cited to explain why Canadian students are scoring as *less engaged* academically in the NSSE surveys than American students in comparable universities, as discussed in chapter 1. However, these comparable American schools actually show relatively high levels of disengagement, so the fact that Canadian schools show *more* disengagement tells us that we should be paying very close attention to factors other than state funding. In the case of data on student engagement, our use of American data is extremely instructive and useful, and we would be negligent not to discuss them in this book. This is even more so the case now that more Canadian universities are participating in the NSSE surveys.

Two other points of comparison can be mentioned to address this concern. First, at the high school level, it appears that Canadian and American students do about the same amount of homework, as discussed in chapter 1 (and both Canadian and American students do very little homework by international standards). Thus, the level of preparation for university is about the same on average, although the quality of American high schools varies somewhat more than that of Canadian high schools because of the reliance on local tax bases to fund schools in the United States. Variation does exist in Canada, but it tends to be based more on social class.

And second, when it comes to the amount of work for pay that university students take on during the school year, as examined in chapter 4, the average amount of time spent working for pay by Canadian university students is seventeen to eighteen hours per week – a doubling of the percentage working during the school year over the past thirty years. This is bringing Canadian students in line with American students, who have been working at least this much over that same period.[2] The average Canadian university student who takes on work during the school year now spends about as much time studying as working for pay, a development that can contribute to the disengagement problem, as pointed out in chapter 4. However, working for pay during the school year cannot be the root cause of disengagement because about half of Canadian students do not work for pay during the school year (compared to one-quarter in the United States), yet many of them can exhibit a similar pattern of disengagement.

On our primary points of comparison, then, Canadian and American university students, especially those in four-year state universities, experience many of the same things. In fact, it is not that difficult for these students to transfer schools if they so wish. Still, when drawing on American sources in this book, we shall remind readers that there may be some differences to take into account, and there may be more variation in conditions in U.S. schools.

The second concern is that we are too hard on the contemporary cohort of students and are blaming them for the circumstances in which they find themselves that are not of their doing. They didn't set the curriculum or water down the standards, volunteer to pay more tuition so that they would have to work more for pay during the school year, or assign themselves inflated grades. No, these are all traceable to the wards of the education system, from teachers through to policymakers. Today's students have inherited a system that is in many ways irrational, but necessary for many of them to follow if they are to find their way to make a relatively high standard of living. However, as we do with students in our classes, we take them to task in this book, because as actors in the system they have certain responsibilities, in spite of what the system will let them get away with or cajole them to do. Life is about taking responsibility and doing what is right, regardless of how screwed up the society is around us. This is not to endorse, however, an ultra-voluntaristic view of social change, for we are patently aware that there are many structural obstacles in the path of all human actors that go beyond mere individual will or desire.

The fact is that we like most of our students, and most of them like us: we are popular teachers who regularly get high teaching scores. One of us has even won numerous teaching awards over the years.[3] We have spent our adult lives first as students and then as mentors to them. But good mentors are honest with their students and do not flatter them with false praise. At the same time, we are known to be demanding teachers with high standards, and that elicits the respect of engaged students and the dismay of disengaged students. And we are as frank with our students in class and in conversations with them as we are in this book; engaged students know exactly what we are talking about and support our efforts to write this book in the hopes of improving the quality of education for them and others.

The third concern has to do with the fact that we draw heavily from our experiences at the University of Western Ontario, including its official statistics and publications. While it is true that we draw from our experiences in a single institution, it is what we know best, and Western is one of the most transparent and accessible universities when it comes to obtaining many institutional statistics. We attribute this to strong leadership at this university over the years. We cannot say the same for some other Canadian universities that carefully guard institutional indicators. We do not apologize for this reliance on our experience at Western, but simply invite those from other universities to tell their stories in the debate we would like to see happen. Still, we caution readers that schools do differ in sometimes significant ways, and what goes on at a large university like Western may not be happening in other institutions, at least to the same degree, especially in smaller ones. Western is one of the most popular universities in Canada, so there must something noteworthy here about which readers would like hear.

And fourth, there is a concern about the thorny issue of grade inflation. We personally know of no experienced teachers who are informed about the history of grading practices who do not think it exists and is a problem. It appears to be those who are relatively new to the system, or who are unaware of the history of grading practices, who either deny it exists or deny that it is a problem even if they admit it exists. The chief difficulty we encounter in writing about grade inflation is that it has been discussed far more than it has been systematically studied. Part of the problem is that institutions that engage in it most egregiously do not want to advertise the fact, and it can be very difficult to obtain their institutional data. From our investigation of this problem, which spans a good number of years, there is no question that it exists, but it is also clear that it varies from teacher to teacher, department to department, faculty to faculty, and school to school, as discussed in several chapters.

In addition, some people ask why grade inflation matters, and why we shouldn't just get used to it. Throughout this book, we went into great detail about why it does matter. To provide readers who are interested in learning more about why grade inflation matters and needs to be dealt with, we offer next a brief discussion of the historical and comparative dimensions of grade inflation. In doing so, we provide readers with a background knowledge that should help them appreciate our grave concerns with this problem, which we see to be a major threat to the integrity of educational system.

Defining and Measuring Grade Inflation

Both the Canadian and American university systems are historically rooted in the British system (and to some extent the German system), which traditionally had a rigorous system of standards, including assigning very few of the highest grades (usually about 5% As) and having examiners other than teachers in a given course evaluate students in standardized examinations. This type of system is still in place in some British and commonwealth universities, although they too have experienced pressures to inflate grades by assigning more of the highest grades.[4]

American universities began to deviate from this more rigorous system as private, for-profit universities emerged in the late 1800s and early 1900s. These institutions needed to have more mass appeal, as discussed in chapter 5, and thus developed a more popular curriculum and handed the examination of students over to teachers themselves. In Canada, the move to satisfy mass appeal happened somewhat later, but with many of the same consequences: grades rose as teachers were put in a position of both evaluating their students and being evaluated by them.

Although the rigorous British system has been influential in the commonwealth nations, other university systems around the world have been equally rigorous, specifying grade distributions that would recognize excellence (i.e., restricting the percentage of high grades that are assigned) while distributing grades in ways that reflect the belief that abilities are distributed along a normal curve: most students will lie within an average category (the C), a lesser number will be above average (the B), and a minority will be outstanding (the A). Likewise, lesser numbers will be below average (the D), and a minority will be inadequate (the E and/or F).

A grading distribution system recently developed by the European Commission to facilitate student exchange programmes illustrates both this logic and the fact of grade variation among nations, with some university systems allowing grades to inflate and others not doing so. This system – the European Credit Transfer System (ECTS) – was originally set up in 1989 to coordinate student exchange programmes among institutions in some thirty countries. Now in use by thousands of universities, it allows participating universities in each country to convert grades to a common, non-inflated standard, as follows:[5]

- A (10 per cent) = Excellent – outstanding performance with only minor errors
- B (25 per cent) = Very Good – above the average standard but with some errors
- C (30 per cent) = Good – generally sound work with a number of notable errors
- D (25 per cent) = Satisfactory – fair but with significant shortcomings
- E (10 per cent) = Sufficient – performance meets the minimum criteria
- FX = Fail – some more work required before the credit can be awarded
- F = Fail – considerable further work is required

Note that in this grading system the highest grade is limited to 10 per cent of students, and the next highest grade defines 25 per cent of students, such that a maximum of one in three students comes to be identified as above average. This system is somewhat more inflated than the traditional British system when it comes to awarding As, but is apparently palatable to these European universities.

We bring this to the reader's attention because this is the standard that we use when we speak of grade inflation. Our personal experience as students is rooted in the pre-credentialist era when standards rewarded excellence and gave honest feedback to students on where their performance lay relative to their classmates'. Thus, by this standard, when more than 35 per cent of students receive either an A or a B in a given class, grade inflation is clearly taking place. Of course, the odd class could obtain such results if by chance a large number of exceptional students happened to be enrolled in it. But statistically it is just as likely that over time an equal percentage of classes will have large numbers of inadequate students in them, so in the long run, and when dealing with large numbers of courses, the distribution of grades should correspond to this normal distribution.

There is little question that grade inflation is systemic in American high schools and universities, as discussed in this book to illustrate how severe the problem can become and how serious the consequences can be. On the question of grade inflation in Canadian secondary schools and universities, it appears that the situation is not as severe in some cases, but there is also evidence that grades have already crept up – or are in the process of creeping up – in various institutions, and if we do not recognize the problem and do something about it, we shall soon be in the same position as American schools. Indeed, the situation may well already be upon us in the case of many of our universities.

If we take the case of Ontario, we find that grade inflation began with the transformation of secondary schools to mass institutions in the 1960s. Educational researchers Alan King and Marjorie Peart trace the evolution of the grading system in Ontario in *The Numbers Game*, where they describe the turning point as follows: 'When the [standardized] grade 13 departmental exams were discontinued in 1967, failure rates dropped from a ten-year average of 20 percent ... to 6 to 8 percent over the next few years ... More higher marks were given to students and average marks moved slowly up in the 1970s.'[6]

With final marks being 'teacher assigned' in the 1970s, the percentage of students registering in universities with averages higher than 80 per cent grew to about 38 per cent in 1983 and 44 per cent in 1992.[7] This percentage has increased almost every year since. According to the Council of Ontario Universities,[8] in 1995 52.6 per cent of secondary school graduates applying to Ontario universities had As, while 61 per cent did so in 2004. Moreover, those reporting A+s increased from 9.4 per cent in 1995 to a high of 14.9 in 2003. The average grade of university applicants hit the 80 per cent mark in 1997 and has steadily increased each year since.

King and Peart attribute the increase in grades to the change to teacher-assigned grades and to some students taking the same courses several times to increase their marks in courses necessary for the university programme to which they were applying. But they also found that many teachers were raising grades to allow a student to graduate (32%), improve a student's chances of acceptance to a post-secondary institution (16%), or to help a student qualify for designation as an Ontario scholar (16%).[9]

In sum, there is no question that grade inflation exists in Ontario high schools in both historical and comparative terms. It appears that Ontario is one of the worst offenders among Canadian provinces, although it also seems to be the most scrutinized, with some 40 per cent of its graduates leaving with A averages (eight times as many as would be awarded in the traditional British system and four times as many as would be awarded using the ECTS system). Schools in some other provinces are not so promiscuous with their grades. For example, Alberta and Quebec apparently have higher standards,[10] such that Ontario high school graduates transferring to those provinces routinely have the average on their transcripts reduced by universities to make them more compatible with local graduates. But even these other provinces have inflated grades by the historical and comparative standards (e.g., Alberta graduates just over 20% of its high-school students with As). According to a newspaper article from the University of Calgary reporting the difficulties this trend is posing for students there, 'grade inflation is skewing high school achievement results, which in turn affects university entry standards.'[11]

The situation affecting Canadian universities evolved somewhat differently, but a rise in grades also began in the 1970s, according to educational researchers King and Peart. It is quite possible that it occurred in part as result of more students entering with higher grades and thus bringing with them expectations of higher grades in university. Exactly what happened between the 1970s and the present is somewhat difficult to piece together, in part because grade inflation has rarely been studied in Canada. The situation has received much more scrutiny in the United States, as discussed in chapters 1 and 5.

According to the only academic journal article published in Canada on this topic, the percentage of As and Bs increased in all of a sample of Ontario universities between 1973–4 and 1993–4.[12] This study found that in first-year courses As in particular increased (by 5%), while Fs decreased (by 3%). Unfortunately, this study did not look at upper-year courses, which undoubtedly would have had significantly higher grades, and perhaps more inflation over that period. What is more telling is that in the first period, the mid-1970s, 48.2 per cent of courses awarded As and Bs, while in the second period, this figure increased to 53.3 per cent. Thus, these Ontario universities were already giving inflated grades in the 1970s, by more than 10 per cent above what the ECTS now recommends.[13] In addition, this study reports that average grades increased over this time, with the variation in grades decreasing, producing a 'grade compression' around those higher means. Further evidence suggests that this was just the start of a trend that has continued since the early 1990s,[14] as examined in detail in chapter 1. To further document this trend, we now provide a brief summary of the situation found in some Canadian universities to illustrate the extent of grade inflation that appears to have occurred.

Because this issue has not been systematically studied, it is necessary to dig into the records of individual universities. Some universities do post their grade distributions on their websites, but most apparently do not, unless they are deeply buried somewhere away from their search engines. If we look at a couple of universities outside Ontario that post their grade distributions, we find that Simon Fraser University (SFU) in British Columbia awarded, campus-wide, 60.5 per cent As and Bs in 1995–6 in their lower courses and 77.2 per cent in their upper courses.[15] Thus, Simon Fraser University appears to have been awarding about 10 per cent more As and Bs than those awarded during the same period in the Ontario universities discussed, and about twice as many as recommended by the ECTS. On a positive note, there does not seem to have been increased inflation at SFU since the mid-1990s, according to these institutional figures.

The University of Calgary has also posted statistics on grade distributions, in a piece titled 'Grade Inflation at the U of C: Is It an Issue?' which indicates that the percentage of As and Bs increased from 60 per cent in 1992–3 to 69 per cent in 2001–2 in their 'junior level' courses.[16] In senior-level courses, these figures were 75 per cent and 80 per cent, respectively. The percentage of Cs and Ds/Fs also decreased, except in senior courses. Thus, both universities outside of Ontario give grades that are inflated by historical and comparative standards.

Other data on grade distributions have recently become available from the NSSE research. In 2004, eight Canadian universities participated in this U.S.-based survey (472 universities did so in the United States). The Canadian universities are from among the 'G10,' considered to be Canada's oldest and best schools: Western, Waterloo, Queen's, Ottawa, McGill, University of British Columbia, Calgary, and University of Toronto.

According to the annual report summarizing these results for all 160,000 students surveyed in 2004 in American and Canadian institutions, about 40 per cent of respondents reported receiving As in response to the question 'What have most of your grades been up to now at this institution?' An additional 40 per cent reported receiving mainly Bs. Thus, for all institutions, 80 per cent report being awarded mostly As and Bs, more than twice the standard set by the ECTS. It is possible that this figure is an overestimate because these figures are based on self-reports from samples of students rather than institutional records of entire student populations, as represented by data collected by universities (e.g., those with higher grades may be more likely to fill out the surveys). Nevertheless, these figures allow a comparison with Canadian universities, because Canadian students were asked the same question.

As noted, results from the NSSE indicate that Canadian students are actually less academically engaged, on average, than American students. Results from the question about grades are equally surprising: Canadian students in our best schools are reporting percentages of As and Bs at levels just slightly below those in equivalent schools in the United States. The averages for the Canadian G10 schools show that 78 per cent of first-year students report being awarded As and Bs, while 89 per cent of seniors claim to be so blessed. Among equivalent 'doctoral-extensive' universities in the United States these figures are only slightly higher at 90 and 94 per cent, respectively, but at this level there is no question of a glut of high grades.[17] The two Canadian schools for which we found complete access to their NSSE results ranged from reports of 79 per cent As and Bs from first-year students to 96 per cent from seniors. Note that half of these universities are outside Ontario, so we can no longer point only to Ontario schools as culpable.

Again, although these sample-based estimates may be higher than institutional data based on all marks awarded because a different methodology was used, this comparison is relative and speaks strongly against claims that Canadian universities have not inflated their grades the way American schools have. Besides, the University of Calgary participated in the NSSE, and their official institutional data show only about a 10 per cent lower grade distribution than the G10 averages (69 and 80% in 2002 for Calgary, versus 78 and 89% in 2004 for the G10). However, we could not find the University of Calgary's NSSE results on their university website to determine an exact comparison of the 2004 NSSE results with their institutional reporting.

Thus, although it takes considerable digging, we find significant evidence of grade inflation in Canadian universities in both historical and comparative terms, as well as evidence that it is continuing beyond these levels at some universities so as to be comparable with levels found in some American universities. It is also apparent that the inflated grades at Canadian universities are now taken for granted as normal, or as non-inflated, by many people, including professors who never knew the traditional system, have forgotten it, or are in denial. Moreover, when we look to views from outside of North America, we can find considerable alarm at the influence of our grading promiscuity on their own standards. For example, referring to the high incidence of As and Bs awarded in North American universities, a researcher at the University of the West Indies in Jamaica is concerned about a possible change of the grading system there to the North American GPA method, and its effect on student reactions to the looser standards:

> Within this grade inflated system of GPAs, students complain if they receive a B and consider it a failed grade. Currently, a B is considered a good pass in the Caribbean. However, although examination marking in the Caribbean is likely to stay as stringent as it is now is for many years to come, students with B grades will be judged by the common GPA system to be equivalent to U.S. students with B grades. The American university accredi-

tation system has been unable to contain grade inflation. Although U.S. university courses are often accredited by more than one agency, these agencies turn a blind eye to the problem.[18]

That researcher's own university system (the University of the West Indies) has also been fighting grade inflation, but on a different scale, as the number of As awarded increased from the historical norm of 5 per cent to 10 per cent between 1997 and 2002, while Bs increased from 30 per cent to 40 per cent over the same period.

As discussed in detail in chapter 1, grade inflation is also occurring at our own university, although the history of Western's experience may be somewhat different in that it affirmed in the 1970s standards like those of the ECTS, but let standards slip in the 1990s. This slippage, and its effect on faculty at Western, were discussed in detail in chapter 2, where we described both our own experiences with it and the results of a survey we conducted among our colleagues there. How much the same slippage is happening at other universities is difficult to say, but the NSSE results suggest it is substantial. We thus call upon our colleagues to discuss this issue and pressure their administrators to systematically study the grade distributions in their own institutions, and to make them public, so that this information can be added to the debate that is needed on the state of our universities.

We leave readers with our concern that grade inflation is at the heart of the crisis universities are currently experiencing, and that we should look at the high participation rate in Canadian and American universities in a light different from that promoted by our governments. If we have been giving so many inflated grades throughout the recent past in our secondary and tertiary education systems, it is little wonder that we are producing the most graduates in international terms. However, it is a hollow achievement because the greater the grade inflation, the less we require of students, so the less they learn.[19]

Consequently, our universities may not be producing the highly skilled labour force that we are told is needed for our future prosperity. Not coincidentally, other countries that are following suit and providing this sort of 'education-lite' are expressing the same complaints about declining standards and grade inflation.

Notes

Introduction

1 Warren Clark, '100 Years of Education,' *Canadian Social Trends* (Winter 2000): 2–7. A recent and ongoing Statistics Canada study – the Youth in Transition Study (YITS) – found that 43% of twenty- to twenty-two-year-olds were in some form of postsecondary education in 2001, and 35% had graduated, with a total of 76% having participated in some form of postsecondary education, including community college and trades programmes (Klarka Zeman, Tamara Knighton, and Patrick Bussière, *Education and Labour Market Pathways of Young Canadians between Age 20 and 22: An Overview.* Education, Skills, and Learning: Research Papers, cat. no. 81-595-MIE2004018 [Ottawa: Statistics Canada, 2004]).

2 Statistics Canada, *Education in Canada: Raising the Standard,* 2001 Census: Analysis Series (Ottawa: Minister of Industry, 2003), 10. An additional 21% have community college credentials, making Canada the world leader when both forms of postsecondary education are considered, with the United States in second place when two-year and four-year degrees are counted.

3 See, for example, Swedish Institute, *The Swedish Economy* (Stockholm: Author, 2004). See also Alison Wolf, *Does Education Matter? Myths About Education and Economic Growth* (London: Penguin, 2002).

4 See Wolf, *Does Education Matter?*

5 Statistics Canada, 'Working Teens,' *Canadian Social Trends* (Winter 1994): 18–22, emphasis added.

6 Statistics Canada, *The Changing Profile of Canada's Labour Force 2001 Census,* Analysis Series (Ottawa: Author, 2003). It is not difficult to find totally erroneous accounts of how higher education is related to the labour force. For example, writing for *Maclean's* magazine annual university edition, Ann

Dowsett Johnston wrote in 2002 (18, 23 Nov.) that between '1990 and 2001, 1.1 million jobs were created in Canada for those with a university education.' In fact, according to this Statistics Canada analysis of census data, only about half that number of jobs requiring university credentials was created. The real news is that 1.2 million university graduates came onto the job market during that period – twice the number of full-employment jobs available for them.

7 Statistics Canada, *Canada's Labour Force 2001*.

8 James E. Côté and Anton L. Allahar, *Critical Youth Studies: A Canadian Focus* (Toronto: Pearson Education, 2006).

9 Gene I. Maeroff, 'The Media: Degree of Coverage,' in *Declining by Degrees: Higher Education at Risk*, ed. Richard H. Hersh and John Merrow (New York: Palgrave, MacMillan, 2005), 11–22.

10 Ibid., 13.

11 Ibid., 21.

12 This change in approach by *Maclean's* continues at the time of writing with their annual rankings issue of 2006 (13 November). This issue includes articles giving voice to complaints by professors similar to those we report in this book (e.g., a lack of preparedness among many students, the necessity of dumbing down courses, the sense of entitlement among some students for As with little effort, students' sense that they can 'purchase' their degree, inappropriate use of email, and so forth). Other articles note the decline in the relative value of the bachelor's degree and the associated underemployment experienced by many graduates, and the widespread cheating, much of which is not defined by students as such.

13 National Survey of Student Engagement, *Student Engagement: Pathways to Collegiate Success; 2004 Annual Survey Results* (Bloomington, IN: Center for Postsecondary Research, Indiana University, 2004). Since 1999, this survey has been administered annually at hundreds of institutions in the United States, and increasingly in Canada. In 2006, all universities in Ontario were compelled to participate in it, as a result of recommendations by Bob Rae after his review of Ontario universities; Jeffery R. Young, 'Homework? What Homework?' *Chronicle of Higher Education* (6 Dec. 2002): A35; Harriet Eisenkraft, 'Students Have Their Say,' *University Affairs* (Mar. 2006): 28–32. For Rae's review, see http://www.edu.gov.on.ca/eng/document/reports/postsec.pdf.

14 Bob Rae, *Ontario: A Leader in Learning Report & Recommendations* (Toronto: Ministry of Training, Colleges and Universities, 2005), 53.

15 Peter Sacks, *Generation X Goes to College* (Chicago: Open Court, 1996). This source describes the experiences of an American journalist who changed careers to that of a professor, only to find that he needed the approval of his

mainly disengaged students – as a result of the student evaluation system – to obtain tenure and keep his job. To be granted tenure, he was told he needed to improve his teaching evaluations, so he conducted what he calls the 'Sandbox Experiment,' in which he unashamedly pandered to his students' whims and wishes, as if he were teaching kindergarten students. It worked, and he got tenure, but he laments the poor education his students received in the process. Note that Sacks wrote about 'Generation X,' the cohort preceding the millennial generation, supporting the view that the problems we see now did not begin with the current cohort of students, but more likely grew over several cohorts.

16 Thomas J. Collins, *The High School / Post-secondary Education Transition*, Council of Ministers of Education, 1998, http://www.cmec.ca/postsec/transitions/en/431.collins.pdf (accessed 8 Aug. 2006).

1 Troubles in Paradise

1 Cooperative Institutional Research Program (CIRP), 'The American Freshman: National Norms for Fall 2001.' UCLA Graduate School of Education and Information Studies, Higher Education Research Institute, http://www.gseis.ucla.edu/heri/norms_pr_01.html (accessed 15 Feb. 2006).

This is the oldest and largest survey of university students, conducted first in 1967. Each year the survey includes several hundred thousand freshmen at hundreds of higher-education institutions in the United States. Data for the fall 2001 survey were 'culled from 281,064 of those students at 421 baccalaureate institutions [and] have been statistically adjusted to be representative of the 1.2 million freshmen entering four-year colleges and universities as first-time, full-time students' (¶10).

2 James Côté and Anton Allahar, *Generation on Hold: Coming of Age in the Late Twentieth Century* (Toronto: Stoddart, 1994).

3 Both the National Survey of Student Engagement (introduction, note 13) and CIRP (note 1 above) studies clearly show this. The fact that these are longitudinal studies, one dating back to the 1960s, adds to the strength of the claim about the trend. As we shall see, numerous other studies also support this claim.

4 Several terms have been coined recently to describe this growing phenomenon. For example, some psychologists are using the term *emerging adults*. See Jeffery Arnett, 'Emerging Adulthood: A Theory of Development from the Late Teens through the Twenties,' *American Psychologist* 55 (2000): 469–80. A journalist coined the term *twixters* to describe those in their twenties: Lev Grossman, 'Grow Up? Not so Fast,' *Time*, 25 Jan. 2005, 42–53.

5 James E. Côté and Anton L. Allahar, *Critical Youth Studies: A Canadian Focus* (Toronto: Pearson Education, 2006). This book examines theories about the increasingly prolonged transition to adulthood and explanations for it, including the collapse of the youth labour market.

6 Arthur Levine and Jeanette S. Cureton, *When Hope and Fear Collide: A Portrait of Today's College Students* (San Francisco: Jossey Bass, 1998).

7 National Survey of Student Engagement, *Student Engagement: Pathways to Collegiate Success; 2004 Annual Survey Results* (Bloomington, IN: Center for Postsecondary Research, Indiana University, 2004).

8 U.S. Census Bureau, *Statistical Abstract of the United States: 2004–2005* (Washington, DC: Author): 173.

9 See also Henry Rosovsky and Matthew Hartley, *Evaluation and the Academy: Are We Doing the Right Thing?* (Cambridge, MA: American Academy of Arts and Sciences, 2002).

10 Tony Bastick, 'Commonwealth Degrees from Class to Equivalence: Changing to Grade Point Averages in the Caribbean,' *Journal of Studies in International Education* 8, no. 1 (2004): 86–104.

11 University of Western Ontario, *Performance and Activity Indicators: Annual Report to the Board of Governors*, 28 Apr. 2005, http://www.ipb.uwo.ca/documents/2005_performance_indicator.pdf (accessed 1 Feb. 2006); Paul Mayne, 'Western Promises Greater Accountability, Transparency,' *Western News*, 12 May 2005, 3.

12 Kevin McQuillan, 'Evaluations, Admissions, and the Quality of Ontario Universities,' COU Colleagues Working Papers Series 2 (Feb. 2004), http://www.cou.on.ca/content/objects/AC%20Working%20Papers%202004.pdf (accessed 4 June 2006).

13 Human Resources Development Canada, *Measuring Up: The Performance of Canada's Youth in Reading, Mathematics and Science* (Ottawa: Minister of Industry, 2001), http://www.pisa.gc.ca/what_pisa.shtml (accessed 31 May 2006).

14 National Center for Educational Statistics, *Youth Indicators, 2005: Trends in the Well-being of American Youth.* http://nces.ed.gov/pubsearch/pubsinfo.asp?pubid=2005050 (accessed 22 May 2006).

15 Human Resources Development Canada, *Measuring Up.*

16 For example, referring to the PISA, Marita Moll reports that 'one day my daughter came home from high school saying the teachers were really angry at her and a few of ... friends for skipping a test that "didn't even count" ('Who's Keeping Tabs on Global Tests?' *Our Schools, Our Selves* 14, no. 2 [2005]: 34–7.)

17 The Ontario Secondary School Literacy Test (OSSLT) is designed to assess the reading and writing skills that students should have acquired with a

grade 9 education. Passing this test is now required to graduate from high school in Ontario, suggesting that a rather low standard has been set to obtain a high school diploma there. According to a 2004 report, while some 90% of students in academic programmes had passed this test at that time (after some jigging of the test), only about half of those in applied programmes had done so. A significant number of students have been avoiding or deferring the test. Education Quality and Accountability Office, Ontario Secondary School Literacy Test, October 2003: Report of Provincial Results (Toronto: Queen's Printer, 2004), http://www.eqao.com/pdf_e/04/ 04P002e.pdf (accessed 31 May 2006). Another 2004 source noted that 120,000 students had failed the test to date (Carlo Ricci and Steven Taylor, 'Challenging the Validity of Standardized Testing,' *Our Schools, Our Selves* 14, no. 1 [2004]: 63–73).

18 National Center for Educational Statistics, *Youth Indicators, 2005.* In the highest-scoring country, Finland, only 15% were capable of Level 5 literacy, and in the United States, 9% scored at this level.

19 Level 5 is defined as the ability process 'a complex and unfamiliar set of instructions about how to make telephone calls from a hotel room, and a letter with the phone number of a friend in a different country. They were required to find and organize in correct sequence four pieces of information and to draw inferences to work out exactly how to dial the number.' Level 3 literacy simply involves the ability to compare and contrast information, as in understanding a timetable (Human Resources Development Canada, *Measuring Up*, 24).

20 Moll, 'Who's Keeping Tabs on Global Tests?'

21 Howard S. Becker, Blanche Geer, and Everett C. Hughes, *Making the Grade: The Academic Side of College Life* (New York: Wiley, 1968).

22 Thomas J. Collins, *The High School / Post-secondary Education Transition,* Council of Ministers of Education, 1998, http://www.cmec.ca/postsec/transitions/ en/431.collins.pdf (accessed 8 Aug. 2006). Collins provides samples from two essays showing what was being handed in and the extent of correction each sample needed.

23 Ibid., 4.

24 John Goyder and Susan Miller report a parallel decline in mathematics skills among students entering the University of Waterloo, as well as at Western, during this same time: 'The Eroding Standards Issue: A Case Study from the University of Waterloo,' *Canadian Journal of Higher Education* 30 (2000): 57–86.

25 Collins, *The High School / Post-secondary Education Transition,* 4.

26 Ibid.

27 Credential inflation continues in these professions, with more and more stu-

dents applying with master's degree, making the bachelor's degree less useful as an entry requirement to medical programmes.

28 The figure for the proportion of unskilled jobs in the United States and Canada ranges from about 50 percent to 70 percent, depending on how the count is made. As noted in the introduction, according to a Statistics Canada recent count, only about 46% qualify as 'skilled' or 'highly skilled,' meaning that they required some form of post-secondary education (Statistics Canada, *Education in Canada: Raising the Standard*, 2001 Census: Analysis Series [Ottawa: Minister of Industry, 2003]). See, for instance, Ivar Berg, *Education and Jobs: The Great Training Robbery* (New York: Praeger Publishers for the Centre for Urban Education, 1970); Alfred A. Hunter and Jean McKenzie Leiper, 'On Formal Education, Skills and Earnings: The Role of Educational Certificates in Earnings Determination,' *Canadian Journal of Sociology* 18 (1993): 21–42; David W. Livingstone, *The Education-Jobs Gap: Underemployment or Economic Democracy* (Boulder, CO: Westview, 1998).

29 Randall Collins, *The Credential Society: A Historical Sociology of Education and Stratification* (New York: Academic, 1979).

30 Livingstone, *The Education-Jobs Gap*.

31 This figure is adapted from table 3.2 in Côté and Allahar, *Critical Youth Studies*.

32 Warren Clark, '100 Years of Education,' *Canadian Social Trends* (Winter 2000): 2–7.

33 Canadian Association of University Teachers, *CAUT Almanac of Post-secondary Education in Canada 2005* (Ottawa: Author, 2005); Statistics Canada, 'University Enrolment 2003/04,' *Daily*, 11 Oct. 2001.

34 See, for instance, James Côté and Charles Levine, 'The Genesis of the Humanistic Academic: A Second Test of Erikson's Theory of Ego Identity Formation,' *Youth & Society* 23 (1992): 387–410.

35 According to Levine and Cureton, *When Hope and Fear Collide*, only about one-third of first-year students intend to stop with a BA. Forty per cent plan for a master's degree, 15% hope for a PhD or equivalent, and 10% expect to receive an MD or equivalent. While the ranks of graduate schools have increased, they have not accommodated this demand. For example, only 15% of those who graduated with BAs in 1999 went on to graduate or professional school. An equivalent percentage went on to obtain certificates of some sort (e.g., accounting); Warren Clark, 'University Graduates at College,' *Canadian Social Trends* (Autumn 1999): 18–19.

36 Canadian Association of University Teachers, *CAUT Almanac*, table 2.1, 3; this figure for the United States is 9.3%, according to the U.S. Census Bureau, *Statistical Abstracts of the United States: 2004–2005*, table 214, 142.

37 Mayne, 'Western Promises Greater Accountability, Transparency,' 3.

38 See also McQuillan, 'Evaluations, Admissions, and the Quality of Ontario Universities.'

39 Richard H. Hersh and John Merrow, 'Introduction,' *Declining by Degrees: Higher Education at Risk* (New York: Palgrave, MacMillan, 2005), 8. They produced a PBS documentary of the same title and witnessed the range of student talent from the best and most motivated, to the worst and least motivated, but they were disheartened by the widespread disengagement. In some of the footage, students were asked how much time they spent on their studies, and in one case students in a senior-level macroeconomics class said that on a typical day more than half spent an hour or less preparing for *all* of their classes combined, citing a lack of expectations from faculty to do more. What was uncovered corresponds closely with what we discovered in the literature, in our own experiences with students, and in the study we report in the next chapter.

Recent findings from the Youth in Transition Survey (YITS) conducted by Statistics Canada suggest that, while more fully engaged high school students go on to attend university than alternatives such as community college, among those who do attend university, only about one quarter were 'very engaged' in high school and about 6% were 'not very engaged,' with the reminder falling into a category that corresponds with our designation of partially engaged (Mylène Lambert, Klarka Zeman, Mary Allen, and Patrick Bussière, *Who Pursues Postsecondary Education, Who Leaves and Why: Results from the Youth in Transition Survey* (Ottawa: Statistics Canada, 2004) (Culture, Tourism and the Centre for Education Statistics, research paper, catalogue no. 81-595-MIE2004026).

40 James E. Côté and Charles Levine, 'Attitude versus Aptitude: Is Intelligence or Motivation More Important for Positive Higher-Educational Outcomes?' *Journal of Adolescent Research* 15 (2000): 58–80.

41 See Paul M. Anglin and Ronald Meng, 'Evidence on Grades and Grade Inflation at Ontario's Universities,' *Canadian Public Policy / Analyse de Politiques* 26 (2000): 361–8.

42 Hal Niedzviecki, *Hello, I'm Special: How Individuality Became the New Conformity* (Toronto: Penguin Canada, 2004).

43 Charles E. Phillips, *The Development of Education in Canada* (Toronto: Gage, 1957).

44 Ibid.

45 Daniel K. Lapsley, Robert D. Enright, and R.C. Serlin, 'Toward a Theoretical Perspective on the Legislation of Adolescence,' *Journal of Early Adolescence* 4 (1985): 441–66.

46 Lawrence Steinberg, *Beyond the Classroom: Why School Reform Has Failed and What Parents Need to Do about It* (New York: Simon & Schuster, 1996).

47 Côté and Levine, 'Attitude versus Aptitude.'

48 Mark Bauerlein, 'A Very Long Disengagement,' *Chronicle of Higher Education*, 6 Jan. 2006, B6.

49 George Kuh, 'What We're Learning about Student Engagement from NSSE,' *Change* (March/April 2003): 28. Also phrased as 'If you don't bother me too much, I won't bother you too much – I'll trade you a B if you trade me some piece of mind' in Jeffery R. Young, 'Homework? What Homework?' *Chronicle of Higher Education*, 6 Dec. 2002, A35.

50 Kuh, 'What We're Learning about Student Engagement,' 28.

51 Hersh and Merrow, *Declining by Degrees*, 4.

52 Young, 'Homework? What Homework?'

53 National Survey of Student Engagement, *Student Engagement*.

54 Young, 'Homework? What Homework?' A35.

55 Cooperative Institutional Research Program (CIRP), 'The American Freshman: National Norms for Fall 2002,' UCLA Graduate School of Education and Information Studies, Higher Education Research Institute, http://www.gseis.ucla.edu/heri/02_press_release.pdf (accessed 15 Feb. 2006).

56 American Diploma Project, *Ready or Not: Creating a High School Diploma that Counts* (Washington, DC: Achieve, 2004). This report charges that the high school diploma in the United States is little more than an attendance certificate at most schools.

57 National Survey of Student Engagement, *Student Engagement*.

58 University of Western Ontario, *Performance and Activity Indicators: Annual Report to the Board of Governors*; Harriet Eisenkraft, 'Students Have Their Say,' *University Affairs* (Mar. 2006): 28–32 ; University of Western Ontario Senate Agenda, *Institutional Benchmark Report, University of Western Ontario (Exhibit III, Appendix 2)* (18 Mar. 2005), prepared by the National Survey of Student Engagement, Indiana University.

59 Paul Mayne, 'Poor Results Blamed on Too-Few "Resources."' *Western News*, 24 Mar. 2005, 3.

60 The University of Waterloo has posted its NSSE reports on its website, as have Queen's University and the University of Ottawa. At Waterloo, 15% of students appear to fall into the 'fully engaged' category, while the Queen's figure of 10% is identical to the NSSE average among American students. The University of Ottawa reported its results differently, so no direct comparisons can be made here. http://www.analysis.uwaterloo.ca/docs/NSSE/U%200f%20Waterloo%20Means%20and%20Frequencies%20Report%20FREQENG.pdf; http://www.queensu.ca/irp/pdfiles/nsse/Frequencies_core.

pdf; http://www.uottawa.ca/services/irp/eng/NSSE%202005%20Report.
pdf (accessed 14 Aug. 2006).

61 James E. Côté and Charles Levine, 'Student Motivations, Learning Environments, and Human Capital Acquisition: Toward an Integrated Paradigm of
Student Development,' *Journal of College Student Development* 38 (1997): 229–
43; Côté and Levine, 'Attitude versus Aptitude.'

62 Catherine Tylee, 'Grade Expectations: When Is an "A" Not Quite an "A"?' *New-
media Journalism,* http://www.fims.uwo.ca/newmedia2006/default.
asp?id=424 (accessed 15 Nov. 2006).

63 Statistics Canada is studying student engagement-disengagement as part of a
large-scale longitudinal study of young Canadians in the National Longitudinal Survey of Children and Youth (NLSCY). This study began in 1994–5
and re-interviews some 23,000 children aged eleven years and younger every
two years. Initial findings suggest that academic disengagement among children has an impact on grades, truancy, juvenile delinquency, and early
school leaving (Christina Norris, Jean Pignal and Garth Lipps, 'Measuring
School Engagement,' *Education Quarterly Review* 9, no. 2 [2003]: 25–34). We
await the publication of the full set of results following the impact of disengagement on young Canadians through their transition from school to
work.

64 Steinberg, *Beyond the Classroom.*

65 Ibid., 67.

66 Ibid.

67 Ibid., 68.

68 In fact, over the past thirty years, more young Americans are quitting high
school and opting for the later GED equivalent. This makes the overall U.S.
high-school completion statistics look good, but speaks to a decline in the
overall quality of education. See Stephen F. Hamilton and Mary Agnes
Hamilton, 'School, Work, and Emerging Adulthood,' in *Coming of Age in the
21st Century: The Lives and Contexts of Emerging Adults,* ed. Jeffery J. Arnett and
Jennifer L. Tanner (Washington, DC: American Psychological Association,
2006).

69 Alan King and Marjorie Peart, *The Numbers Game: A Study of Evaluation and
Achievement in Ontario Schools* (Toronto: Ontario Secondary School Teachers'
Federation, 1994).

70 Ibid.

71 Céleste M. Brotheridge and Raymond T. Lee, 'Correlates and Consequences
of Degree Purchasing among Canadian University Students,' *Canadian Journal of Higher Education* 35 (2005): 71–97.

72 Ibid., 79, 91.

73　Côté and Allahar, *Critical Youth Studies.*

74　Ibid.

75　Compare Scott Davies, who writes, 'A universal post-secondary system will absorb much of the selection and streaming functions that have been historically performed by high schools ... Colleges, it appears will increasingly become like the lower streams of high school.' ('A Revolution in Expectations? Three Key Trends in the SAEP Data,' in *Preparing for Post-secondary Education: New Roles for Governments and Families,* ed. Robert Sweet and Paul Anisef (Montreal and Kingston: McGill-Queen's University Press, 2005), 160.

76　Reginald W. Bibby and Donald C. Posterski, *Teen Trends: A Nation in Motion* (Toronto: Stoddart, 1992).

77　For a well-argued case that the proliferation of university degrees has not directly contributed to prosperity and economic growth in Britain, see Alison Wolf, *Does Education Matter? Myths about Education and Economic Growth* (London: Penguin, 2002).

78　Collins, *The High School / Post-secondary Education Transition.*

79　Compare Laurence J. Peter and Raymond Hull, *The Peter Principle* (New York: Morrow, 1969).

80　Harvey C. Mansfield, 'Grade Inflation: It's Time to Face the Facts,' *Chronicle of Higher Education,* 6 Apr. 2001, B24.

81　Davies, 'A Revolution in Expectations?'; Mansfield, 'Grade Inflation'; Rosovsky and Hartley, *Evaluation and the Academy*; Bradford P. Wilson, 'The Phenomenon of Grade Inflation in Higher Education,' *Association of American Educators,* 24 Oct. 1998, http://aaeteachers.org/gradeinflation.htm (accessed 24 Mar. 2003).

82　Professors face a similar levelling experience when they are rated against each other in the annual performance appraisals that determine their 'merit.' For example, in many departments most faculty members are leaders in their respective fields, but when leaders are compared with each other using these higher standards, most will be average and only a few will stand out.

83　Richard Kamber and Mary Biggs, 'Grade Conflation: A Question of Credibility,' *Chronicle of Higher Education,* 12 Apr. 2002, 14.

84　*Economist,* 'Finance and Economics: An Eye for an A,' 9 Mar. 2002, ¶4, http://proquest.umi.com/pqdlink (accessed 25 Mar. 2003); McQuillan, 'Evaluations, Admissions, and the Quality of Ontario Universities.'

85　See McQuillan, 'Evaluations, Admissions, and the Quality of Ontario Universities.'

86　Ibid.; Kelly Marcella, 'Grade Inflation Questioned: Universities Lack Compensation Method,' *Gazette* (University of Western Ontario), 16 Jan. 2003, 1.

87 McQuillan, 'Evaluations, Admissions, and the Quality of Ontario Universities.'

88 Alan Finder, 'Schools Avoid Class Ranking, Vexing Colleges,' *New York Times*, http://nytimes.com, accessed 6 Mar. 2006.

89 Ibid.

90 University of Calgary, 'National Grading Differences Short Change Alberta Students,' *In the News*, 6 Nov. 2003, http://www.ucalgary/ca/news/nov03/grading.html (accessed 31 Dec. 2003).

91 Rosanna Tamburri, 'Some Universities Tighten Admission Standards,' *University Affairs* (Dec. 2005): 29; *Globe and Mail*, 'Johnny Can't Read, and He's in College,' 26 Sept. 2005, A-16.

92 *Globe and Mail*, 'Universities Trying to Cope with Students Lacking Basics,' http://www.theglobeandmail.com (accessed 22 Sept. 2005).

93 Collins, *The High School / Post-secondary Education Transition.*

94 Davies, 'A Revolution in Expectations?'

95 To Western's credit, these figures are in the public domain and can be readily accessed in its 'databook.' At the time of writing, data are available for 2001 through 2005, and each databook provides data for the ten previous years: see, for instance, http://www.uwo.ca/ipb/databk01/toc_text.html; http://www.uwo.ca/ipb/databk05/toc_text.html.

96 'Minutes of the Committee on Academic Policy,' Department of Economics, University of Western Ontario, http://www.ssc.uwo.ca/economics/newsletter/misc/octoberCAPminutes.pdf (accessed 15 Feb. 2006).

97 'Undergraduate Grade Distribution,' UWO Databook 2005, http://www.uwo.ca/ipb/databk05/econtb09.html (accessed 15 Oct. 2006).

98 See the U of T website for its plan to maintain standards: http://www.steppingup.utoronto.ca (accessed 21 Feb. 2006). Curiously, however, it has no posted written policy about grade distributions. In it official document, 'University Grading Practices Policy,' it is simply stated that 'the distribution of grades in any course shall not be predetermined by any system of quotas that specifies the number or percentage of grades allowable at any grade level.' http://www.utoronto.ca/govcncl/pap/policies/grading.html (accessed 12 Aug. 2006). Apparently, an informal culture of consensus preserves these standards. At the same time, we were unable to find their 2004 NSSE results for the grades their students reported, so we do not know if the U of T average is actually lower than the high level found for Canada's G10 universities (i.e., 80–90% As and Bs), as we discuss in the appendix.

99 'Psychology A01: Defense of the University of Toronto Marking Philosophy,'

University of Toronto–Scarborough, http://www.utsc.utoronto.ca/ ~psya01/MarkingPhilosophy.htm (accessed 15 Feb. 2006).
100 See Randle W. Nelson, *Schooling as Entertainment: Corporate Education Meets Popular Culture* (Kingston, ON: Cedarcreek, 2002).
101 'Psychology A01.'
102 Virginia Galt, 'Canada's Youth Feeling Weight of the Working World,' *Globe and Mail,* 16 Feb. 2005, B1, B6; Mel Levine, *Ready or Not, Here Life Comes* (New York: Simon & Schuster, 2005).
103 Cheating among college and university students has been extensively studied in the United States. Findings indicate that most students admit to some form of cheating, and that the practice of cheating on exams has become more widespread (Kevin Bushweller, 'Generation of Cheaters,' *American School Board Journal,* Apr. 1999, http://www.asbj.com/199904/ 0499coverstory.html (accessed 1 June 2006). The vast majority of those admitting to this offence say that they have never been caught, and half did not believe what they did was wrong (Carolyn Kleiner and Mary Lord, 'The Cheating Game: "Everyone's Doing It," from Grade School to Graduate School,' *U.S. News & World Report,* 2 Nov. 1999, 55–66). Plagiarism on essays has become a particularly serious problem, and many universities are taking great measures to deal with it (Ronald B. Standler, 'Plagiarism in Colleges in USA,' 2000, http://www.rbs2.com/plag.htm) (accessed 1 June 2006). The anti-plagiarism software provided by the website turnitin.com has become especially popular among university faculty for discouraging and detecting plagiarism in essays. With the recent availability of the Internet, e-cheating has taken on major proportions, either through the cut-and paste form where portions of essays are plucked from various sources, or from the dozens of websites where essays are available, usually for a small fee (e.g., phuckschool.com – note the mocking of standards in the name of this website). For further information on this topic, see Lisa Renard, 'Cut and Paste 101: Plagiarism and the Net.' *Educational Leadership* 57, no. 4 (Dec. 1999/Jan. 2000): 38–42; Kim McMurtry 'e-cheating: Combating a 21st Century Challenge,' *Journal,* Nov. 2001, http://www.thejournal.com/articles/15675_1 (accessed 1 June 2006). For a recent Canadian study of the problem, see Julia M. Christensen Hughes and Donald McCabe, 'Academic Misconduct within Higher Education in Canada,' *Canadian Journal of Higher Education* 36 (2006): 1–21.
104 Compare Anglin and Meng, 'Evidence on Grades and Grade Inflation at Ontario's Universities.'

2 The Professor as Reluctant Gatekeeper

1 CBC News, 'University Students Offered a B-Minus to Stay Away,' http://www.cbc.ca (accessed 5 Feb. 2006).

2 David Livingstone and Doug Hart, 'Hedging Our Bets on the Future,' *Academic Matters: The Journal of Higher Education* (Fall 2005): 6, 8–9, 13–14.

3 James E. Côté and Charles Levine, 'Genesis of the Humanistic Academic: A Second Test of Erikson's Theory of Ego Identity Formation,' *Youth & Society* 23 (1992): 387–410.

4 National Survey of Student Engagement, *Student Engagement: Pathways to Collegiate Success; 2004 Annual Survey Results* (Bloomington, IN: Center for Postsecondary Research, Indiana University, 2004), 22.

5 Harvey C. Mansfield, 'Grade Inflation: It's Time to Face the Facts,' *Chronicle of Higher Education*, 6 Apr. 2001, B24.

6 See Western's public databook: http://www.uwo.ca/ipb/databk05/toc_text.html.

7 Hal Niedzviecki, *Hello, I'm Special: How Individuality Became the New Conformity* (Toronto: Penguin Canada, 2004).

8 For example, techniques for 'mastery learning' have been developed in which all students are brought to a certain level of competency before progressing to the next level of difficulty. This 'outcome-based' learning prevents those with low grades from being left to lag behind in a manner that compounds over time, rendering them incompetent at higher levels: Benjamin S. Bloom, *All Our Children Learning: A Primer for Parents, Teachers, and Other Educators* (New York: McGraw-Hill, 1981).

9 Recently, there has been a dramatic increase in interest in criminal-investigations careers as a result of numerous TV shows now glamorizing those rather uncommon but tedious jobs. This trend has been referred to as the 'CSI effect' and is thought to be behind increased enrolments in criminology courses. See, for instance, 'CSI Effect,' in *Wikipedia*, http://en.wikipedia.org/wiki/CSI_effect (accessed 16 Feb. 2006).

10 Alan King and Marjorie Peart, *The Numbers Game: A Study of Evaluation and Achievement in Ontario Schools* (Toronto: Ontario Secondary School Teacher's Federation, 1994); Lawrence Steinberg, *Beyond the Classroom: Why School Reform Has Failed and What Parents Need to Do about It* (New York: Simon & Schuster, 1996)

11 Reginald W. Bibby and Donald C. Posterski, *Teen Trends: A Nation in Motion* (Toronto: Stoddart, 1992).

12 There are various academic formulations of credentials constituting a form

of 'exchangeable' capital. See, for example, Pierre Bourdieu and Jean-Claude Passeron, *The Inheritors: French Students and Their Relations to Culture*, trans. Richard Nice (Chicago: University of Chicago Press, 1979); James E. Côté, 'Sociological Perspectives on Identity Formation: The Culture-Identity Link and Identity capital,' *Journal of Adolescence* 19 (1996): 419–30; Tom Schuller, John Preston, Cathy Hammond, Ann Brassett-Grundy, and John Bynner, *The Benefits of Learning: The Impact of Education on Health, Family Life and Social Capital* (London: RoutledgeFalmer, 2004).

13 King and Peart, *The Numbers Game.*

14 Other professors, who grade by the old standards, think that handing out easy grades cheapens their own credentials and causes students to respect them less.

15 Multiple-choice tests introduce a random factor into grades that artificially produces a normal curve with reduced variation around the average, pulling up the marks of poorer students, but pulling down the marks of stronger students. They thus have a 'basement effect' preventing students with no knowledge in the area from getting extremely low marks (e.g., 20–25% of answers will be correct by chance). Tests with a number of easy questions can also be passed with little or no involvement in the course, with either educated guesses or general knowledge. One of our colleagues conducted an experiment in which he administered the multiple-choice test he had used regularly in Introductory Sociology to his daughter. She was in junior high school, but earned a C without doing any of the reading ostensibly required to pass it. Thereafter, he subtracted wrong answers from correct ones, producing a more realistic assessment of his students' knowledge of the material in the readings, but reducing both the grades in the course and his teaching scores.

16 Laurence J. Peter and Raymond Hull, *The Peter Principle* (New York: Morrow, 1969).

17 Valen Johnson, *Grade Inflation: A Crisis in College Education* (New York: Springer, 2003).

18 James G. Hutton, *The Feel-Good Society: How the 'Customer' Metaphor Is Undermining American Education, Religion, Media, and Healthcare* (West Paterson, NJ: Pentagram, 2005).

19 Lawrence M. Friedman, *The Horizontal Society* (New Haven, CT: Yale University Press, 1999).

20 James Côté, *Arrested Adulthood: The Changing Nature of Identity and Maturity in the Late-Modern World* (New York: New York University Press, 2000).

21 For example, Western's motto is 'Major in yourself.'

22 Howard Adelman, *The Holiversity* (Toronto: New Press, 1973).

23 Ibid., 42.

24 David W. Livingstone, *The Education-Jobs Gap: Underemployment or Economic Democracy* (Boulder, CO: Westview, 1998); Alexander Lockhart, 'Future Failure: The Unanticipated Consequences of Educational Planning,' in *Socialization and Values in Canadian Society*, ed. Robert M. Pike and E. Zureik (Toronto: McClelland-Stewart, 1975).

25 Scott Davies examines how heightened expectations for post-secondary education are merely repositioning the population to higher levels of education, with dubious consequences for enhanced social equality. He notes, for example, that many parents are pushing their children to pursue a post-secondary education even though their children do not like school, get low grades, and do little homework. In contrast, he notes that 'whereas in previous eras a student who disliked school, fared poorly, and did no homework would seldom be encouraged to pursue advanced studies, now many of their parents expect them to at least attend community college.' Scott Davies, 'A Revolution in Expectations? Three Key Trends in the SAEP Data,' in *Preparing for Post-secondary Education: New Roles for Governments and Families*, ed. Robert Sweet and Paul Anisef (Montreal and Kingston: McGill-Queen's University Press, 2005), 158.

26 Interestingly, the NSSE recently reported that almost two-thirds of students feel that their coursework emphasizes memorization, while fewer than one-third of professors do so; National Survey of Student Engagement, *Student Engagement*, 22.

27 In top universities in countries like the United States and the United Kingdom with endowed chairs, accomplished professors do little or no teaching, and if they do, it is at the graduate level with a few students in small seminars.

28 Compare Thomas J. Collins, *The High School / Post-secondary Education Transition*, Council of Ministers of Education, 1998, http://www.cmec.ca/postsec/transitions/en/431.collins.pdf (accessed 8 Aug. 2006).

29 See, for example, Hutton, *The Feel-Good Society*.

30 Howard Tennen and Glenn Affleck, 'The Puzzles of Self-esteem: A Clinical Perspective,' in *Self-esteem: The Puzzle of Low Self-Regard*, ed. Roy Baumeister (New York: Plenum, 1993).

31 See, for example, Albert Bandura, *Self-Efficacy: The Exercise of Control* (New York: Freedman, 1997).

32 Compare Niedzviecki, *I'm Special*.

33 See the National Center for Policy Analysis website for numerous bulletins on this problem: www.ncpa.org. The U.S. Department of Education has also published a guide for ending social promotion: 'Taking Responsibility for

Ending Social Promotion: A Guide to Educators and State and Local Leaders,' http://www.ed.gov/pubs/socialpromotion (accessed 12 Feb. 2003).

34 Student interest in 'keeping up with political affairs' from the 1960s to the present, has been traced by the Cooperative Institutional Research Program (CIRP), which found that it had dropped from an important concern for two-thirds of students in the sixties to fewer than one-third of students by 2000. In recent years, a minor increase (6%) in interest in politics has been detected. See CIRP, 'The American Freshman: National Norms for Fall 2001,' UCLA Graduate School of Education and Information Studies, Higher Education Research Institute, http://www.gseis.ucla.edu/heri/findings.html (accessed 15 Feb. 2006).

35 All full-time faculty members in the Faculties of Arts & Humanities, Social Science, and Science were sent email messages via the public mailing lists for each faculty. Questionnaires were attached as PDFs and Word files, and respondents were free to complete the questionnaire on-screen and return the email attachment electronically, or print it out, and return the completed hardcopy questionnaire by campus mail. The estimated total sampling frame, net of cross-listings and incorrectly listed addresses on the lists, was 585. We received fifty-nine completed questionnaires, a 10% response rate, a rate that is comparable with mail-out surveys (Angus Reid, cited by Ann Dowsett Johnston, 'How Grads Grade Their Schools,' *Maclean's*, 15 Nov. 2005, 28).

Given the small population we surveyed, we were hoping for a higher response rate. The low response rate we got may have been due to the fact that we sent the questionnaire as an email attachment, rather than as hardcopies. It may be easier to dismiss such requests with the 'Delete' button, especially in an era when people receive a lot of irrelevant email messages and spam. At the same time, a software error occurred when the original message was sent to the public mailing lists that provided the email addresses in the various faculties. Unfortunately, the message got 'stuck' in the outbox and was sent four to five times before the error was corrected (this is a flaw with a certain common email programme). To rectify the situation, the questionnaires were placed on the Sociology Department homepage for people to download on their own, but it was apparent that a number of prospective respondents had been annoyed by the error and were hostile to the subsequent opportunity to retrieve the message from the department homepage.

It is also possible that the lower-than-desired response rate was affected by the very faculty disengagement we are trying to study, for disengaged faculty would be less likely to care about these issues or perhaps did not want to draw attention to their situation. While this number of responses is too low to draw firm conclusions about characteristics of the faculty at Western or elsewhere at a population level, the findings are taken as merely suggestive of how some faculty members feel about these issues, and are subject to external verification and replication. We note in the text where our findings are externally verified by other studies, and we call for a large, random survey of faculty members across Canada and the United States, using our questionnaire as a starting point. Faculty associations would be the most likely sponsors of these surveys, and we would be happy to help out.

36 Sometimes large numbers of students in a class will try to form a critical mass to pressure professors to raise grades for the entire class on a test. Often professors will relent, and students know it. We have had students complain in class, when class averages have been two low, and we have refused to raise the grades. In one recent case, a student who received a C stomped out of class, stating on the way that she was dropping the course. Because there were persistently low grades in that course, during the next year the two-hour rule was explicitly stated in a course outline. This is a senior course, where many of the students are in their fourth year and expecting to graduate with an honours BA. One-quarter of the students dropped the course immediately after receiving the course outline in the first class. Another quarter, apparently not taking us seriously, either failed or got Ds. The reasons for the poor performances ranged from not attend classes with any regularity, failing to prepare for classes or study for tests, not writing essays suitable for an honours-level university course, or simply not completing the assignments.

37 See Western's public databook: http://www.uwo.ca/ipb/databk05/toc_text.html.

38 Jonathan D. Glater, 'To: Professor@University.edu Subject: Why It's All about Me,' *New York Times*, http://nytimes.com (accessed 22 Feb. 2006).

39 According to Western educational psychologist Harry Murray, some three-quarters of professors surveyed in studies across North America feel that student evaluations provide useful feedback on their teaching, with about two-thirds reporting that they have used them to improve their teaching. Still, Murray admits that there is evidence that they contribute to grade inflation and lower standards, and he suggests that they be used in conjunction with other indicators, such as how much students are engaged in the course being evaluated (Paul Mayne, 'Student Evaluations Helpful but Limited as Teaching Tool,' *Western News*, 11 May 2006, 1, 10).

40 'Instructor & Course Evaluation,' http://www.ipb.uwo.ca/evaluation/search.php.

41 For a quick review of these complaints, see Robin Wilson, 'New Research Casts Doubts on Value of Student Evaluations of Professors: Studies Find

That Faculty Members Dumb Down Material and Inflate Grades to Get Good Reviews,' *Chronicle of Higher Education*, 16 Jan. 1998, A12.

42 Peter Sacks, *Generation X Goes to College* (Chicago: Open Court, 1996); Wilson, 'New Research Casts Doubts.'

43 Items used in Western's evaluations include criteria such as 'Displays Enthusiasm,' 'Shows Concern,' and 'Good Motivator,' which are highly subjective and closely tied to how much the particular student might 'like' the professor. Another item, 'Provides Fair Evaluations,' will obviously be closely tied to the grade a student receives, and given that some 90% of students begin courses expecting As or Bs, the more that students receive less than these grades, the more likely the professor will be given a poor evaluation in this category. In all these items, there is likely a carry-over effect to other items that are potentially less affected by the professor's personality or grade earned, such as 'Course as Learning Experience' or 'Grades Work Promptly.'

44 George Kuh, 'What We're Learning about Student Engagement from NSSE,' *Change* (March/April 2003): 28.

45 See Ernest T. Pascarella and Patrick T. Terenzini, *How College Affects Students: Findings and Insights from Twenty Years of Research* (San Francisco: Jossey-Bass, 1991).

46 See, for example, Sacks (*Generation X Goes to College*), a journalist who changed careers to professor, but who found it was easier to pretend to know less than he actually did about what he was teaching so he would get higher teaching evaluations from his students. He did this because his students said they felt intimidated by his knowledge and preferred to relate to him more as a co-learner of the material; see also Arthur Levine and Jeanette S. Cureton, *When Hope and Fear Collide: A Portrait of Today's College Students* (San Francisco: Jossey Bass, 1998).

47 George D. Kuh, George D., Jillian Kinzie, John H. Schuh, Elizabeth J. Whitt, and Associates, *Student Success in College: Creating Conditions That Matter* (San Francisco: Jossey-Bass, 2006).

48 Ibid.

49 Ibid., 24.

50 National Survey of Student Engagement, *Student Engagement*, 20.

51 See, for example, Steve Alsop, Larry Bencze, and Erminia Pedretti (eds.), *Analysing Exemplary Science Teaching* (London: Open University Press, 2005); Kirsti Lonka, Erkki Olkinuora, and Jarkko Mäkinen, 'Aspects and Prospects of Measuring Studying and Learning in Higher Education,' *Educational Psychology Review* 16, no. 4 (2004): 301–23. Journals such as *Teaching Sociology* have also taken up this issue: Angela Coco, Ian Woodward, Kirstyn Shaw, Alex Cody, Gillian Lupton, and Andrew Peake, 'Bingo for Beginners: A Game Strategy for Facilitating Active Learning,' *Teaching Sociology* 29 (2001):

492–503; Jocelyn A. Hollander, 'Learning to Discuss: Strategies for Improving the Quality of Class Discussion,' *Teaching Sociology* 30 (2002): 317–27; David Horton Smith, 'Encouraging Students' Participation in Large Classes: A Modest Proposal,' *Teaching Sociology* 20 (1992): 337–9.

3 The Student as a Reluctant Intellectual

1 James E. Côté and Anton L. Allahar, *Critical Youth Studies: A Canadian Focus* (Toronto: Pearson Education, 2006).
2 The following account was provided for the Call for Papers for the conference 'Getting It Right for Adolescent Learners,' sponsored by the Canadian Education Association in May 2006, http://www.cea-ace.ca/dia.cfm (accessed 15 Jan. 2006):

> As the requirement for education has grown, young people may find themselves in systems of learning where their input is not welcomed; where curricula are established in advance by people they never meet; where deference to authority is expected; where insubordination can result in suspension; and where disengagement can lead to jeopardized futures. In an era when education is critical yet drop out rates sometimes approach 30%, a new focus on adolescent learners is imperative. Can the high school be transformed in such as way as to facilitate the inputs of adolescents and accommodate their demand for self-determination? Can such a transformation be the key to increasing young people's interest in learning? What do we know about learning in adolescence and what are we doing about it?

3 Statistics Canada, 'University Enrolment 2003/04,' *Daily*, 11 Oct. 2001. Participation in post-secondary education ranges from 70% for those from families in the highest income quartile, and 50% in the lowest income quartile. Note that although about 60% attempt a post-secondary education, only about 45 per-cent of young people currently earn some sort of post-secondary credential.
4 Barry Schwartz, *The Paradox of Choice: Why More Is Less* (New York: Harper Collins, 2004); James E. Côté, 'Identity Capital, Social Capital, and the Wider Benefits of Learning: Generating Resources Facilitative of Social Cohesion,' *London Review of Education* 3 (2005): 221–37.
5 Mel Levine, *Ready or Not, Here Life Comes* (New York: Simon & Schuster, 2005); 'College Graduates Aren't Ready for the Real World,' *Chronicle of Higher Education*, 18 Feb. 2005, B11.
6 Levine, 'College Graduates,' B11.
7 Compare with Hal Niedzviecki, *Hello, I'm Special: How Individuality Became the New Conformity* (Toronto: Penguin Canada, 2004).

8 Levine, 'College Graduates,' B11.
9 Ibid.
10 Côté, 'Identity Capital, Social Capital.'
11 Levine, 'College Graduates,' B11.
12 Neil Howe and Bill Strauss, *Millennials Rising: The Next Great Generation* (New York: Vintage Books, 2000).
13 Mark Edmundson, 'On the Uses of a Liberal Education, *Harper's*, Sept. 1997, 39–49.
14 Ibid., 49.
15 Ibid., 41.
16 Ibid., 45.
17 'Johnny Can't Read, and He's in College,' *Globe and Mail*, 26 Sept. 2005.
18 Caroline Alphonso, 'Universities Trying to Cope with Students Lacking Basics,' http://www.theglobeandmail.com (accessed 22 Sept. 2005).
19 Ibid.
20 Students and parents can visit his website for advice and to order his guides: http://www.profsecrets.com.
21 Rosanna Tamburri, 'Some Universities Tighten Admission Standards,' *University Affairs* (Dec. 2005): 29.
22 Ibid.
23 To the contrary, our research shows that grades are not correlated with IQ at this university; rather, motivations associated with the desire for self-development are one of the few factors examined that were found to be correlated with grades. See James E. Côté and Charles Levine, 'Attitude versus Aptitude: Is Intelligence or Motivation More Important for Positive Higher-Educational Outcomes?' *Journal of Adolescent Research* 15 (2000): 58–80.
24 Cooperative Institutional Research Program (CIRP), 'The American Freshman: National Norms for Fall 1999,' UCLA Graduate School of Education and Information Studies, Higher Education Research Institute, http://www.gseis.ucla.edu/heri/norms_pr_99.html (accessed 12 Sept. 2005). Paradoxically, this same report shows record high levels of academic disengagement, grade inflation, and academic confidence among this cohort. A study by this same centre released in 2005 found 70 percent of first-year students rate themselves as 'above average' or among the 'highest 10 percent.'
25 CIRP, The American Freshman: National Norms for Fall 2004,' UCLA Graduate School of Education and Information Studies, Higher Education Research Institute, http://www.gseis.ucla.edu/heri/findings.html (accessed 17 Feb. 2006).
26 Mark Edmundson, 'On the Uses of a Liberal Education,' *Harper's*, Sept. 1997, 45.

27 David Livingstone and Doug Hart, 'Hedging Our Bets on the Future,' *Academic Matters: The Journal of Higher Education* (Fall 2005): 6, 8–9, 13–14.

28 Roger Shattuck, 'From School to College: We Must End the Conspiracy to Lower Standards,' *Chronicle of Higher Education*, 18 July 1997, http://chronicle.com/che-data/articles.dir/art-43.dir/issue-45dir/45b00601.htm (accessed 13 Jan. 2003).

29 Ibid., ¶2, ¶8.

30 'All Shall Have Prizes,' *Economist*, 14 Apr. 2001, http://proquest.umi.com, ¶5 (accessed 25 Mar. 2003).

31 Bradford P. Wilson, 'The Phenomenon of Grade Inflation in Higher Education,' *Association of American Educators*, 24 Oct. 1998, http://aaeteachers.org/gradeinflation.htm (accessed 24 Mar. 2003) ¶1.

32 We saw this in our study of Western professors reported in chapter 2. Wilson puts it bluntly: 'Thanks to student evaluations ... and the decline in respect for authority, students have learned the not-so-subtle art of blackmail,' which they use against professionally inexperienced TAs and insecure junior professors. (Wilson, 'Grade Inflation in Higher Education,' ¶16).

33 Jane F. Gaultney and Arnie Cann, 'Grade Expectations,' *Teaching of Psychology* 28 (2001): 84–7.

34 Zachary Karabell, *What's College For? The Struggle to Define American Higher Education* (New York: Basic Books, 1998), xxi.

35 Ibid., 11.

36 Ibid.

37 Céleste M. Brotheridge and Raymond T. Lee, 'Correlates and Consequences of Degree Purchasing among Canadian University Students,' *Canadian Journal of Higher Education* 35 (2005): 71–97.

38 Ibid., 83.

39 Edmundson, 'On the Uses of a Liberal Education,' 44.

40 Karabell, *What's College For?* 5.

41 Ibid., 11.

42 Ibid., 5.

43 Denis Hayes and Robin Wynyard, *The McDonaldization of Higher Education* (Westport, CT: Greenwood, 2002).

44 George Ritzer, *The McDonaldization of Society* (Thousand Oaks, CA: Pine Forge, 2000), 11–12.

45 David K. Brown. 'The Social Sources of Educational Credentialism: Status Cultures, Labor Markets, and Organizations,' *Sociology of Education*, extra issue (2001): 19–34.

46 Ibid., 27.

47 Winston Churchill, 'Speech to the House of Commons, 11 November

1947,' *Oxford Dictionary of Quotations* (New York: Oxford University Press, 1999),

48 Benjamin D. Singer, 'Standards from a Distance: The Graduate Scholarship Process,' in *Sociology of Education in Canada*, ed. Lorna Erwin and David MacLennan (Toronto: Copp Clark, 1994), 253–62.

49 Ibid., 261.

50 Ibid., 256.

51 Michael Locke, 'The Decline of Universities with the Rise of Edubis,' *Society/Société* 14 (1990): 8–16.

52 Quoted in Jeffery R. Young, 'Homework? What Homework?' *Chronicle of Higher Education* (6 Dec. 2002): A35.

53 Locke, 'The Decline of Universities,' 11.

54 Edmundson, 'On the Uses of a Liberal Education,' 48.

55 Graduate surveys like those reported in *Maclean's* can have response rates lower than 20% (Ann Dowsett Johnston, 'How Grads Grade Their Schools,' *Maclean's*, 15 Nov. 2005, 28), while Western's own survey has been about 25% (Office of the Provost and Vice-President [Academic], *Report on the Survey of Graduating Students: 2003–04*, Nov. 2004, 2). Several universities opted out of the *Maclean's* survey in 2006, 'citing a host of reasons including inaccurate research methods' associated with a small sample size and low response rate (Emily Senger, '*Maclean's* Denied,' *University of Calgary Gauntlet*, 25 May 2006, http://gauntlet.ucalgary.ca/story/10123 (accessed 31 May 2006). An indication of potential methodological problems is significant variability from survey to survey, indicating that estimates are unreliable. In the case of Western's scores, satisfactions ratings dropped as much as 20% on some indicators in just two years (*Maclean's*, '2006 Graduate Survey: Graduate Satisfaction,' http://www.macleans.ca/universities/index.jsp [accessed 22 June 2006]). For example, in 2004, 66% of respondents rated Western's 'teaching and instruction' in the highest two levels of satisfaction, but in 2006, only 46% did so. Likewise, satisfaction with student services dropped from 56 to 42%, and recommending the university to a friend from 79 to 66%. While we readily admit there are problems at Western and have provided evidence for this, these problems predate the 2004 survey and could not have been exacerbated so drastically in just a two-year period. The 2006 survey had a 21% response rate and claims accuracies of plus/minus 2.7–6.8%, nineteen times out of twenty-nine, depending on the school, but these estimates do not seem to account for the significant drop in scores at schools like Western.

Western cautions that its 'methodology permits only relatively global generalizations' (Office of the Provost and Vice-President [Academic], *Report on the Survey of Graduating Students: 2003–04*, Nov. 2004, 2). In *Performance and*

Activity Indicators Annual Report to the Board of Governors, Western claims that its satisfaction rating is 90%+. However, the question used to assess this apparent level of satisfaction is biased toward obtaining more positive ratings because the midpoint on the five-point scale used is 'somewhat satisfied' rather than 'neutral' or 'neither satisfied nor dissatisfied,' leaving disproportionately more response categories to reflect satisfaction than dissatisfaction. Only about 25% of respondents to Western's graduation survey report being 'very satisfied' with the education they received there.

56 There is not much published on this in the academic literature, but results of these surveys can be readily accessed on the Internet. In Canada, *Maclean's* and the *Globe and Mail* provide ratings, as does the *Sunday Times* in the United Kingdom (http://www.timesonline.co.uk/section/0,,8404,00. html) (accessed 2 Feb. 2006).

57 Arthur Yehle, business consultant, personal communication, 22 Jan. 2004.

58 Gene I. Maeroff, 'The Media: Degree of Coverage,' in *Declining by Degrees: Higher Education at Risk*, ed. Richard H. Hersh and John Merrow (New York: Palgrave, MacMillan, 2005), 11–22.

4 Parents as Investors and Managers

1 Generalizations are useful to the extent that they apply to trends characterizing common experiences among large numbers of people. Generalizations thus deal with probabilities and possibilities, for which exceptions exist. However, by definition, exceptions do not invalidate probabilities. In fact, the social sciences are built on probabilities and the use of statistics to establish and report probabilities.

2 Professors who give some reflection to this matter may realize that they are determining the fate of their individual students each time they assign final grades, hence the enticement to give high grades. However, this is a positional issue, as already noted: they are simply changing a standard and leaving the sorting to someone else. Still, who wants to deal with students who think that by arbitrarily receiving a low grade in a course the professor is 'ruining' their future by 'condemning' them to unskilled work and denying them hundreds of thousands of dollars in potential wages?

3 See http://www.collegeparents.org/cpa/index.html (accessed 16 Feb. 2006).

4 For a critique of school rankings written by David Naylor, see 'The Trouble with Maclean's,' *Ottawa Citizen*, 22 Apr. 2006, http://www.canada.com/ottawacitizen/news/opinion/story.html?id=adc4a1df-d148-484f-a569–80c18039f7c6&p=1 (accessed 25 May 2006).

5 Compare Gene I. Maeroff, 'The Media: Degree of Coverage,' in *Declining by Degrees: Higher Education at Risk*, ed. Richard H. Hersh and John Merrow (New York: Palgrave, MacMillan, 2005), 11–22.

6 Marilyn Montgomery and James E. Côté, 'The Transition to University: Outcomes and Adjustments,' *The Blackwell Handbook of Adolescence*, ed. Gerald Adams and Michael Berzonsky (Oxford: Blackwell, 2003); Ernest T. Pascarella and Patrick T. Terenzini, *How College Affects Students: Findings and Insights from Twenty Years of Research* (San Francisco: Jossey-Bass, 1991).

7 According to findings from the Youth in Transition Survey (YITS), those who drop out of university are less likely to earn high grades in high school and be engaged in high school, and more likely to feel that the university programme they undertook 'wasn't for them' or 'they didn't like it' (Mylène Lambert, Klarka Zeman, Mary Allen, and Patrick Bussière, *Who Pursues Postsecondary Education, Who Leaves and Why: Results from the Youth in Transition Survey* (Ottawa: Statistics Canada, 2004).

8 This is a reason why the teaching competencies of professors are not seen by many universities as crucial – students are expected to meet professors halfway by actively linking with the professor's expertise, rather than being passively spoon-fed; see James E. Côté and Charles Levine, 'Student Motivations, Learning Environments, and Human Capital Acquisition: Toward an Integrated Paradigm of Student Development,' *Journal of College Student Development* 38 (1997): 229–43.

9 Compare Tom Schuller, John Preston, Cathy Hammond, Ann Brassett-Grundy, and John Bynner, *The Benefits of Learning: The Impact of Education on Health, Family Life and Social Capital* (London: RoutledgeFalmer, 2004).

10 Côté and Levine, 'Student Motivations.'

11 Cooperative Institutional Research Program (CIRP), 'Degree Attainment Rates at Colleges and Universities,' UCLA Graduate School of Education and Information Studies, Higher Education Research Institute, http://www.gseis.ucla.edu/heri/darcu_pr.html (accessed 17 Feb. 2006). This has been called 'the dirty little secret of college' by Lynn Olson, *The School-to-Work Revolution* (Reading, MA: Perseus Books, 1997).

12 The Education Trust, 'College Results Online,' http://collegeresults.org/mainMenu.aspx (accessed 1 Feb. 2006). Some of the data provided there are striking. For example, Florida International University in Miami has a four-year graduation rate of only 18%, a five-year rate of 37%, and a six-year rate of 47%. This university would be comparable to York University in Toronto in terms of the constituency served, and its role as a satellite university in a large city with a world-class university (the University of Miami) in the city proper. The University of Miami would be comparable to the University of Toronto in these terms and has four-, five-, and six-year graduation rates of 53, 65, and 67%, respectively. Florida State University, which would be roughly comparable to Western in geographical and status terms (i.e., it has

a good academic reputation *and* is considered the number-one party university in the United States), has graduation rates for these time spans of 42, 62, and 66%.

13 Some data suggest that Canadian universities have a better record of completion rates, with estimates putting completion within *five years* at between 40 and 80%, but these figures are not believed to be very reliable (Sean Junor and Alex Usher, *The Price of Knowledge 2004: Access and Student Finance in Canada* [Montreal: Canada Millennium Scholarship Foundation, 2004], 88). We agree that there is reason to suspect statistics released by individual institutions, because it is difficult to separate the public-relations spin put on institutional data from objective data collection and reporting. Western reports its rate at about 73% within five years in one source, but 76% for *seven years* in another source. Compare University of Western Ontario, *Performance and Activity Indicators: Annual Report to the Board of Governors*, 28 Apr. 2005, http://www.ipb.uwo.ca/documents/2005_performance_indicator.pdf (accessed 1 Feb. 2006) with *Graduation Rates, Employment Rates, and OSAP Default Rates*, http://www.uwo.ca/western/MTCU/MTCU2003oct.html (accessed 5 Nov. 2006). Still, these rates are only slightly better than those reported for comparable American universities (e.g., as in note 12, the six-year rate for Florida State University is reported to be 66%), and lower than those for the average of the top five research-intensive universities in the United States (78.5%); http://collegeresults.org/mainMenu.aspx (accessed 5 Nov. 2006). The overall seven-year rate for Ontario universities is 73%.

14 Ministry of Training, Colleges and Universities, 'Choosing a School and Program Wisely,' http://osap.gov.on.ca/eng/not_secure/choose.htm (accessed 21 Feb. 2006).

15 Statistics Canada, 'University Tuition Fees,' *Canadian Social Trends* (Spring 2005): 33; Ontario Ministry of Education, 'Students' Costs,' http://www.edu.gov.on.ca/eng/general/postsec/costs.html (accessed 20 Oct. 2006); for this breakdown for Western, see 'Tuition and Ancillary Fee Schedule of 2005–2006,' http://www4.registrar.uwo.ca/FinancialServices/2005_2006FeeScheduleUGRDFT.pdf (accessed 15 Jan. 2006). Specialized programmes can be much more expensive. At Western, for example, professional programmes charges fees of up to about $25,000 in dentistry, $20,000 in (undergrad) business, $15,000 in medicine, and $10,000 in law. Averaged from universities across Canada, between 1995 and 2002, tuition rose 132% in medical programmes, 168% in dentistry, and 61% in law, with the impact of reducing the number of middle-income students entering these programmes (defined as those whose parents had only a community college diploma or BA). See Marc Frenette, *The Impact of Tuition Fees on Uni-*

versity Access: Evidence from a Large-scale Price Deregulation in Professional Pro-grams, Analytic Studies Research Paper Series, cat. no. 11F0019MIE (Ottawa: Statistics Canada, 2005).

16 Ontario Ministry of Education, 'Student Costs'; Junor and Usher, *The Price of Knowledge 2004*, 136, cite housing expenses of about $500 per month for those living independently.

17 Junor and Usher, *The Price of Knowledge 2004*.

18 See Ibid., 191–2, for the eligibility criteria tied to expected parental contri-butions.

19 Ibid., 4. As reported by Leo Charbonneau, 'Financial Barriers Likely Not Hurting Access,' *University Affairs* (Dec. 2003): 36, students from families earning more than $90,000 per year are expected by the loan system to get $10,000 from their parents, when the actual contributions from such fami-lies are between $2,500 and $4,000. These students can accumulate the most debt and are forced to take on jobs if they cannot get a student loan.

20 Sophie Lefebvre, 'Saving for Postsecondary Education,' *Perspectives* (July 2004): 5–12. See also Mary Allen and Chantal Vaillancourt, 'Class of 2000: Student Loans,' *Canadian Social Trends* (Autumn 2004): 18–21.

21 Junor and Usher, *The Price of Knowledge 2004*.

22 Michael Doucet, 'The Tuition Squeeze: A Trans-Generational Perspective,' *OCUFA Forum* (Ottawa: Ontario Confederation of University Faculty Associa-tions, 2000), 16–21.

23 Doucet, 'The Tuition Squeeze,' estimates that tuition could be covered with about 250 hours of work in the mid-1970s when tuitions were about $700 and the minimum wage was $2.65. By the late 1990s, tuition of $4,500 would take 660 hours of employment to cover at a minimum wage of $6.85. At thirty-five hours per week, this is about nineteen weeks, while the summer 'work season' spans only the four months of May through August.

24 Junor and Usher, *The Price of Knowledge 2004*, 149.

25 Ibid., 19–24.

26 Sophie Lefebre, 'Saving for Postsecondary Education,' *Perspectives* (Statistics Canada cat. no. 75-001-XIE) (July 2004): 5–12. A sponsor (parent, grandpar-ent, relative, or friend) can put money into a Registered Education Savings Plan (RESP) to a maximum of $4,000 per year, which grows tax free until used by a post-secondary student. Through the Canadian Education Savings Grant (CESG), the government ponies up 20% of the amount saved, to a maximum of $400 per year, or $7,200 lifetime limit.

27 Junor and Usher, *The Price of Knowledge 2004*.

28 Lefebvre, 'Saving for Postsecondary Education.'

29 Junor and Usher, *The Price of Knowledge 2004*.

30 Lefebvre, 'Saving for Postsecondary Education.'

31 Junor and Usher, *The Price of Knowledge 2004*.

32 Ibid.; Alex Usher, *A Little Knowledge Is a Dangerous Thing: How Perceptions of Costs and Benefits Affect Access to Education* (Toronto: Education Policy Institute, 2005), http://www.educationalpolicy.org/pdf/littleknowledge.pdf (accessed 15 Dec. 2005).

33 Junor and Usher, *The Price of Knowledge 2004*, 111.

34 Copy machines commonly charged 25 cents per page in the mid-1970s, which would be about 92 cents per page in 2006 inflation-adjusted dollars. To make such conversions visit, http://www.bankofcanada.ca/en/rates/inflation_calc.html.

35 Those who took math and science courses in the pre- and early-computer era will remember similar experiences with assignments. Math and statistics work was done by hand, using memorized multiplication and long division – hand calculators were expensive and a luxury when they first came out. Those who took advanced courses in statistics when mainframe computers became available for student use needed to punch all commands out on cards, run them through a reader, and wait while the job was placed in a queue for time-share processing and printout (sometimes for hours). If even one typo had been made, the offending card would have to be corrected, but all cards would have to be reread, with an additional wait, such that assignments could take days just to compute the statistical analysis portion. Statistical and other specialized programmes for a number of fields are now available for PCs, with drop-down menus that allow computations to be set up and run in a fraction of the time – minutes rather than hours. This is a different and potentially less transforming experience.

36 Peg Tyre, 'Bringing up Adultolescents,' *Newsweek*, 22 Mar. 2002, http://www.hyper-parenting.com/newsweek5.htm#BODY (accessed 16 Jan. 2006).

37 'Helicopter parent,' *Wikipedia*, http://en.wikipedia.org/wiki/Helicopter_parent (accessed 16 Jan. 2006), ¶1.

38 Ibid., ¶4 and ¶6.

39 We urge parents interested in honing their communication and emotive effectiveness to consult some parenting literature, like that on authoritative parenting and intensive parenting. Authoritative parenting gives children firm guidelines for maturity, but grants them the psychological autonomy to direct their own development, while intensive parenting provides activities that help children to engage themselves in the school system. See, respectively, Laurence Steinberg, *The Ten Basic Principles of Good Parenting* (New York: Simon & Schuster, 2004), and Robert Sweet and Nancy Mandell, 'Exploring Limits to Parents' Involvement in Homework,' in *Preparing for Post-secondary Education: New Roles for Governments and Families*, ed. Robert Sweet and Paul Anisef (Montreal and Kingston: McGill-Queen's University Press, 2005), 273–88.

40 Unless otherwise indicated, the statistics reported in the remainder of this chapter are taken from Junor and Usher, *The Price of Knowledge 2004*.

41 According to Junor and Usher, *The Price of Knowledge 2004*, 5, 93% of parents do so.

42 Ibid., 5.

43 David Livingstone and Doug Hart, 'Hedging Our Bets on the Future,' *Academic Matters: The Journal of Higher Education* (Fall 2005): 6, 8–9, 13–14. Compare Scott Davies, who cites research indicating a doubling in the percentage of grade 12 students expecting to graduate university from the 1970s to the 2000s, from one-third to almost two-thirds. Scott Davies, 'A Revolution in Expectations? Three Key Trends in the SAEP Data,' in *Preparing for Post-secondary Education: New Roles for Governments and Families*, ed. Robert Sweet and Paul Anisef, 149–65 (Montreal and Kingston: McGill-Queen's University Press, 2005)

44 Ross Finnie, Eric Lascelles, and Arthur Sweetman, *Who Goes? The Direct and Indirect Effects of Family Background on Access to Post-secondary Education*, Analytic Studies Branch Research Paper Series (Ottawa: Statistics Canada, 2005).

45 We do not have comparable data for the myriad immigrant cultures in Canada, but it is well known that parents from many of these cultures who do not have higher levels of education themselves nevertheless push their children harder and farther, and the latter are out-performing the children of more complacent parents, who have been here longer and are more settled (e.g., Anglo-Canadians).

46 All findings reported in this paragraph are from Finnie, Lascelles, and Sweetman, *Who Goes?*

47 This problem is not restricted to Canada. Even in England, where social class distinctions are more evident, the government is attempting to counteract this bias in parental reasoning while it introduces apprenticeship programmes in which students can enrol when as young as fourteen years of age (Sarah Cassidy, 'Parents Must Drop Prejudices Make Apprenticeship Scheme Work, Says CBI,' *Independent*, 11 May 2004, A16). In these programmes, students substitute two days per week of regular school with on-the-job training in engineering, business, or the arts. An official with the programme called for parents to 'drop their "dreadful and old-fashioned" prejudices' to help the programme get off the ground, further noting that 'parents were keen for other people's children to train as plumbers, [but] were determined that their own offspring would go to university.' Those completing these programmes have good prospects of financial independence by the time they are twenty. At the time of writing, several provincial governments in Canada have launched advertising campaigns to encourage young people to undertake apprenticeships.

48 Barbara Schneider and David Stevenson, *The Ambitious Generation: America's Teenagers, Motivated but Directionless* (New Haven, CT: Yale University Press, 1999).

49 Junor and Usher, *The Price of Knowledge 2004*, 10.

50 Ibid., 14.

51 Compare, European Group for Integrated Social Research (EGRIS), 'Misleading Trajectories: Transition Dilemmas of Youth Adults in Europe,' *Journal of Youth Studies* 4 (2001): 101–18.

52 Schneider and Stevenson, *The Ambitious Generation*.

53 Ibid., 83.

54 Ibid.

55 Ibid., 86.

56 We have systematically investigated this at the more general level of identity formation theory, with an approach called the identity capital model. This model theorizes that young people who 'agentically' (proactively and with reflection) invest in 'who they are' as they undertake higher-educational routes to adulthood have better eventual outcomes, especially in terms of non-monetary, personal benefits. Support was found for this proposition in a ten-year longitudinal study that tracked students from their first year of university through to six years after graduation (James E. Côté, 'An Empirical Test of the Identity Capital Model,' *Journal of Adolescence* 20 (1997): 577–97; James E. Côté, 'The Role of Identity Capital in the Transition to Adulthood: The Individualization Thesis Examined,' *Journal of Youth Studies* 5 (2002): 117–34.

57 Côté and Levine, 'Student Motivations.'

58 While the accessibility ranking looks good, it is measured by the number of graduates, so countries that 'pump them out' will rank higher, regardless of the quality of their systems.

59 Educational Policy Institute, 'Education Report: Global Study Ranks Canadian Higher Education 11th in Affordability, 5th in Accessibility,' http://www.educationalpolicy.org/globalhigheredrank.html (accessed 15 Apr. 2005).

60 Junor and Usher, *The Price of Knowledge 2004*, 159. This is up from one-third in the early 1980s; Canadian Association of University Teachers, *CAUT Almanac* 40, table 5.29.

61 Jeanine Usalcas and Geoff Bowlby, 'Students in the Labour Market,' Statistics Canada, http://www.statcan.ca/english/freepub/81-004-XIE/2006001/market.htm (accessed 20 Oct. 2006). The trend is even greater for female students.

62 Franke reports that female post-secondary students with jobs devote over an hour less per day on their education (from 6.4 to 5.1 hours). Males appear not to be affected by their jobs in this way, but males spend less time on their

education to begin with (about five hours). Franke also reports that both
males and females in post-secondary institutions spend more time on leisure
than on their education. See Sandra Franke, 'Studying and Working: The
Busy Lives of Students with Paid Employment,' *Canadian Social Trends*
(Spring 2003): 22–5.

63 The survey showing this was based on responses from 12,695 students from
thirty universities across Canada: Junor and Usher, *The Price of Knowledge
2004*, iv.

64 Usalcas and Bowlby, 'Students in the Labour Market.'

65 Junor and Usher, *The Price of Knowledge 2004*.

66 Arthur Levine and Jeanette S. Cureton, *When Hope and Fear Collide: A Portrait
of Today's College Students* (San Francisco: Jossey Bass, 1998).

67 National Center for Education Statistics, 'The Condition of Education 2002,'
section 37, http://nces.ed.gov/pubs2002/2002025.pdf (accessed 22 Feb.
2006).

68 Philip Giles and Torben Drewes, 'Liberal Arts Degrees and the Labour Market,' *Perspectives* (Autumn 2001): 33.

69 Levine and Cureton, *When Hope and Fear Collide*, 118.

70 James E. Côté and Charles Levine, 'Attitude versus Aptitude: Is Intelligence
or Motivation More Important for Positive Higher-Educational Outcomes?'
Journal of Adolescent Research 15 (2000): 58–80.

71 For more on the topic of parental financial support and the difficulties
experienced by the millennial generation, see Anna Bahny, 'The Bank of
Mom and Dad,' *New York Times*, 20 Apr. 2006, http://nytimes.com (accessed
21 Apr. 2006); Tamara Draut, *Strapped: Why America's 20- and 30-Somethings
Can't Get Ahead* (New York: Doubleday, 2006); Anya Kamentz, *Generation
Debt* (New York: Riverhead Books, 2006).

5 Policy Implications

1 Parents reading this who did go on to college or university were clearly the
exceptional 10% of their generation in terms of their interests or abilities,
and were likely 'pulled' into higher education. Their children, however, are
much more likely to be running with the pack, so to speak, and are being
pushed along by the momentum of the economic forces affecting their
generation. As a result, students today are much more extrinsically motivated than were the more intrinsically motivated students of their parents'
generation.

2 For thorough treatment of the history of credentialism in the United States,
see Thomas J. Collins, *The High School / Post-secondary Education Transition*,

Council of Ministers of Education, 1998, http://www.cmec.ca/postsec/
transitions/en/431.collins.pdf (accessed 8 Aug. 2006).

3 Ibid., 123.

4 Conversely, if the undergraduate population dropped precipitously, departments would be closed and the viability of these disciplines would be seriously affected, in part because there would be no students to help pay the
bills and in part because there would be fewer recruits to each discipline.

5 Randall Collins, *The Credential Society: An Historical Sociology of Education and
Stratification* (New York: Academic Press, 1979).

6 Richard H. Hersh and John Merrow, *Declining by Degrees: Higher Education at
Risk* (New York: Palgrave, MacMillan, 2005).

7 The assumption was that the skills transmitted through higher education –
human capital – would meet the needs of an advanced industrial economy
and generate economic wealth for the individual graduate and for the society as a whole. This human capital assumption has been borne out to some
extent, but has also been found faulty as a full explanation of educational
outcomes (Alfred A. Hunter and Jean McKenzie Leiper, 'On Formal Education, Skills and Earnings: The Role of Educational Certificates in Earnings
Determination,' *Canadian Journal of Sociology* 18 [1993]: 21–42). In particular, beyond achieving widespread literacy and numeracy (which used to be
achieved with a grade 9 education), generic skills do not generate economic
activity on their own, and certainly abstract academic knowledge in most
fields does not. Most university graduates have skills that can make them
good employees, not entrepreneurs, so if positions are not available, there is
little most university graduates can do except take a position not requiring a
university degree. This is precisely what many graduates do, as we have discussed throughout this book.

8 Alexander Lockhart, 'Future Failure: The Unanticipated Consequences of
Educational Planning,' in *Socialization and Values in Canadian Society*, ed. Robert M. Pike and E. Zureik (Toronto: McClelland-Stewart, 1975).

9 Lucie Nobert, Ramona McDowell, and Diane Goulet, *Profile of Higher Education in Canada: 1991 Edition* (Ottawa: Department of the Secretary of State of
Canada, 1992).

10 Association of Universities and Colleges of Canada, *Trends 1996: The Canadian University in Profile* (Ottawa: Association of Universities and Colleges of
Canada, 1996).

11 Association of Universities and Colleges of Canada, *Trends in Higher Education* (Ottawa: Association of Universities and Colleges of Canada, 2002).

12 Statistics Canada, 'University Enrolment 2003/04,' *Daily*, 11 Oct. 2001.

13 Association of Universities and Colleges of Canada, *Trends in Higher Educa-*

tion. This report predicts that between 2001 and 2011, some 1.6 million BAs and 330,000 graduate degrees will be produced.

14 Statistics Canada, *Education in Canada: Raising the Standard,* 2001 Census: Analysis Series (Ottawa: Minister of Industry, 2003).

15 Ivar Berg, *Education and Jobs: The Great Training Robbery* (New York: Praeger Publishers for the Centre for Urban Education, 1970).

16 Another 30% were classed as skilled, but they required largely blue-collar and technical skills picked up in apprenticeships or at community colleges (i.e., trade workers, technicians, low-level managers, and semi-profession-als). It is now very difficult to define skill levels of jobs independent of educational attainment. Statistics Canada defines skills in terms of educational attainment, but in doing so renders the question of changes in skill level required by the labour force inseparable from the output of higher educational credentials.

17 Statistics Canada, *Education in Canada,* 5.

18 Based on his extensive analysis of this problem, Livingstone argues that the primary cause of underemployment is not inadequate education so much as a lack of decent jobs to match the high levels of education now achieved. Livingstone identifies six dimensions of underemployment, which if all applied, would make everyone underemployed in some way: a talent-use gap, structural unemployment, involuntary reduced employment, the credential gap, the performance gap, and subjective underemployment. However, Livingstone argues that these dimensions are not additive. Still, he concludes that 'it is safe to say that over half of the potential U.S. and Canadian adult workforces have experienced some of the overlapping dimensions of objective underemployment, and that significantly less have a coherent sense of their underemployment.' We refer mainly to credential underemployment in this book. See David W. Livingstone, *The Education-Jobs Gap: Underemployment or Economic Democracy* (Boulder, CO: Westview, 1998), 95.

19 Wolf makes a strong case for this point in reference to the U.K. educational system. See Alison Wolf, *Does Education Matter? Myths about Education and Economic Growth* (London: Penguin, 2002).

20 See, for example, Robert C. Allen, 'The Employability of University Graduates in the Humanities, Social Sciences, and Education: Recent Statistical Evidence,' http://ideas.repec.org/p/ubc/bricol/98-15.html (accessed 15 Nov. 2006).

21 Zachary Karabell, *What's College For? The Struggle to Define American Higher Education* (New York: Basic Books, 1998).

22 Peter Shawn Taylor and Ian McGugan, 'Devoured by Degrees,' *Canadian Business,* September 1995, 26–36.

23 '"What's Up" What's New at University?' *London Free Press*, http://www. fyilondon.com (accessed 17 Jan. 2004).

24 Taylor and McGugan, 'Devoured by Degrees,' 30.

25 Although the dropout rate in Canada declined in the first part of the 1990s (Statistics Canada, 'Dropping Out of High School on the Decline,' *Update on Family and Labour Studies* 1 [2002], http://www.statcan.ca [accessed 1 Feb. 2004), it increased between 1997 and 2003. Excluding Ontario (because of its elimination of grade 13 and the 'double-cohort' issue), the overall completion rate across the country is about 75 percent, with females graduating at a higher rate than males (by 10 percentage points) ('High School Dropout Rate Rises,' *CAUT Bulletin*, February 2005, A11). Ontario's rate now appears to be about 70 percent.

More recent results from the Youth in Transition Study (YITS) conducted by Statistics Canada provide a focus on a random sample of young people studied over time, first when they were eighteen to twenty (in 1999) and then when they were twenty to twenty-two (in 2001). This study, which is open to certain biases in sample selection when it comes to tracking down and getting young people to participate repeatedly, found that by age twenty-two, only 9% of respondents re-contacted did not have high school diploma or greater (some left and then returned to high school or took advantage of a 'second chance' opportunity by getting admitted to a post-secondary programme without a high school diploma). See Klarka Zeman, Tamara Knighton, and Patrick Bussière, *Education and Labour Market Pathways of Young Canadians between Age 20 and 22: An Overview*. Education, Skills, and Learning: Research Papers, cat. no. 81-595-MIE2004018 (Ottawa: Statistics Canada, 2004).

26 This is what the NSSE calls 'DEEP Learning.'

27 John Gravois, 'Professor Sues Wisconsin College,' *Chronicle of Higher Education*, 28 Jan. 2005, A11.

28 Scott Smallwood, 'Faculty Group Censures Benedict College Again over "A for Effort" Policy,' *Chronicle of Higher Education*, 21 Jan. 2005, A12.

29 Harvey C. Mansfield, 'Grade Inflation: It's Time to Face the Facts,' *Chronicle of Higher Education*, 6 Apr. 2001, B24.

30 Ibid.

31 Ibid.

32 Ibid.

33 Rebecca Aronauer, 'Princeton's War on Grade Inflation Drops the Number of As,' *Chronicle of Higher Education*, 30 Sept. 2005, A41.

34 Office of the Dean of the College, Princeton University, 'Grading Overview,' http://www.princeton.edu/odoc/faculty/grading/ (accessed 5 Nov. 2006).

For further information about their grading proposals, see 'Grading Proposals,' http://www.princeton.edu/~odoc/grading_proposals/01.html (accessed 5 Nov. 2006).

35 Ibid.

36 Valen Johnson, *Grade Inflation: A Crisis in College Education* (New York: Springer, 2003).

37 Ibid., 9.

38 Mansfield, 'Grade Inflation,' B24.

39 Johnson, *Grade Inflation*, 9.

40 Correlations averaged over a number of studies are in the magnitude of .2 and .3 (p. 81), and professors can 'double their odds of getting high evaluations from students simply by awarding As rather than Bs or Cs' (ibid., 83).

41 Ibid., 237.

42 This has been established in experimental studies where student decision-making in course selection was examined at various points in time.

43 Johnson, *Grade Inflation*, 237.

44 These conclusions were confirmed with various forms of evidence, an important one of which was a study that compared grades received by the same students taught in different departments. This study showed that differences in grades are due to systematic differences in the grading practices of the departments studied, not the ability level of students. Little wonder, then, that students can be confused by what constitutes the various grade levels and that students gravitate to departments and faculties that grade more leniently.

45 George Kuh, Jillian Kinzie, John H. Schuh, Elizabeth J. Whitt, and Associates, *Student Success in College: Creating Conditions That Matter* (San Francisco: Jossey-Bass, 2006) 9.

46 Johnson, *Grade Inflation*, 246.

47 Ministry of Training, Colleges and Universities, 'University Links to Key Performance Indicators,' http://osap.gov.on.ca/eng/not_secure/urlsuniv.htm (accessed 14 Aug. 2006).

48 The research that will be discussed is based mainly on the 'pre-inflation years' when higher standards were enforced and students were more engaged. Accordingly, it should be noted that the benefits associated with having a university education might be in jeopardy. It is possible that future research will need to differentiate disengaged students from engaged ones when assessing benefits.

49 Ernest T. Pascarella and Patrick T. Terenzini, *How College Affects Students: Findings and Insights from Twenty Years of Research* (San Francisco: Jossey-Bass, 1991).

50 Accordingly to the 2001 Canadian Census, 60% of those making $100,000 or more had a university degree. This means that 40% did not, indicating that non-university means to affluence are still common. See Statistics Canada, *Earnings of Canadians: Making a Living in the New Economy*. 2001 Census Analysis series (Ottawa: Statistics Canada, 2001), 9.

51 Pascarella and Terenzini, *How College Affects Students*.

52 Allen, *The Employability of University Graduates*.

53 The French sociologist Pierre Bourdieu has written extensively about the politics of education and social reproduction – the ways in which social class background will determine rates of educational success. His approach goes further than simply saying that children of the rich do better than children of the non-rich merely because their parents can buy them a better education at private schools with private tutors and so on. That much is taken for granted. Instead, Bourdieu looks at the latent benefits of being rich; the so-called non-specific and unarticulated benefits of coming from a class background that sets the tone for the culture of the classroom. In short, youths from privileged families do better in school than other youths because the values, assumptions, and expectations of educational institutions, their definitions of what constitutes learning, and how knowledge is transmitted or acquired are the same values, assumptions, expectations, and definitions as those found in the families of the privileged classes or 'cultivated classes.' See Pierre Bourdieu and Jean-Claude Passeron, *The Inheritors: French Students and Their Relations to Culture*, trans. Richard Nice (Chicago: University of Chicago Press, 1979), 22.

54 See, for example, Wolf, *Does Education Matter?*

55 Pascarella and Terenzini, *How College Affects Students*, 557.

56 In statistical language, average net change is about one-quarter to one-third of a standard deviation. Assuming a normal distribution, this would mean that about half of students change less than this, and some would experience no change, especially, we would add, those who put minimal effort into their courses. See Pascarella and Terenzini, *How College Affects Students*, 566–73.

57 Ibid., 575–7.

58 Compare Brotheridge and Lee's concept of 'degree purchasing,' from 'Correlates and Consequences of Degree Purchasing among Canadian University Students,' *Canadian Journal of Higher Education* 35 (2005): 71–97.

59 Philip Giles and Torben Drewes, 'Liberal Arts Degrees and the Labour Market,' *Perspectives* (Autumn 2001): 33.

60 According to Statistics Canada (*Education in Canada*, 9), among men who were working on a full-year, full-time basis in 2000, those without a university degree had average earnings of less than $50,000. In contrast, earnings for

men with a university degree (including postgraduate degrees, so these figures are higher than those with just a BA) have been above this level in each
census since 1980, and surpassed $70,000 on average for the first time in
2000. In fact, university-degree holders were the only group of men to earn
significantly more than they did two decades earlier.

61 Human Resources Development Canada, *Profile of Canadian Youth in the
Labour Market* (Ottawa: Human Resources Development Canada, 2000), 58.
Estimates for personal rates of return on an undergraduate degree com-
pared to a high school diploma vary slightly in how they are calculated, but
are now at least 10%, with estimates in some countries topping 30%. See
Elchanan Cohn and John T. Addison, 'The Economic Returns to Lifelong
Learning in OECD Countries,' *Education Economics* 6 (1998): 253–63. Recent
estimates for Canada put the private rate of return at 15–28% for community
college graduates and 12–20% for university graduates (Sean Junor and Alex
Usher, *The Price of Knowledge 2004: Access and Student Finance in Canada* [Mon-
treal: Canada Millennium Scholarship Foundation, 2004]). For U.S. estimates, see Pascarella and Terenzini, *How College Affects Students.*

62 Human Resources Development Canada, *Profile of Canadian Youth in the
Labour Market.*

63 James E. Côté and Anton L. Allahar, *Critical Youth Studies: A Canadian Focus*
(Toronto: Pearson Education, 2006). Direct costs include tuition and sup-
plies, while indirect costs include lost wages while in school, also known as
opportunity costs.

64 Lester C. Thurow, *Building Wealth* (New York: HarperCollins, 1999).

65 Human Resources Development Canada, *Profile of Canadian Youth in the
Labour Market*; Junor and Usher, *The Price of Knowledge 2004.*

66 Compare Wolf, *Does Education Matter?*

67 Considering all universities, the student-to-teacher ratio increased from 17.5
to 22.9 between 1991 and 2001 (Canadian Association of University Teachers, *CAUT Almanac* [Ottawa: CAUT], 4, figure 3.1). In some faculties (like
Arts, Humanities, and Social Sciences) and some schools, it is much higher,
reaching into the hundreds of students per faculty member.

68 Paul Davenport, 'Universities and the Knowledge Economy,' in *Renovating
the Ivory Tower*, ed. David Laidler (Toronto: C.D. Howe Institute, 2002), 39–
59.

69 Junor and Usher, *The Price of Knowledge 2004.*

70 Association of Universities and Colleges of Canada, *Trends in Higher Education*, 2002.

71 Fred Hemingway and Kathryn McMullen, *A Family Affair: The Impact of Paying
for College or University* (Montreal: Canada Millennium Scholarship Foundation, 2004).

72 Statistics Canada, *Earnings of Canadians*.

73 Martina Morris and Bruce Western, 'Inequality in Earnings at the Close of the Twentieth Century,' *Annual Review of Sociology* 25 (1999): 623–57.

74 Samuel Halperin, 'Today's Forgotten Half: Still Losing Ground,' in *The Forgotten Half Revisited: American Youth and Young Families, 1998–2008*, ed. S. Halperin (Washington: American Youth Policy Forum, 1998).

75 Morris and Western, 'Inequality in Earnings,' 633. The 'college premium' is the salary and employability advantage that a college/university degree has over a high school diploma. The National Center for Policy Alternatives estimates that in the United States, the premium of having a college (or university) degree over a high school diploma increased from 1.43 to 1.82 between 1972 and 1992. The premium of having an advanced degree over high school increased from 1.72 to 2.54 over the same period (http://www.ncpa.org/bg/gif/bg138fig5.gif, accessed 2 Feb. 2003). In Canada, this figure was recently calculated to have risen from 1.34 for males in 1980 to 1.51 in 2000, but to have stayed stable for females (at 1.62) over this period (presumably because of the lower relative wages of females at both points). Daniel Boothby and Torben Drewes, 'Post-secondary Education in Canada: Returns to University, College and Trades Education,' Feb. 2005, http://www.trentu.ca/academic/economics/documents/Drewes-Boothby-Paper.doc (accessed 15 Aug. 2006).

76 Anton Allahar and James Côté, *Richer and Poorer: The Structure of Social Inequality in Canada* (Toronto: Lorimer, 1998).

77 Marilyn Montgomery and James E. Côté, 'The Transition to University: Outcomes and Adjustments,' *The Blackwell Handbook of Adolescence*, ed. Gerald Adams and Michael Berzonsky (Oxford: Blackwell, 2003).

78 Herman G. Van de Werfhorst and Robert Andersen, 'Social Background, Credential Inflation and Educational Strategies,' *Acta Sociologica* 48, no. 4 (2005): 322–3.

79 Robert C. Allen, 'The Employability of University Graduates in the Humanities, Social Sciences, and Education: Recent Statistical Evidence,' http://ideas.repec.org/p/ubc/bricol/98-15.html (accessed 15 Nov. 2006).

80 For example, Allen claims that 70% of employed university grads are in professional/managerial positions (although admitting to a 12% drop between 1970 and 1995), leaving fewer than one in five in sales or clerical positions. Problems with his data and argument include the problem that certain sales and clerical job titles have been changed to managerial-types jobs to make those jobs sound more prestigious and skilled than they really are, as we noted earlier in this chapter (e.g., being manager of a small chain store). His data are also for all university graduates, not just those with a liberal arts BA – a common error in these types of analyses due in part to Statistics Canada's

habit of reporting data for all university grads and not separating the levels of graduates, who have very different experiences.

81 Hunter and McKenzie Leiper, 'On Formal Education, Skills and Earnings'; Wolf, *Does Education Matter?*

82 Graham Lowe, 'Youth, Transition, and the New World of Work,' in *Restructuring Work and the Life course,* ed. Victor W. Marshall, Walter R. Heinz, Helga Kruger, and Anil Verma (Toronto: University of Toronto Press, 2001), 23–44; R.A. Teixeira and L. Mishel, 'Skills Shortages or Management Shortage?' in *The New Modern Times: Factors Reshaping the World of Work,* ed. D. Bills (Albany, NY: State University of New York Press, 1995), 193–206.

83 Garnett Picot, John Myles, and Ted Wannell, *Good Jobs/Bad Jobs and the Declining Middle: 1967–1986.* Analytic Studies Branch research paper series no. 028. (Ottawa: Statistics Canada, 1990).

84 Scott Davies, Clayton Mosher, and B. O'Grady, 'Trends in Labour Market Outcomes of Canadian Post-Secondary Graduates, 1978–1988,' in *Sociology of Education in Canada,* ed. Lorna Erwin and David MacLennan (Toronto: Copp Clark Longman, 1994), 39–59.

85 Nobert, McDowell, and Goulet, *Profile of Higher Education;* Marc Frenette, 'Overqualified? Recent Graduates and the Needs of Their Employers,' *Education Quarterly Review* 7 (2000): 6–20.

86 For example, about one-third of those aged twenty to twenty-nine with bachelor's degrees feel they are overqualified for their jobs, compared with 22% for all Canadian workers with college or university degrees; Karen Kelly, Linda Howatson-Leo, and Warren Clark, 'I Feel Overqualified for My Job,' *Canadian Social Trends* (Winter 1997): 11–16. See also Mary Allen, Shelley Harris, and George Butlin, *Finding Their Way: A Profile of Young Canadian Graduates.* Education, Skills and Learning: Research Papers, cat. no. 81-595-MIE, no. 3 (Ottawa: Statistics Canada, 2003).

87 Susan Crompton, 'I Still Feel Overqualified for My Job,' *Canadian Social Trends* (Winter 2002): 23–6.

88 Using a skills-use index based on whether their current job required the skills acquired from their post-secondary programme, Ross Finnie reports that 35%–41% of graduates of all levels were overqualified in the period from the mid-1980s to the mid-1990s ('Graduates' Earnings and the Job Skills–Education Match,' *Education Quarterly Review* 7, no. 2 [2001]: 7–21).

89 Côté and Allahar, *Critical Youth Studies.*

90 Julian Betts, Christopher Ferrall, and Ross Finnie, *The Transition to Work for Canadian University Graduates: Time to First Job, 1982–1990.* Analytic Studies Branch research paper series no. 141 (Ottawa: Statistics Canada, 2000).

91 Frenette, 'Overqualified?'

92 Ibid., 9.
93 Chris Li, Ginette Gervais, and Aurélie Duval, 'The Dynamics of Overqualification: Canada's Underemployed University Graduates,' Statistics Canada
cat. no. 11-621-MIE2006039 (Ottawa: Minister of Industry, 2006), http://
www.statcan.ca/english/research/11-621-MIE/11-621-MIE2006039.pdf
(accessed 7 Apr. 2006).
94 George Butlin, 'Bachelor's Graduates Who Pursue Further Postsecondary
Education,' *Education Quarterly Review* 7, no. 2 (2001): 22–41.
95 Warren Clark, 'University Graduates at College,' *Canadian Social Trends*
(Autumn 1999): 18–19. Some 70% of college applicants over the age of
twenty-five have a university degree, according to Junor and Usher, *The Price
of Knowledge 2004.*
96 Statistics Canada, *Income of Canadian Families. 2001 Census Analysis Series*
(Ottawa: Statistics Canada, 2003), 30.
97 Junor and Usher, *The Price of Knowledge 2004;* John Zhao and Patrice de
Broucker, 'Participation in Postsecondary Education and Family Income,'
Daily, 7 Dec. 2001; Miles Corak and John Zhao, 'Family Income and Participation in Postsecondary Education, *Daily,* 3 Oct. 2003). Compare Atiq Rah-
man, Jerry Situ, and Vicki Jimmo, *Participation in Postsecondary Education:
Evidence from the Survey of Labour and Income Dynamics* (Ottawa: Statistics Canada, 2005) (Culture, Tourism and the Centre for Education Statistics,
Research Paper, cat. no. 81-595-MIE2005036).
98 Ross Finnie, Eric Lascelles, and Arthur Sweetman, *Who Goes? The Direct and
Indirect Effects of Family Background on Access to Post-secondary Education,* Analytic Studies Branch Research Paper Series (Ottawa: Statistics Canada,
2005). This is controlling for other factors like parental and student attitudes toward education, urban/rural residence, etc.
99 Watson Scott Swail and Donald E. Heller, *Changes in Tuition Policy: Natural
Policy Experiments in Five Countries* (Montreal: Canada Millennium Scholarship Foundation, 2004); Canada Millennium Scholarship Foundation, *Is
University Education in Canada More Affordable Than in the United States? A
Review of the Argument Presented in the Affordability of University Education; A
Perspective from Both Sides of the 49th Parallel* (Montreal: Canada Millennium
Scholarship Foundation, 2004).
100 Junor and Usher, *The Price of Knowledge 2004.*
101 CEISS – Research & IT Solutions, *The Millennium Bursary in British Columbia:
Exploring Its Impact* (Montreal: Canada Millennium Scholarship Founda-
tion, 2004). Each dropout is estimated to cost the institution over $4000
according to J. Paul Grayson and Kyle Grayson, *Research on Retention and
Attrition* (Montreal: Canada Millennium Scholarship Foundation, 2003).

102 EKOS Research, *Making Ends Meet: The 2001–2002 Student Financial Survey* (Montreal: Canada Millennium Scholarship Foundation, 2003); Fred Hemingway, *Pressure Points in Student Financial Assistance: Exploring the Making Ends Meet Database* (Montreal: Canada Millennium Scholarship Foundation, 2004).

103 Junor and Usher, *The Price of Knowledge 2004,* postulate that such students have 'horizons' that are different from those of more affluent and advantaged students, which deeply affect their conceptions of their possible futures and life plans. In a similar analysis, the concept of 'horizons for action' has described perceptions of labour-market opportunities and what people perceive to be appropriate for themselves in relation to those opportunities in terms of their family of origin and experiences while growing up (Phil Hodkinson, Andrew C. Sparkes, and Heather Hodkinson, *Triumphs and Tears: Young People, Markets and the Transition from School to Work* (London: Fulton, 1996).

104 R.A. Malatest & Associates, *Aboriginal Peoples and Post-secondary Education: What Educators Have Learned* (Montreal: Canada Millennium Scholarship Foundation, 2004). This study found that 'personal reasons' are more responsible for dropout from university among Aboriginal youth than all other factors (p. 16).

105 Association of Universities and Colleges in Canada, *Trends in Higher Education,* 2002, 10; Personal reasons that may be more important than financial barriers can include indecision, other interests, or a lack of interest at the time, as well as more deep-seated factors like self-regard, self-confidence, and other identity-related factors.

106 Junor and Usher, *The Price of Knowledge 2004*; Alex Usher, *A Little Knowledge Is a Dangerous Thing: How Perceptions of Costs and Benefits Affect Access to Education* (Toronto: Education Policy Institute, 2005), http://www.educationalpolicy.org/pdf/littleknowledge.pdf (accessed 15 Dec. 2005).

107 Pascarella and Terenzini, *How College Affects Students.*

108 Andy Furlong and Fred Cartmel, *Young People and Social Change: Individualization and Risk in Late Modernity* (Buckingham, UK: Open University Press, 1997).

109 This figure is based on Vladimir Shubkin, 'Sociology of the Educational System: Society's Requirements and the Career-Choice Attitudes of Young People,' *Political Economy, Sociology and Anthropology* (1984): 187–200.

110 The history of the '11 plus' exams in the United Kingdom is a case in point. These exams have been used for decades to sort students at age eleven, sending the brighter students to 'grammar schools,' and lower-performing students to 'secondary school.' There are still complaints that they favour students from more affluent backgrounds, but then again, all known educa-

tional systems do this. The question becomes, then, how to establish a system that maximizes the chances that academically brighter children from all backgrounds will be given the opportunities to realize the potential of this aspect of their intelligence. Children with other potentials should then be assisted in maximizing those non-academic potentials.

111 In the traditional German apprenticeship system, high school ends with grade 10 and entails a three-year contract for extensive on-the-job vocational training by working three days per week in a specific job like mechanic or bank clerk, along with two days per week in-class education in subjects related to that vocation (e.g., engineering for mechanics and accounting for bank clerks). Until recently, this provided a reliable route to full employment and a secure basis for the financial independence upon which to move into adulthood. However, as in other countries, the forces of globalization that permit the penetration of transnational corporations in local economies have reduced the cooperation of the business sector in this arrangement. These corporations do not want to share in the cost for worker training, and in fact make efforts to deskill the jobs available locally. Consequently, this apprenticeship system is in decline in the private sector. See, for example, Kai U. Schnabel, Corinne Alfeld, Jacquelynne S. Eccles, et al., 'Parental Influence of Students' Educational Choices in the United States and Germany: Different Ramifications – Same Effect?' *Journal of Vocational Behavior* 60 (2002): 178–98.

112 Organisation for Economic and Cooperative Development, *From Initial Education to Working Life: Making Transitions Work* (Paris: OECD, 2001).

113 Swedes are eligible for study allowances when they are sixteen, so long as they remain studying in upper secondary school (Swedish National Board for Youth Affairs, *Youth in Progress: The Transition to Adulthood in Sweden in the 1990s* [Stockholm: Swedish National Board for Youth Affairs, 1999). This amounts to about 950 Swedish kronas per month, or about 165 Canadian dollars, which is worth about twenty hours of work at minimum wage. The vast majority of young Swedes take advantage of this, accounting for the high retention rates in Swedish school (over 90% of eighteen-year-olds are in some form of schooling in Sweden, compared to about 75% in Canada); Swedish National Board for Youth Affairs, *Statistics on Young People in Sweden – Tables* (Stockholm: Swedish National Board for Youth Affairs, 1999).

114 As noted in chapter 4, working excessive hours during secondary school is related to a variety of problems, including early school leaving. See, in addition, Jeffery J. Arnett, *Adolescence and Emerging Adulthood: A Cultural Approach*, 2nd ed. (Upper Saddle River, NJ: Pearson Education, 2004).

115 Swedish Institute, *Upper Secondary and Adult Education in Sweden* (Stockholm: Swedish Institute, 2000).

116 Alberta, British Columbia, and Quebec have systems that are more sequential, where community college and related education can count toward a university degree, as in the United States with the associate's degree.
117 Swedish Institute, *Higher Education in Sweden* (Stockholm: Swedish Institute, 2004).
118 Compare Dave Armishaw, 'A Response to William Humber's Article "Intellectual and Utilitarian Identities,"' *College Quarterly* 8, no. 4 (Fall 2005), http://www.collegequarterly.ca/2005-vol08-num04-fall/armishaw.html (accessed 4 Mar. 2006).
119 Further reading that can constitute the basis for this discussion and debate is Paul Axelrod, *Values in Conflict: The University, the Marketplace, and the Trials of Liberal Education* (Montreal and Kingston: McGill-Queen's University Press, 2002).
120 For an excellent treatise on the merit of lifelong learning inside and outside of academia, see Charles Hayes, *The Rapture of Maturity: A Legacy of Lifelong Learning* (Wasilla, AK: Autodidactics, 2004). For further readings from this press on lifelong learning and reflections on deriving deeper meaning in life through intellectual activity, see http://www.autodidactic.com/index.html.
121 Paul Davenport, 'The Liberal Arts and Social Progress,' Western Matters, accessed 2 Jan. 2006, reprinted from the *National Post's Business* magazine, November 2005.

Appendix

1 Paul Davenport, 'Universities and the Knowledge Economy,' in *Renovating the Ivory Tower*, ed. David Laidler (Toronto: C.D. Howe Institute, 2002), 39–59.
2 U.S. Department of Education, National Center for Education Statistics, 'The Condition of Education 2002,' http://nces.ed.gov/pubsearch/pubsinfo.asp?pubid=2002025 (accessed 3 Aug. 2006).
3 'Allahar 3M Teaching Winner,' Western News, 26 May 2005, http://communications.uwo.ca/western_news/story.html?listing_id=18722 (accessed 7 Aug. 2006).
4 Tony Bastick, 'Commonwealth Degrees from Class to Equivalence: Changing to Grade Point Averages in the Caribbean,' *Journal of Studies in International Education* 8, no. 1 (2004): 86–104.
5 See 'ECTS: European Credit Transfer and Accumulation System,' http://ec.europa.eu./education/programmes/socrates/ects/index_en.html#5.

6 Alan King and Marjorie Peart, *The Numbers Game: A Study of Evaluation and Achievement in Ontario Schools* (Toronto: Ontario Secondary School Teacher's Federation, 1994), 218.

7 Ibid.

8 See 'Facts and Figures 2006: A Compendium of Statistics on Ontario Universities,' http://www.cou.on.ca/ (accessed 8 Aug. 2006).

9 King and Peart, *The Numbers Game*, 169. The Ontario Scholar programme began in the early 1960s when standardized exams were still in place, and needless to say, only a few qualified because few students earned As. Now, as the figures reviewed in the text suggest, the programme lacks its original meaning because of the large number of As awarded.

10 Catherine Tyler, 'Grade Expectations: When Is an "A" Not Quite an "A"?' New Media Journalism, http://www.fims.uwo.ca/newmedia2006/default.asp?id=424 (accessed 8 Aug. 2006).

11 University of Calgary, 'National Grading Differences Short Change Alberta Students,' In the News, 6 Nov. 2003, ¶2, http://www.ucalgary.ca/news/nov03/grading.html (accessed 23 Dec. 2003).

12 Paul Angling and Ronald Ming, 'Evidence on Grades and Grade Inflation at Ontario's Universities,' *Canadian Public Policy / Analyse de Politiques* 26 (2000): 361–368.

13 The first author attended an Ontario undergraduate university during the early to mid-1970s, and it was made explicit to students that the 5% rule for As applied to all courses. The university, Trent, was still following the British model at the time, replete with its don structure and tutorial system. The sort of grade inflation reported by Anglin and Meng was apparently not affecting Trent at that time.

14 T. Frank, 'New Study Says Grades Are Inflated at Ontario Universities,' *University Affairs* (February 2001): 29.

15 Office of Analytical Studies, Simon Fraser University, 'Historical Distribution of Undergraduate and Graduate Course Grades 1995/96 to 2004/05,' http://www.sfu.ca/analytical-studies/GradesReport/grades.html (accessed 8 Aug. 2006).

16 Office of Institutional Analysis, 'Grade Inflation at the U of C: Is It an Issue?' *Fact Files* 1, no. 2 (2003): 3, http://www.oia.ucalgary.ca/FactFiles/2003March.pdf (accessed 25 Oct. 2006).

17 'National Survey of Student Engagement,' http://www.queensu.ca/irp/pdfiles/nsse/Frequencies_background.pdf; 'National Survey of Student Engagement (NSSE),' http://www.analysis.uwaterloo.ca/docs/pi.html (accessed 14 Aug. 2006).

18 Tony Bastick, 'Commonwealth Degrees from Class to Equivalence: Changing

to Grade Point Averages in the Caribbean,' *Journal of Studies in International Education* 8, no. 1 (2004): 90.

19 See chapter 1 for the reactions of an administrator who returned to the classroom: Thomas Collins, *The High School / Post-secondary Education Transition*, Council of Ministers of Education, 1998, http://www.cmec.ca/postsec/transitions/en/431.collins.pdf (accessed 8 Aug. 2006).

Index